Raleigh

An Unorthodox History of North Carolina's Capital

Marshall Lancaster

Copyright 1992 by Marshall Lancaster

First Printing, October, 1992

All rights reserved.
No part of this book may be reproduced
by any means without permission of the publisher,
except for brief passages in reviews and articles.

ISBN
1-878086-15-4

Library of Congress Catalog Number
92-072660

Printed in the United States of America

Cover and book design:
Elizabeth House

Down Home Press
P.O. Box 4126
Asheboro, N.C. 27204

"Ill fares it with a (city) whose history is written by others than her own sons."
— Prescott, 1851.

For David Brinkley

Contents

Prologue ix

Introduction xiii

He That Hath No Ear Will Hear No Evil 1

Dead Horses Wheresoever They May Be 32

Take Two With Meals (And Get Right With God) 64

All Pistols, Cards And Likker
Must Be OK'd By The Teacher 87

No Balm In Gilead 103

Hands Off Our Weak-Brained Women 122

Nothing Is Too Much Of A Humbug 143

Fetch My Squirrel-Gun, Ma!
They're A'Pavin' Our Poppy Patch! 166

Indecent Exposure 196

Of Hootch And Bawds And Chicken Pecks,
And Cards and Frolicking 214

Our Special Guests 231

Bibliography 255

Prologue

Fayetteville Street is overbuilt for tenant demand and has a lagging occupancy rate. The newest building is outsized compared to its neighbors and strikes traditionalists as being just the least bit ugly.

Real estate speculators worry about whether they paid too much for their lots, which lately have been difficult to resell. Banks holding real estate loans are uneasy about further lending.

The city's infrastructure needs serious work, but city fathers say they lack the revenues even for repairs, much less for improvements.

A debate simmers about the need for a civic center where meetings and performances could draw visitors from around North Carolina and be competitive with facilities of neighboring cities.

Raleigh's students rank somewhere toward the bottom of the nation, yet it is difficult to get parents to attend meetings on how to better education.

Liquor is fast becoming a problem throughout the citizenry, even among young people. Adults sell narcotics openly in some parts of the state capital.

Infant mortality and pregnancies among unmarried teenagers are at unacceptably high rates.

People in Raleigh despair that religion has lost hold in many families and needs to be reemphasized along with traditional values.

Raleigh

Citizens disagree about whether the taxpayers can afford more correctional facilities versus the societal cost of having criminals loose on the streets.

Raleigh is not even close to a consensus on how or where to shelter the homeless and mentally disturbed. Nor is there unanimity on whether to resort to a lottery and use the proceeds for education.

Businessmen in town want to privatize certain governmental functions or at least to realize more profit from them as a means of allaying taxes.

Civil libertarians are adamant against capital punishment.

Getting along with city government, according to widespread gossip, is more a matter of who you are and who you know than it is based on impartiality. Whole categories of citizens are certain they are being discriminated against. The ordinary wage-earner in particular bears a disproportionate share of civic obligations.

Proposed ordinances for gun and dog control have the public acting like pit bull terriers, a breed which prompted much of the discussion.

Raleigh's two principal news outlets have open contempt for each other, offer more advertising and recycled news from other media than they do local coverage, and agree only in deploring the low voter turnout in recent elections.

What with a soft economy, tax foreclosure notices seemed especially thick last year.

City government says that it would like to plan farther ahead, but that the General Assembly keeps changing the groundrules and will not grant Raleigh enough authority to make decisions.

Each week, the residents of Raleigh lug their garbage to the streets, separated into special containers, for municipal pickup.

It is business as usual in the year 1800.

Raleigh

The evolution of the City of Raleigh, North Carolina – which was essentially a busted-out field, woodland and some swamps when the State paid Joel Lane for 1,000 acres and named it the new State Capital – was a process which never lacked intrigue.

In many ways, it is startling that Raleigh reached its position today as the second most populous city in the State, all in the absence of waterfront property and balmy weather.

How did Raleigh manage to grow from 669 inhabitants in the first census to more than 208,000 in 1992? How did it manage to grow in square miles by more than 3,200 percent in this century alone, if the word "manage" is at all appropriate?

How, given its early disregard for schools, health care and public improvements, did Raleigh attain its status today as a center of higher education, beaucoup hospital beds, and a road network which threatens to strangle the city with its own cars?

Raleigh, after all, is a city which lagged behind its sisters in North Carolina in nearly every urban category, from fire protection to urban renewal to infrastructure to the form of its government. How did it end up with an amphitheater and auditoriums and sports arenas, even though some consider them behind the times and call for more public expenditures to keep up with Charlotte?

Looking at Raleigh's economy in 1992 – service industries, government and education dominate it along with the ever-present real estate speculators who have been in the capital since the beginning – raises the question of why, despite repeated campaigns, the city never developed into a manufacturing center. And what kinds of "progress" would have been visited upon the capital if the boosters had prevailed?

How did Raleigh get all those shopping centers and why are there people who want still more?

Why do the citizens of Raleigh enjoy bashing the State government, which is singly responsible for the existence of the city? What happened to Raleigh's founders – men with names like Lane, Haywood, Boylan, Bloodworth, Jones and Hinton – who drank and smoked seegars and bought on credit and would try most anything to get the city to expand? Does their spirit survive them?

Who was trampled under in the growth of the capital? What little-known characters managed in their own ways to thrive, and what pillars of the community were not, as the State motto cautions, exactly what they seemed to be?

Did the latest influx of population from the North beginning in the 1950s make a difference in outlook as well as wage levels?

Are the suburbs inside the Beltline as highfalutin' as some of their residents believe them to be? And incidentally, when the phrase "inside the Beltline" is invoked, why does it refer to Raleigh's largely segregated white neighborhoods to the north and west and not to its largely segregated black neighborhoods to the south and east which lie within the same loop of highway?

How, over some 200 years, have the citizens of Raleigh treated each other? How have they been treated by their own municipal government? How, in general, do the myths of the State Capital correspond with the facts?

It is an intriguing city, the Raleigh which began with a roadhouse to get drunk in and a jail to house the results. But then, any city which was named to honor a man who got himself beheaded for treason and perjury has to be an interesting place.

Introduction

RALEIGH: The Unorthodox History. A title such as that requires at least a perfunctory brush by old Truth in Packaging.

Here are a few observations about this work:

- It is a history only in the sense that each event described in the book did occur in Raleigh during the last 200 years.
- Each incident was confirmed by more than one source. Either the events in the book are true or diverse people in Raleigh – over generations – were *non compos mentis* or perpetuated lies.

This book does *not* embrace the ancient doctrine which says to "never let the truth stand in the way of a good story."

- To gain admission to the book, an event had to be interesting, or outrageous, or humorous, or represent trends and forces larger than itself, or preferably all of the above.
- Although the book draws parallels between episodes in Raleigh's history and its present, it reaches no conclusions about the city. Readers are welcome to form their own judgments.
- Because no chronological account can supply the flavor of what was really transpiring in the city, this book tends to skip around. The chapter groupings are arbitrary for good reason: an act of entertainment, for instance, could as easily have been classified under "vice" or "crime and punishment."
- In response to one previewer's question – "Didn't anything ever go *right* here in 200 years?" – the answer is yes.

How else can one explain the book's congratulatory passage about the Jaycees, who are the patron target of journalists?

• In answer to other comments – "You can't print that s___" is an expurgated example – complainers should see the material which did *not* pass muster for the book. Much of it is as steamy as daytime television.

• The book contains little about "what goes on behind closed doors," as Charlie Rich and Clarence Thomas so eloquently phrased it. Unless a peccadillo spilled into a booking office or courtroom and unless it stood for something larger than the beleaguered participants, it is excluded.

That injunction eliminates some of Raleigh's most cherished rumors: the stories about incest; or who parented what child; or who had a relative secreted for years in the attic; or who tore what funeral home apart one night; or what former taxi driver took prostitutes to whose residence; or even the brand name of the preferred cooking oil one afternoon at the Triangle Motel. (Hint: there were no arteries clogging in Room 47.)

The principle which underlies all these omissions is called the right to privacy. Any reader who really needs to know that kind of trash should – as was suggested to a North Carolina congressman several generations ago – take the fatback out of his or her mouth, walk up to the alleged malefactors, and ask point-blank what happened. (Editor's note: And then for goodness' sake tell the rest of us!) With a little advance notice, an action such as that might sell more tickets than minor-league basketball at the Cow Palace.

• Certain names are omitted from the book. The descendants of persons involved in these cases will probably appreciate it.

• Last, the book makes no attempt to bring every theme up to date. For one thing, the more current the event, the more likely that people already know about it. For another, it is the task of another researcher 50 years from now to size up Raleigh today. And of course, libel suits have gotten expensive to defend.

So with all of those exclusions, are there any lip-smacking activities still available to chronicle?

Well, there are the murders, rapes, arsons and maimings – good old family-style fare. Or embezzlements, frauds and crooked politicians.

Or public hangings, or train wrecks as popular entertainment, or what the city fathers used to regard as indecent shows.

Or the unending efforts to contend with – not eradicate, mind you – gambling, bootlegging and prostitution in the capital. Or the pervasion of drug traffic in Raleigh since 1792.

A balanced account of the city's panorama should compare its actual experience to its myths. The Civil War turned out to be a fertile place to start.

A balanced account should examine the city's discrimination against blacks and women. It should discuss what money has been able to buy in this town. It might even reflect on a few examples of hypocrisy.

A balanced view requires a discussion of the evolution of the city's health care, schools and churches and even what we antiseptically refer to as "infrastructure." (That last topic was not so antiseptic on the evening when one of Raleigh's downtown streets caught on fire.)

The rise of city hall; how Raleigh has gotten its information over 200 years; how development occurred – the book examines each of them. It discusses what many believe to be the whopper of all whoppers: the notion that if the city grew fast enough, growth would reduce or stabilize taxes.

There is even a survey of Raleigh's special guests: Dorothea Dix Hospital, Central Prison and the Legislature.

So let this "history" of Raleigh begin.

Do not expect to learn the identity of the local man whose

Raleigh

impulses led the State Supreme Court to add chickens to its list of beasts which were covered by a certain criminal law.

But do expect to learn, for example, that if Raleigh celebrated its birthday on the same basis as other cities in the United States – by the date of its charter – we would not have a bicentennial until 1995. What the city is celebrating in 1992 is a real estate deal. It somehow seems appropriate.

He That Hath No Ear Will Hear No Evil

"I've come down here to give all you guilty bastards a fair trial."
Superior Court judge, 1977

One jurist's sense of humor notwithstanding, during the past two centuries Raleigh has grown positively slack in the way it treats criminals.

It is just as well – no one in this city would want to be sentenced by one of our founding fathers.

Imagine the atmosphere on the Fayetteville Street mall today if the old whipping post were still in operation at the courthouse, vying for attention with the hot dog vendors, occasional musicians and street people. Or the city's pillory.

"And the criminal shall stand in the pillory for one hour," one old law went, "at the expiration of which time both ears... shall be cut off and severed entirely from the head, and the ears so cut off shall be nailed to the pillory by the officer, and there remain until the setting of the sun."

Fewer people would sit outside for lunch. ("Well, where shall we eat, Mildred?" a conversation might go. "Down by the whipping and maiming, or just up here where we can watch the rats?")

Raleigh's founders may have had their shortcomings – such as failing to provide a water supply, neglecting to fund schools, tolerating abysmal sanitation, and doing nothing about street clearance – but they leapt into action when it came to criminals.

Raleigh

When the whipping post literally wore out in the early 1800s, they replaced it with an improved model. Nor did the founders hesitate to define criminal conduct when they thought they saw it.

To examine the history of crime and punishment in Raleigh – from hangings and worse to today's alternative sentencing programs and house arrests – it is necessary to trace the criminal laws of the State, then the evolving Raleigh municipal code, and then all brands of court records.

Several trends emerge which look suspiciously like facts: a criminal in Raleigh today is treated better than at any time in the city's history and is physically safer until he or she comes into contact with other criminals; the well-off in Raleigh have generally come out ahead in the justice system as compared to the city's disadvantaged; the chances of a prisoner escaping are minimal compared to those in the past; public punishments – the most gruesome of early deterrents – seem to have done nothing to reduce crime on a per capita basis; and courts have suffered backlogs since before Chief Justice John Marshall held occasional sessions in the city.

What follows are some little-known aspects of law and a sampler of how Raleigh citizens over the years have managed to get into trouble.

Consider the ink-stained counterfeiter. He may think that he has problems today, what with the U.S. Secret Service on his tail, but the penalty for being a counterfeiter in Raleigh in the early 1800s was something more than a term in a minimum-security federal prison.

"... He shall for the first offense stand in the pillory three hours," the law read, "and have his right ear nailed to the pillory and cut off, and receive on his or their bare back thirty-nine lashes, and be branded with a red hot iron on the right cheek with the letter C, and on the left cheek with the letter M (which brands shall be at least one inch in length) and be imprisoned not exceeding one year, and forfeit one half of all his goods and chattels, lands and tenements, whereof he or she was seized or possessed at the time the offence was committed...."

(If that seems like a strong penalty for a first offense, the second-time counterfeiter was sentenced to death. Suffice it to say that if someone were counterfeiting money in Raleigh in the early 1800s, it was not low-denomination bills.)

Well, the General Assembly just doesn't write statutes like that anymore. Nor does the Legislature enact laws today such as the one under which Treasurer John Haywood issued this voucher:

"To the burning of a Negroe Fellow, Toney... he being condemned for murder, £500... To provision found six men for two Days as a Guard; and cutting wood holling and erecting and fixing the place of Execution--£200."

Toney had committed the State's most heinous crime, that of *petit treason*. The crime occurred when a slave killed a master or a wife killed her husband, even if the husband, at the time of his death, was exercising his "right of correction" by beating her. Treasurer Haywood's voucher paid for the slave to be burned at the stake.

Maiming, burning at the stake, hanging, branding, whipping, the pillory, the stocks, forced labor, banishment, debtor's prison, even being forced into slavery – Raleigh was the locale for all of these governmental sanctions during its first 30 years as a city. Many of them persisted for generations after that.

The city usually managed to keep its public hangings off of Fayetteville Street unless they were notorious cases with a great viewing demand by spectators.

An oak tree between South and Lenoir streets was a favorite place for hangings, as was a crossbeam which was nailed up from time to time at the old city cemetery. The corner of South and West streets, where a beam was erected between two pine trees, got sufficient business so that it was named "Gallows Hill." And towards the end of the 19th century, when the Wake County sheriff at last obtained a formal gallows, it was built at the state quarry east of the old city limits.

Other gallows were built as needed in the courthouse yard.

At the city's centennial celebration in 1892, historian Kemp P. Battle described some of the public executions which had taken place in Raleigh. (His address, delivered on Fayetteville Street to an audience of thousands, runs to 84 pages of single-spaced type. The city fathers in 1892 may have given up their pillory, but they still knew how to punish the ears.)

As Dr. Battle depicted a local hanging, the condemned person –almost certainly a male – was taken by cart from the jail. He wore a white shroud and rode atop his own coffin, surrounded by guards and accompanied by ministers. When the condemned man arrived at the crossbeam and had the noose tightened around his neck, the officers simply whipped the horses to pull the wagon out from under him. This technique, to quote Dr. Battle, prompted "the criminal to struggle to keep his feet on the moving vehicle as long as possible in a manner horrifying to the spectators."

Local officials responded to Battle's description by building the quarry gallows with a trap. But amateur inventors got into the act, and by the time Central Prison took over executions in 1910 the gallows in Raleigh was outfitted with heavy weights which were dropped in order to snatch the prisoner upwards. The resulting strangulations reportedly took time.

What could an inhabitant of Raleigh do over the years to merit the rope?

In addition to the crimes of murder with malice, arson of a dwelling house, and felonious burglary – offenses regarded as repugnant even into recent decades – the possibilities were almost endless.

A Raleigh man was hanged for burning a barn which contained a grain crop; others died for burning store houses, grist mills, and saw mills; in fact, the death penalty applied to a person who burned a building for the manufacture "of any article whatsoever."

(These laws not only reflected a desire to industrialize, but they certainly raised the stakes for insurance fires.)

A robbery "in or near any public highway" also resulted in hanging, although presumably it did not if the felon mugged his victim a safe distance into the woods.

If a man took part in a duel and survived, he was subject to be hanged for participating in the contest. (This law may have been a deterrent.) Anyone involved in castrating, maiming or disfiguring another's genitals was supposed to be hanged. (So much for calling up a surgeon and scheduling a 19th century sex-change operation.)

Rape of a female over 10 years old would get a man hanged, as would consensual intercourse with females under the age of 10.

In case there were any dreaded gays in the City of Oaks, a noose was ready for "any person who shall commit the abominable and detestable crime against nature, not to be named among Christians, with either man or beast." (Unrequited gays apparently were safe.)

The threat of being hanged did not end there. Whoever burned down a government office containing public records was to be hanged. Any Raleigh resident who broke into an occupied place to steal more than two dollars was liable to be hanged.

And in general, the perpetrator of each of these crimes might have had company under the crossbeam, because those who aided and abetted were also executed.

In a law which might bring a smile to retired Superior Court Judge Pou Bailey, an accused person was also hanged "if he peremptorily challenged more than thirty-five jurors" in a capital case, whether he might have been convicted in a trial or not. (Presumably, somewhere around challenge No. 34, the prisoner would make forceful efforts to silence his attorney.)

Speaking of attorneys, the laws in effect in early Raleigh permitted only one lawyer per side in a case because, the statute read, "the frequent abuses of attornies have occasioned distresses to many of the good people of this state."

Raleigh

There were certain nuances to capital crimes in the city.
Find yourself standing over the body of a slave with a smoking pistol in your hand? In that case, you usually would receive a branding. But if instead of killing that slave you stole him or helped him to escape, you faced a felony charge and the rope.

The complexities and fear inherent in slavery led to a number of capital offenses: concealing a slave; or transporting one to freedom; or removing one from the State with the intention of selling him; or making a speech which would agitate the slaves; or printing up a pamphlet which might make them discontented. (So much for the First Amendment in Raleigh. But how were the slaves supposed to read the pamphlets?)

The march of death penalties continued. Steal a horse, mare, gelding, jackass or mule? Hanging. Embezzle $10.01 of your master's goods? Hanging. Second offense for maiming, forgery or larceny? Hanging.

Bigamists could be hanged, although the Wake County courts preferred public whippings and branding with the letter "B." (One blacksmith's shop in Raleigh offered branding irons covering the entire alphabet, and the sheriff was a customer.) In a sexist policy, women were exempted from this particular barbarity.

Once past the dozens of capital offenses, the laws in Raleigh became innovative.

Take manslaughter, for instance: although the statutory penalty was for the letter "M" to be branded on the left thumb, the judge had discretion to let a killer off with a fine and a public whipping.

For someone who said, "I'll kill the little bastard" and did exactly that, the penalty was a fine of up to $500 and jail for up to 12 months.

(In a case which does not fit neatly into today's discussions of choice in childbearing, a woman in Raleigh served only six months in jail for killing her unwanted newborn baby. She had beaten, choked and knifed the infant and then made sure it was dead by submerging it in Crabtree Creek. That was the regard which Raleigh's founders had for unwanted children after their birth.)

For trying to break up an election, the penalty was three months in jail and a fine of not more than $100, whether the effort succeeded or not.

Fornication and adultery carried fines of not more than $200.

Marrying a 14-year-old girl without the written consent of her father brought a sentence of six months and a fine – but the marriage stood.

If a person were "found sauntering about" without applying himself "to some honest calling," the opening penalty was a bond plus ten days in jail plus costs. If the "vagrant" could not raise the money, find work or leave Raleigh, the penalties escalated to a month in jail, and then six months, and then being hired out as forced labor. (Of course, the prisoner could opt for 39 lashes at the Fayetteville Street whipping post in exchange for his liberty.)

Consider for a moment the context of these punishments: only white male property-owners or poll tax payers could vote and serve on juries; the city had multiple layers of law enforcement; and if women were second-class citizens by law, the slaves and even free negroes had it worse.

A stranger in town, or a newcomer, or one of the city's legally or economically disadvantaged, needed to play it by the book.

It is important to realize that while some laws in early Raleigh would be unthinkable today, by no means were all of the old laws enforced.

Chief Justice John Louis Taylor in 1821 called for a general relaxing of the State's criminal code. He said that juries were increasingly unwilling to convict someone of stealing two dollars when it meant a public hanging.

Taylor was concerned that the laws had lost meaning and were being applied unevenly, and the General Assembly eventually heeded his advice.

Meanwhile, many Raleigh criminals were "transported"; that is, shipped out of the State with instructions never to come back.

For those in early Raleigh who blanched at the sight of court-ordered mutilations, there was always the hope that the Intendant (the title of Raleigh's early Mayor-Police Chief) might round up a Common Scold.

As Chief Justice Taylor explained it, a Scold was "a term which our discourteous ancestors have limited to the fair sex." Taylor wrote that it applied to women who were shrewish on a habitual basis, since "there is no great harm in scolding once or twice."

For this offense, our forefathers roped the Scold to a dunking stool and plunged her repeatedly into the water until she nearly drowned.

John Haywood had reservations about the punishment. He wrote that it did not "exhibit a very charitable indulgence towards their (women's) infirmities...." Haywood added that "those men who abandon themselves to beastly intoxication and every sort of loathsome sensuality, who, by blasphemous language and obstreperous mirth, offend the pious and disturb the peaceful, are fitter objects for some such striking and exemplary punishment."

Raleigh

Raleigh's founding fathers may have been unable to make the streets passable and unwilling to pay for schools, but they had some ideas for protecting their property on the cheap.

(Some might call it vigilantism, others simply overkill, but Raleigh in 1800 had enough strata of law enforcement to please the average third-world strongman.)

First was the Intendant of Police. John Haywood was the original Intendant, and he also acted as chief executive of the city and as its judge, but in 1800 who cared about the fad known as separation of powers? Haywood also had the power to summon up *posses comitatus.*

Next, Raleigh had standing companies of armed militia, dressed out in uniforms with plumes, fifes, drums and assorted firearms. Headed by the esteemed Captains of Wake County, the 120 men in the militia were compelled by law to serve unless they were well off enough to hire substitutes.

However, in 1800 the Intendant, Sheriff, posses, courthouse crowd and militia were not considered adequate to protect Raleigh's population of 669 whose only Indian problem was local jealousy when the Governor put up a Catawba Indian delegation in first-class quarters. So the city also established a compulsory Night Watch.

If the militia's main purpose was to fend off foreign invaders such as a resurgent England or other states which were peeved at North Carolina's cattle-drive laws, the Night Watch had a different mission: to collar those dastardly residents who might be afoot after the city bell rang. Most of their energy was directed at enforcing myriad laws concerning the conduct of slaves and at running in common drunks. The two classes were exclusive and the Night Watch was busy.

But were five layers of law enforcement sufficient to guard the city's 669 residents who lived, after all, in pretty much open field? Probably, but Raleigh took no chances and created the Patrol, composed of men who fanned out through the 400 platted acres at least twice per month – anything to get out of the house – to make certain that public morals and calm prevailed and that the Sabbath was preserved. The Patrol was empowered to arrest people and to whip them on the spot without trial.

In addition, Raleigh had a Ranger who picked up stray animals, sold them if they were edible, and killed them if they were not. The city also had a Warden to see after the poor and assorted Justices of the Peace to keep the machinery going.

One has to wonder who was left in Raleigh in 1800 to commit crimes. (It must have been those bored, confined women who lusted after slaves, strangers, or some of the law enforcement community itself. Either that, or every child in town was a delinquent.)

But a resident of Raleigh in 1800 had one more level of law enforcement to reckon with: the paid Informants.

Given institutional status, the Informants received 50 percent of criminal fines for turning in their neighbors. In so doing, they siphoned off monies which formerly were sent by the counties to the church parishes. (Did someone just mutter "church and state"?)

Haywood Hall is venerated for many splendors: its design, its gardens, its rare survival in its intended plan, and its role in Lafayette's visit to the city in 1825.

(A digression. Of the many descriptions of Lafayette's visit, some of the most pungent are by the General Assembly, which was trying to learn who had authorized what extravagances with the taxpayers' money while Le General was in town. It was a classic exercise in finger-pointing, most of them aimed in the direction of Treasurer Haywood and his house. It appears that the State officials had gladly eaten the hams and drunk the toasts, but none wanted the cost debited to his budget.)

But architecture and Lafayette aside, Haywood Hall has a storied past. It is standing proof of the maxim that a family cannot be considered great unless it has a few characters in its background who become "colorful" only as the passing decades put distance between their actions and today's society. Raleigh had enough Haywoods so that the presence of a few characters is inescapable.

And so in 1827, Haywood Hall became the focus of Raleigh's greatest scandal in its first 35 years as a city.

In that year Treasurer Haywood died after 40 years as the guardian of the State's purse. When grieving state officials looked in his office, they found that his official accounts were short by "$68,631 and some cents."

Officials prized open Haywood's locked desk and the State's "publick chest" and found— besides a shortfall of currency— worthless notes, counterfeit money, and piles of unexplained chits.

There were unauthorized loans to private individuals. On top of that, Haywood's son had been signing State checks in his father's name while the Treasurer had been ill. And Treasurer Haywood had failed to stay bonded according to law. All hell broke loose.

To explain the events which followed is simple but painful: the State sued the Haywood estate and won; when the Wake County sheriff dragged his feet on seizing Haywood property, the General Assembly passed a special law forcing him to act or to be personally liable; and over several years, auctions were held of the late Treasurer's lands and about 105 slaves.

Raleigh

The sales of Haywood property were frequent and detailed enough so that the State Printer finally made up a receipt book with the family's name on each page.

Left with her dower and little else, Haywood's widow Betsey proved resourceful and began to take in boarders at Haywood Hall. She sent solicitations to incoming members of the General Assembly, the very politicians whose presence had exhausted her in years past.

"Mrs. J. Haywood," the formal announcements read, "is prepared to accept Twenty Five or Thirty members of the Legislature. She assures all those who may honor her with their patronage, that no exertions shall be spared to make them comfortable.... Mrs. H. continues to receive Travellers and Boarders by the Week, Month or Year."

But if Betsey Haywood adjusted to reality, other Haywood relatives became despondent as the proceedings dragged on for five years.

One, upon paying a debt related to the State claims, referred to her banker as a "Shylock" who had "the avidity of a hungry constable." (Raleigh's constabulary received its income by the conviction rather than by salary.) She said the obligations "hovered over" her like a "Phantom from Hell" and asked her relatives to burn the satisfied note "1000 times over."

The Treasurer's son John, who had written the checks, was hounded by questions in inquiry after inquiry although they all found him blameless.

Another son, Willitt, writing about his own need to sell stock in the State Bank, said that "the situation of my father's pecuniary affairs... has long afflicted me. This is a heavy blow. I console myself in the conviction that it might have been a lot worse.... A few years more – say, 50 only – and what will it all be to us?" About son Alfred, the less said the better.

As for how Treasurer Haywood died in such a fix, the State's attorney wrote in 1832 that "the Treasurer kept no books."

Noting what he called Haywood's "mismanagement and neglect of economy in his private affairs," Gavin Hogg found that "the defalcations commenced at no very long time after his appointment" as Treasurer in 1787.

"It is pretty certain," Hogg wrote to Haywood's successor, "that except in the year 1819 when an investigation was asked by the Treasurer, no settlement was ever made between him and the State during the forty years he was in office."

(Haywood had requested an audit in 1819 because he said that "impressions and insinuations have gone abroad" concerning his honesty. A joint select committee reviewed the Treasurer's checks "from 1787 to date" and reported that the papers showed "the most minute accuracy" and that Haywood had "the most scrupulous integrity."

The committee concluded that "having found everything perfectly fair and honest about him," any person who questioned Haywood was acting out of "stupid ignorance or... still more detestable malice." The committee called the rumors "base and malicious calumnies." *The Niles Register* reported nationally that "the money matters of this State appear to be very carefully managed.")

Just so. And Haywood, even in declining health, could not let his office transfer to a successor. Armed with the committee's clean bill, he had to stay Treasurer and keep juggling balances until he died.

Hogg found that "there is much reason to believe that even on the scrutiny (of the audit) the true state of the Treasurer's accounts was not ascertained – How it was concealed from the Committee it would be painful and it is now unnecessary to conjecture."

(Among other documents in the State Archives are some warrants by which the Treasurer paid the whiskey bills of the committee which investigated him. He had the panache to pay the tabs with State funds.)

Hogg counseled the State that it was impossible to determine how much money Haywood had diverted in any given year. As a result, he said, it would be fruitless for the State to seek payment from the bonding firms for the scattered years in which Haywood had kept up his insurance policies.

When did Haywood get into the habit of "the frequent misappropriation of small sums to meet the expenses of his private affairs..."? At what point did he come to believe that the State should reimburse him for the steady stream of notables who passed through Haywood Hall?

William and Joseph Peace provided some clues. At the time, they owned a general store. (They had not yet gotten into the business of endowing colleges.) The Peace brothers kept ledgers which are not only meticulous but are legible. Treasurer Haywood's purchases are on record for 16 years, and no modern computer bank can expose a person's private business any more than those fragile ledgers.

Haywood bought items such as quarter casks of aged sherry which today would cost $1,030 each. He graduated to half casks. He bought $120 cheeses. He was fond of Imperial Tea until he switched to Hysong at the time of the War of 1812. He spent a great deal to clothe his family, particularly as his daughter began to mature. The household went through raisins and nutmeg as if they were cheap.

Haywood also had, hands down, the sorriest record of paying the Peace brothers of anyone in Raleigh. The Peaces routinely sued customers for far less than Haywood usually owed.

The Treasurer went for about a year once without paying on his account, charging new purchases all the while, until the Peaces delivered a

Raleigh

bill to Haywood Hall and the Treasurer remitted today's equivalent of $9,790. (Try that at Hudson Belk. And bear in mind that Haywood dealt with many other merchants and was acquiring an out-of-town plantation.)

A few months later, Haywood was $2,740 in arrears in today's money and the Peaces called at Haywood Hall again. About this time, Betsey Haywood began to visit the store in person to pay cash for such items as her daughter's shoes and "eight pairs of fine cotton stockings." After the last major payment, Haywood essentially stopped trading with the Peace brothers, although other relatives in Raleigh continued to shop there.

The ledgers indicate a man with a perpetual cash flow problem and a sporadic approach to paying bills. No one else in Raleigh – not prominent men such as Joseph Gales, or Willie Jones, or Seth Jones, or James Hinton, or William Boylan – had an account like the Treasurer's. Not even Archibald Murphey, the father of education in North Carolina who spent time in debtor's prison, had an account like Haywood's.

Neither did they have the key to the Publick Chest.

Those meticulous Peace brothers who documented Treasurer Haywood's purchases from their store also revealed a few things about themselves in their ledgers.

Keeping in mind that in early Raleigh there were no such things as tight financial regulation or income tax, some of their activities included:

• Usury. (That is, if one considers an effective interest rate of 101 percent per year to be usurious.) The Peaces charged this rate to people who borrowed money from them, including their own employees who might want advances for, say, Christmas. The rate did not apply to their regular customers.

• Charge-offs of personal expenses. Everything from ladies' umbrellas to liquor to the cost of "Supper at the State House" to payment of school tuition was run through the books of the store without reimbursement.

• Resourceful financing. When Capt. Theophilus Hunter got behind in his account in 1802, the Peace brothers accepted as partial payment a two-pound, five-shilling University lottery ticket. (Given the record of the lottery in not paying off, the brothers might as well have written down the debt. But perhaps they knew that.)

The name of Mason Scott heretofore has not graced any histories of Raleigh, but his experience – and the furor it caused – deserve some belated recognition.

Raleigh

Scott, described as "a handsome young man about 18 or 19 years old," was publicly hanged in Raleigh in 1820. In the process, Scott became the first known white person in North Carolina – and perhaps anywhere in the South – to be executed for murdering a slave.

According to the testimony, Scott, under the power of "that demon of destruction, Whiskey," was flashing a dagger around Raleigh's public houses one night. After he got himself tossed out of two bars, he decided to buy a nightcap at Mears' general store.

There Scott encountered a slave named Caleb; an argument developed, most likely when Caleb remarked that Scott was drunk; a boy tending the store ran outside for help; and Caleb ended up face down on the floor, stabbed through the back.

Raleigh police found Scott's "bloody dirk" outside the store and then apprehended Scott himself, who was sleeping it off on a bench near to the old Market-House. Scott had fresh blood on his clothes.

At his trial, Scott maintained that he remembered being at Mears' store and hearing "a terrible scream," but that he knew nothing else until he awoke the next morning in jail. Several defense witnesses said that Caleb had an "insolent" personality.

The jury was not persuaded by Scott's defense. The judge then sentenced him to death, denied him the benefit of clergy and ordered him jailed pending appeal.

Unfortunately for Scott, his appeal went to Chief Justice Taylor, whose remarks about uneven punishment were well known. Mason was denied a new trial. He tried once to escape and was seriously shot. He was confined for 15 "tedious months of an uncommonly severe winter and an excessively sultry summer," and then scheduled for the rope.

At that moment, Raleigh's white citizens became aghast at the precedent which would be set by Scott's hanging. A typeset petition circulated through the city asking for a full pardon from Governor John Branch.

The petition, signed by members of every prominent family in Raleigh, advanced all kinds of arguments as to why Mason should be freed outright: "the high and threatening tone and exultation already manifested by slaves"; the fact that Scott's 15 months in jail had been filled with "exceeding misery and mental desolation"; the allegation that Scott had gotten religion and "received from his Maker pardoning grace"; that one juror had lied when he said he was unprejudiced, another juror was incompetent, the store boy had been clearly hostile to Scott, and the judge had committed errors. Even the dead slave's owner signed the petition.

But Scott's attorneys did not rely on mass petitions alone.

They wrote privately to the Governor about "the very great doubt which exists in the minds of some of our best informed men, and which is daily gaining strength, respecting the *policy* of the law which puts the life of a slave and a freeman upon the same footing."

Praying for time – since the General Assembly convened in four weeks – the lawyers asked Branch to stay the execution so that they could more effectively make their case. "Justice is not satisfied," they wrote in a novel argument, "if the law is mistaken."

Branch granted a three-week reprieve and listened to the arguments.

Then, a week before the Legislature arrived, Mason Scott was stood up on a wagon, bound and fitted with a noose, and "the vehicle was driven from beneath the culprit. A very few seconds terminated his existence." Although Scott broke down sobbing and ministers had to deliver his final remarks for him, newspapers reported that "towards the close... he displayed astonishing firmness."

Raleigh's newspapers interpreted the execution of Scott as proof that "our scales of justice are impartially poised." They also delivered some more realistic advice to the town's young men about their need to avoid "strong passions and intemperate habits" brought on by liquor.

Mason Scott's chagrin when he realized he was nearing the end of his rope is even more understandable in view of another murder in Raleigh five years earlier.

John R. Cooke was an all-American lad who happened across a missing slave named Stephen on the Fourth of July, 1815. Drinking heavily, using a noose, sticks, whips and a wagon, Cooke and several cohorts ran the exhausted slave for an estimated 20 miles around town and into the country. There, in front of Stephen's owner, they tied the slave to a log, garroted him, and stomped him to death.

The murder was foul enough to get Raleigh some national publicity. "Such savage sport as these monsters made of the life of a human being," wrote the *American Magazine,* "would disgrace the veriest savages on earth." Cooke alone was convicted and sentenced to hang.

On execution day, Cooke was brought out of the downtown jail "seated on his coffin in a cart, and carried to the gallows: After remaining there some time and hearing the discourses of some pious men who attended him, a noose was put around his neck and the cap drawn over his eyes."

At that instant, the magazine reported, Cooke "now began seriously to think it was really intended to hang him, which he had not believed before." And Cooke cried out.

Who should then arrive on Fayetteville Street but the personal secretary to Governor William Miller (no relation to Barry Goldwater's running mate). He handed the sheriff not a reduction or commutation of Cooke's sentence, but a full pardon. Cooke got down from the cart and walked free.

(This must have been the incident mentioned by Dr. Battle in his 1892 centennial address. Speaking of the crowds, Battle said that "there were many expressions of disappointment on the part of those who had traveled many miles to witness the consummation." More information on hangings can be found in the chapter on entertainment.)

Rather than showing appreciation or even peeing in his pants, Cooke was reported as "getting drunk and exercising more than brutal rage upon a poor dumb beast (his horse) as soon as he left the gallows."

Governor Miller's pardon excited a second wave of national publicity about justice in the City of Oaks.

"We consider what you call *clemency* as an encouragement to murders," one reader observed.

"This was the first instance in which a white man had ever been convicted for killing a negro," a journal retorted, "and it would have been impolitic to hang him so unexpectedly."

Governor Miller was criticized for not explaining his reasons for the pardon, but critics did not see the petitions which poured in from Raleigh asking that Cooke be spared.

The Grand Jury which had indicted Cooke decided to petition Miller itself, writing that "taking the circumstances in view altogether, they do with sympathizing hearts petition your Excellency in behalf of an unfortunate fellow mortal."

Then came a series of affidavits, taken after the trial by William Boylan and William Peace, which tended to show that Cooke had been less responsible for the murder than others, including Samuel Bailey, the slave's owner.

Bailey swore that he had relied on the doctrine that Stephen's death was "no bodies loss but my own." He said he had agreed to Stephen's being tied to the log and felt that "what they did was done as a neighbourly act."

The owner added that "he never knew of any one being hung for killing their own negroes – and that if he could break two or three more of their damned necks he would be willing to be imprisoned for awhile."

Bailey also mentioned that Cooke and Co. "were intoxicated no doubt."

So Governor Miller, in light of the petitions and affidavits and a question as to intent, pardoned Cooke. He did so, he wrote, with "regard to humanity which is the boast of our law."

Raleigh

The law in early Raleigh had its barbaric aspects – what with hanging, the pillory, stocks, maiming, brandings, disfigurement, fire and stakes (and those were the *sanctioned* punishments, not freestyle productions such as tar and feathers) – but in a few areas, our ancestors' code was positively liberal by today's standards.

For example, if a suspect gave a sworn voluntary confession to the authorities, the statement could not be used in court without his permission.

If any official obtained a confession by using either promises or threats ("Now Theophilus, son, we can go easier on you if you cooperate."), the confession was inadmissible. And in such a situation, if the suspect decided to spill the beans and falsely implicated others, the officer who took the confession could be tried for suborning perjury.

Doctors in Raleigh were required to explain their bills in "plain English words," an early consumer protection measure.

Ministers were banned from serving in the Legislature and other public offices for as long as they retained a congregation.

The right of citizens in Raleigh to bear arms, when they were not out hunting, was specifically linked to defending the State. (As a result, most of the dirty work in the city was done with daggers and clubs.)

No one in Raleigh had to worry about being executed as a witch, but the law did have a provision relating to the practice of occult arts: whoever claimed to be a witch or spellbinder could be prosecuted as a common-law cheat.

Barratry – the crime of stirring up litigation – applied not only to lawyers, but to neighbors who went around fomenting discord. (Of course, in those days, ambulances were easier to chase.)

Adultery became a civil rather than a criminal matter, a condition which changed in later decades when hundreds of Raleighites were jailed for fornication and adultery.

A woman could not be indicted for being a "common bawd"; to run a "bawdy house" or to "haunt" one as a customer was only a misdemeanor.

The fine for selling bootleg liquor was one pence, and a newly-discovered still was not destroyed, but was simply added to the county tax rolls.

In short, it was an excellent legal underpinning for a State Capital.

In early Raleigh, the legal age for marriage was 12 for girls and 14 for boys.

However, young couples were entitled under the law to "disagree" once they reached their "years of discretion" and could declare their own marriages void.

For older married couples who wanted to call it quits, they retained not divorce attorneys, but lobbyists, because they needed a bill of divorce passed by the General Assembly. Petitions for legislative divorces from Raleigh usually had numerous co-signers who avowed that a husband was a drunk, a spendthrift, or had low morals or a social disease, or that the wife had "played the harlot."

Prenuptial agreements, far from being an unromantic modern innovation, existed from the beginning of the capital.

One such agreement, between Catherine Haywood and Edward Yarborough in 1852, provided that Yarborough "shall not, and will not, intermeddle with, or have any right in," the Haywood estate which was to settle on his bride.

In his final mitigating remarks to the judge before he was sentenced to hang in 1859, a Raleigh prisoner said that "he had been wrongly convicted – that if he had had one hundred dollars he would not have been convicted – and he concluded by saying 'give me liberty or give me death.'"

Trust thy employees.... Francois-Xavier Martin, in his manual of directions to the State's sheriffs in 1806, mentioned a particular duty which arose out of a case from Raleigh.

"It is clear," Martin wrote, "that if upon judgment to be hanged by the neck, till he is dead, the criminal not be thoroughly killed, the sheriff must hang him again.

"For the former hanging was no execution of the sentence, and if a false tenderness were to be indulged in such cases, a multitude of collusions might ensue."

The law in force in Raleigh in 1800 reached even the dead.
In the case of a suicide, the deceased was "punished by an ignominious burial in the highway, with a stake driven through the body."

Even that requirement showed leniency by the General Assembly compared to several years before, when the State would also seize the entire estate of a suicide victim, leaving the family potentially destitute.

Unless their remains have been disturbed, several citizens from early Raleigh are buried along present-day roads leading out of town to the east.

Raleigh

"None of that cheap booze, Rick, my body is a temple."

Those were not the exact words of James I. Boylan in the last minutes while he could still voice an opinion, but Boylan did refuse a free drink from Raleigh tavernkeeper Richard Hainds with the comment, "Damn your soul, you know I do not drink gin." Boylan then settled down with a free glass of rum.

Boylan had arrived at Hainds' pool room and grog house in 1824 in search of a card game. He "came in and observed that he had a ten dollar bill and that he would either win or lose that amount before he went away," a witness later recalled.

Hainds, who said he was afraid of being arrested since his establishment was within two blocks of police headquarters, told Boylan that he did not permit cards to be played in his bar.

Boylan responded with a recitation of illegal card games which had been played at Hainds' in the recent past. He punctuated his list with repeated claims that Hainds was "a damn liar." In the scuffle which followed the third such assertion, Hainds slit Boylan's throat with a keg knife.

"Oh my God, I am gone," were his last reported words.

This archetypical incident – all of the elements of crime in early Raleigh were present except for adultery – ended when Hainds' defense team convinced a jury that the diminutive defendant had been trying to keep the hulking Boylan from throttling him when he raked out with his knife. Hainds was branded with an "M" on his right hand.

The case would not be memorable ("A crime of early Raleigh passion, kind of messy and old-fashioned," a lyric might go) except for some details which appear almost as a footnote to the proceedings.

Several months before the slaying, Boylan had lost $17 to Hainds in a card game. The game was played at the pool room.

After badgering Boylan for weeks and receiving only $12, Hainds went to a Raleigh "peace justice" the morning of the killing and asked that a warrant be issued for the arrest of Boylan for failure to pay his debt.

(In early Raleigh, a man – but not a wife – could and did get jailed for nonpayment of debts. Bonds were set at the amount of the debt, plus storage and handling of the prisoner, and those saddled with a debt warrant remained in jail until the costs were paid.)

The peace justice signed the warrant. His compliance placed the city government squarely behind the collection of an illegal gambling debt.

Boylan evaded the Intendant all day. That night, he turned up at Haind's with his ten dollars, hoping to change his luck.

Raleigh

Governor James Martin may refuse to discuss his reasons for not pardoning a death-row prisoner, but Governor David Swain had no such reticence when he allowed the hanging of the man who burned down a square block of Fayetteville Street.

Benjamin F. Seaborn, a counting-room clerk, was convicted in 1833 of setting the fire in order to conceal a theft of money from his employer. The fire consumed not only buildings, but many of the deeds to property in Raleigh dating from 1792. Seaborn maintained his innocence. He claimed that he had only hidden the money for a slave named Harry who had been present at the inferno.

A jury in Fayetteville, where the trial was moved, believed none of it.

As is common to the crimes related in this history, the byplay is as compelling as the incident.

Seaborn's lawyers, for instance, used "every technical objection which cunning and ingenuity could suggest," as Governor Swain described it. Among other things, after Seaborn had petitioned for a change of venue because he could not get a fair trial in Wake County, his lawyers argued that the conviction should be reversed because the court had no power to move the proceedings.

No dice.

Seaborn also advanced what may well be the nation's first argument of reverse discrimination.

Writing from his cell, Seaborn told the Governor that he had seen a number of slaves get arrested for capital offenses, only to have their masters "carry them off" from the jail without so much as a trial. "At least allow me the chance as Negroes has had," wrote Seaborn, who promised that in return for a pardon, he would "goe away" from North Carolina and never come back.

Swain received several petitions on Seaborn's behalf. One asked for Seaborn's "perpetual banishment," which the authors felt would somehow comfort "the agonies of his aged and heart-broken mother whose days may end with his."

The Governor answered that "although the convict is an obscure individual... the example humble as it may be is necessary and must be made... for the safety of the community."

Swain explained that "a pardon would clearly prove the truth of the maxim that mercy to the guilty is cruelty to the community."

He asked Seaborn's attorney, Henry Potter, to tell his client that "no prospect of mercy remains for him on earth and that his best and eternal interest requires that his attention and his hopes should be directed to happiness beyond the grave."

The pleas continued. Seaborn, who still professed his innocence, wrote that "if I can't make men believe it, it does me good to know that God does know it to be the truth and nothing else." He stated that: "God knows the guilty from the innocent."

Simultaneously, Governor Swain began to receive reports that Seaborn had been born again.

Potter, who wrote to the Governor that although he was "at all times slow to credit professions of faith made under such circumstances," he was persuaded that Seaborn was sincere. He had warned his client about "the awful state of that man who should die with a lie in his mouth," Potter said, but Seaborn "repeatedly and solemnly" declared his innocence.

Six ministers from Fayetteville agreed and wrote Swain that the prisoner had had "a change of heart" and asked for mercy. Swain replied that at a minimum, Seaborn showed moral guilt by not informing on the slave Harry until after he had been arrested.

Even if Seaborn were only the accomplice and Harry went free, the Governor wrote, "there is no good reason why justice should be disappointed of both of her victims." (A "victim" of justice; it has an interesting ring to it.)

Meanwhile, Seaborn tried to find corroboration that Harry was the culprit. His defense team came up with the name of a Raleigh prostitute. The Governor interviewed the woman "rigidly" but advised Potter that "she is a courtezan and of course her statements (are) liable to great suspicion." Nor was her information particularly helpful.

The last letter concerning Benjamin Franklin Seaborn, aged 27, was from Potter on May 30, 1834.

"Seaborn is just now launched into eternity," he wrote to the Governor from Fayetteville. "It is evident now, awful as the fact may be, that he lied to the Holy Ghost."

In his final minutes of life, sensing that no pardon was forthcoming, Seaborn wrote a full confession. The clerk had set the fire with a candle. Harry was exonerated. "It was the devil that made me do it and nothing else but the devil," he wrote.

The Fayetteville newspapers lamented the attendance of so many females at the hanging and warned boys that "it is the first act of minor turpitude which is to be avoided, as leading to innumerable others."

As Seaborn was being carted off for burial, Potter wrote to Swain that "his conversion was worse than an empty profession – it was as hypocritical as that of Judas."

Raleigh

In one of the earliest recorded lawsuits involving injuries resulting from the collision of two vehicles, lawyers in Wake County Superior Court sought damages in 1838 for a woman who was knocked off the road by a man in a buggy.

The judge rejected what he termed the "English rule of the road" – which at that time required drivers to keep to the right – and set down the standard for Raleigh. "In this country," the judge held, "every man has the right to travel in any part of the road he pleases."

None of Raleigh's chroniclers ever unearthed a duel in the capital's past.

But in 1838, if the city missed having one, it was only by about two minutes.

In fact, the *Microcosm* newspaper even described the incident in 1838 as a duel, with all of the attendant editorial clucking about how degenerate the practice was. (Degenerate, that is, unless the newspaper was trying to increase its circulation; it would splay reports of duels in other cities across its front pages like they were homicides in today's Durham.)

Two slaves in 1838 began arguing over the possession of 50 cents. They challenged each other to a duel and went, pistols in hand, to the woods at the city cemetery.

Their owners, hearing about the impending gunfire, were alarmed not only about the potential loss of property, but also about how the slaves had managed to obtain weapons. Just as the duel was about to begin, the owners arrived at the cemetery. Using their own guns, they ordered the slaves and their appointed seconds to change the nature of the contest.

Each slave was given a whip. Each one was threatened by his owner with death if he struck the other in the face. Under the owners' rules, the two alternately thrashed each other, until their anger was spent. It reportedly took 39 lashes each.

The *Microcosm* coined the term "cowbat" for the affray. It endorsed the practice because of "its great variety in the choice of weapons... simple hickory, strap, horse-whip, coach-whip, wagon-whip, cowhide and cat of nine tails."

I can explain, Senatuh, why that hammer cost $279.

The State of North Carolina set up a Board of Claims in the Capitol in 1861 to try to assess the tide of invoices which hit the new government in the weeks after secession.

Raleigh

Among the claims from Raleigh, the board discovered instances of double-billing, profiteering, and bills which "intermingled articles allowed and disallowed." The board also found that certain local claimants had taken advantage of the Confederacy's chaos by making repeated sales up the chain of command, so that a unit of 100 men might end up with 300 blankets.

Others in Raleigh "ignored Board rules" by first donating space in their homes to quarter soldiers, and then trying to charge the Army for room and board. Their proposed rates were high.

Most of the flim-flams did not work. Out of the initial $250,000 in claims, the Board allowed $49,390.26.

We have met the enemy and they are us.... As the Confederacy began to suspend the right of *habeas corpus* in order to snatch every man who could walk and thrust him into service, it was left to the N.C. Supreme Court to protect the rights of Raleigh citizens against their new government.

In ordering the release of one J.C. Bryan from Camp Holmes, the Court questioned what the Confederacy was doing.

"Every recent alteration of the Federal constitution by the Confederate states," the Court said, "is made with the purpose to contract the powers of the general government and enlarge those of the states."

Under no circumstances put this in a campaign commercial....
In 1873, a man named Frank B. apparently murdered Joseph Frazier at Milburnie east of Raleigh.

"B. then came at once to Raleigh," a newspaper related, "where he closeted himself in a room in the Yarborough Hotel. Here he remained 24 hours with his attorneys when he was advised to leave for points unknown.

"This he did and from that day until this, B. has never been seen or heard of."

For those who imagine that crimes caused by drug addiction are a new phenomenon, or are limited to persons at the fringe of society, consider a case in Raleigh in 1885.

A prominent citizen was arrested and charged with writing a series of worthless checks and with receiving stolen property. In the hearings and trials which followed and decorated the city's newspapers with the defendant's name, it became apparent that the accused was addicted to morphine.

As Judge Walter Clark expressed it, the defendant was "under the influence of the morphine habit and... would do anything to procure means to gratify it."

The prisoner had the indignity of having a member of his own family plead him as being insane; then having a jury *de lunatico inquirendo* agree; then being wrested from the Asylum for a new trial which resulted in a ten-year sentence in the Penitentiary; and finally, in a third proceeding, being held sane "by a preponderance of the evidence" and sentenced to two years of hard labor on the Wake County roads.

In the course of the trials, Judge Clark observed that it does not require a psychiatrist to diagnose a person as insane, particularly if the expert hedges in his testimony.

"Men every day in all their dealings with others more or less take into consideration the mental capacity of those with whom they deal," he wrote. And many of the defendant's own witnesses "did not believe that he was crazy." Others speculated that if he were insane, his case was only monomania – that he was "insane on particular subjects."

It all made terrific newspaper reading. It would be appropriate to say that the episode ruined the prominent citizen's life, except that his morphine habit and the approach of the authorities in judging and treating it had much more to do with the outcome than did the publicity.

As any observer of Southern religion knows, Messrs. Bakker and Swaggart are by no means the first preachers to get caught with their figurative pants down.

Raleigh had its own clerical sex scandal in 1889, and in sheer ferocity, it made latter-day cases look like misdemeanors. At the time it was agreed that the incident was as close as Raleigh ever came to a lynching.

The city's newspapers reported one morning that Father J.J. Boyle, in charge of the Sacred Heart Church, had been indicted for the rape of a 17-year-old congregant. The scene was upstairs in the church rectory.

(Unlike Raleigh's newspapers in 1889, which salivated over half of their front pages about the case, this history will not identify the victim. Nor will any sport be made over the fact that she was also the church's part-time organ player.)

The case proceeded on a schedule tighter than Amtrak. Father Boyle was convicted and sentenced to be hanged. His automatic appeal to the State Supreme Court succeeded on what the populace believed were technicalities. In his retrial, Boyle was acquitted and caught the 1 a.m. train out of Raleigh an hour after the verdict. Less than a year had elapsed.

The proceedings in the trial are intriguing and instructive.

For instance, there was the language of the indictment: "J.J. Boyle, a man not having the fear of God before his eyes, but being moved and seduced by the instigation of the Devil...." It reads unlike most capital indictments in Wake County and is a throwback to another century and place.

Or, for anyone interested in fairness by the news media, consider their "standards" with regard to presumption of innocence.

The News & Observer, in its first report of the priest's arrest, printed that "Father Boyle it is stated has for several weeks been indulging heavily in drink and for the last week especially he has been constantly under the influence of intoxicants. His fast living has for some time past been a source of concern to members of his church."

But the *N&O*'s coverage was balanced compared to that of the *State Chronicle*. Josephus Daniels opened his news reports of the arrest with the headline, "HANGING TOO GOOD – For the Wolf Among Us in Sheep's Clothing – Father Boyle Ought to Petition the Pope to Give Him a Halter So He Could go Hang Himself."

Even in the face of such reporting, Boyle was refused a change of venue.

In the second trial, Boyle's defense attorneys attacked the victim's character as aggressively as anything complained about 100 years later. (The priest had admitted having intercourse with her but maintained that it was consensual.)

"She knew what she was doing," the defense proclaimed. "Every time she went to that room she went there with as thorough an understanding of what she was going there for as if it had been written down and she had put her signet to it."

In terms reminiscent of Jerry Lee Lewis' discussion of a child bride, Boyle's lawyers asked the jurors to "look at her. She is no girl. She is a woman, with all of a woman's attractions." (This was beside the point; among other things, the age of consent in North Carolina at the time was ten.)

Finally, the prosecutor was moved to shout that "it is high time some voice were raised in behalf of this poor outraged little girl. Three attorneys have been engaged for six hours in denouncing her."

As the second trial began to raise more doubts than the first, Daniels at the *Chronicle* turned up the heat.

"So vile a man as Boyle ought to die," one editorial put it.

Daniels wrote: "with his breath foul of liquor... (Boyle) had hypocritically preached the gospel. There is no sin under the sun so damning and so blasting as for one who claims to be an ambassador for Christ to use his holy office to worm himself into the confidence of an unsuspecting young girl."

The newspaper published a missive from Granville County; the anonymous writer urged Raleigh to "send Boyle to Oxford. Our famous white oak is still flourishing." Daniels demurred at this suggestion, holding that the accused should "die legally." But a clamor began to get Boyle no matter what the second jury decided.

Boyle's attorneys offered a down-home defense against the liquor allegations. Responding to the testimony of a train porter, who said the priest had ordered milk punch ("And make it a strong one.") on the morning of the incident, one lawyer argued that "drunkards do not drink milk punches.

"They take whiskey as near straight as they can get it, and if they want to weaken it, they take a little water."

The defense also alleged that Boyle himself was a victim, in this case of religious prejudice in Raleigh. "It is unfortunate that this man should have been a Catholic," Boyle's counsel said. "Because I feel that if he had been a Protestant he would not be on trial here." (Maybe yes, maybe no, but Catholics all over Raleigh could agree with the lawyer's first sentiment.)

Prosecutors openly played the religious card. They told jurors that since Boyle admitted violating his oath of chastity made before God, nothing else he said or did could be trusted. And Daniels chipped in with the information that Boyle had "expelled himself" as a priest, requiring no further action by the Catholic Church. (It was a tactic of "use his Catholicism if you want to, but if that bothers you, treat him as a pariah.")

"Don't try him as a priest," the defense summarized. "Don't try him as a Catholic. Try him as a man."

The defense introduced 14 new witnesses who reported that the victim had been light-hearted until her father got wind of the episode. But the defense did not challenge the testimony of the examining physician on the condition of the girl.

In a description which may seem quaint to gynecologists today, the doctor said that "she presented just the appearance he would expect to find in a bride on the second or third morning after marriage."

Nor would any newspaper accurately quote the physician. It was one thing to call for Boyle to be hanged before a word of testimony was given, but when it came to printing the word "breast" the editors substituted "chest." (Well, it *was* 1889.)

According to the *N&O*, J.J. Boyle awaited the verdict of the second jury "as cool and unconcerned as any disinterested spectator." When he was found innocent of rape, he shook hands with his attorneys and looked around for his suitcase. He did not say, "Thank God."

Raleigh

Immediately beneath its final story, which described Boyle making tracks in the night for the depot, someone at the *N&O* placed a short item. "Today is the beginning of Holy Week," it started.

Tom Jones – what a splendid name for the unordained preacher who was hanged in 1900 as Raleigh's only mass murderer.

Jones, who described himself as a "storefront 'xhorter," had been summoned one night to the cabin of Ella Jones to discuss the paternity of her infant daughter.

There was evidence, as the State Supreme Court remarked, that Jones had gone beyond the confines of preaching and "had been too intimate with the deceased; that he had gotten a child upon her."

Jones went to the cabin intending to negotiate. He told friends that he had offered his lover $2 per month if she would keep quiet. The negotiations ended when Jones took an axe to her and her oldest daughter, then threw kerosene onto her other five sleeping children, and then lit it.

Two of the little girls escaped; one proved to be a very competent witness at Jones' trial.

Once again, accounts of the trial for the six murders reveal much more than the circumstances of the crime.

The speed of the proceedings was impressive. Jones (who was identified by the ever-restrained *N&O* as "the negro who killed Ella Jones") was brought to trial eight days after the bodies were pulled from the ashes. Less than six months elapsed between the murders and his execution, including time for his unsuccessful appeal.

Equally impressive were the efforts of Jones' defense counsel, who first met his client on the day the trial began.

The defense first tried to obtain leniency on the grounds that Preacher Jones was a half-wit. Not so, said the prosecution, which sponsored witnesses who "testified that his mind was as good as ordinary negroes," as the *N&O* explained it.

Next, the defense sought to prove that Jones was delusional.

"One time I asked him why he tried to preach," offered a defense witness. "He told me that the Lord called him. He said he was going along a path and the Lord called 'Tom'; and he responded, 'Here am I'; and the Lord said, 'Go preach.'"

Cross-examined by the prosecution as to whether "you have known other men who claimed they had been called to preach," the witness responded, "Yes, but none who said they'd had a personal conversation with the Lord on the subject."

Raleigh

(That was too much for Atlas Chavis, clerk of the Raleigh church which had denied Jones any formal credentials. Stating that Jones lacked the mental faculties for investiture, Chavis observed that "Well, he could teach up the New Testament right lively, but he didn't know much about the Old Testament. The boys in the neighborhood made Thomas preach and made much sport of him."

Jones was about to find out what the Old Testament meant at Exodus 21:25.

If the accused (who also proselytized under the aliases of Thomas Farrar, and Pharoah) ever stood a chance of peaceful confinement at the Insane Asylum, his own defense attorney probably foreclosed it. The transcript read:

"These victims – one of them his own blood – were sent to the Shadowy Realm by that *thing...*" He pointed to his client. "...and he has not denied it. I stand by him today because I believe him to be a fool and that being thus irresponsible, his execution would be a shame on Wake County. I stand by him and shall do so until his feet have lost hold on the scaffold."

Fortunately for the attorney, he did not make good on his vow to escort Preacher Jones to the gallows.

"Not less than 1,000 requests (for admission to see the hanging) were made and refused" by the sheriff, wrote the *N&O*. The newspaper reported that on the morning of the execution, "windows, tops of houses, telephone poles, trees and everything that gave a vantage point, bore human fruit."

When the trap door dropped, the crowd closed in on Jones' twitching, gasping body.

"The deputies tried to send the crowd back," reported the *N&O*, "but they paid no attention, and crowded and pushed closer. One man wanted to touch the body, and they were all pushing and struggling to get near to the dangling turning body. One man had a kodak and took picture after picture."

Eventually Jones' corpse was taken to a local undertaker who had paid the prisoner $10 for it. (Jones used the proceeds to buy $4 worth of meals and ice water from a downtown restaurant, designated $2 for the poor, and gave the remainder to his cellmates.)

By the time the story was reprised in 1903, as part of an article in the *N&O* about historic murders in Raleigh, Jones was at last elevated to the status of a licensed minister. The author of that article also digressed to express regret that J.J. Boyle had not been strung up in 1889.

The city guardhouse, the workhouse, Central Prison – all of them had deplorable conditions at the turn of the century. So to make it a

Raleigh

clean sweep, reflect on this petition from 1904, asking the county commissioners to improve the jail between Fayetteville and Salisbury streets.

"There is often not sufficient room for all prisoners to lie down at the same time," wrote a committee chaired by Elvira E. Moffitt.

"There are no beds or bedding in the men's prison, prisoners lying in the iron floor of the cages, be their confinement a week or a year; children from ten years old and upward are confined with the most hardened criminals; no provision for bathing, other than the basins in the cells, is made and the prison is... infested with vermin; the two cells for women are living graves five and a half by six and a half feet...."

The defendant would not have been a woman if she had stood that." Justice Walter Clark issued that dictum in overturning the conviction of a Raleigh woman in 1901 who bashed her husband's creditor with "her little boy's baseball bat."

The creditor had barged into a Mrs. Goode's house with the intention of repossessing a bed which her husband had bought on time payment. Cursing the woman, he went into the bedroom and, as Justice Clark described it, "laid his profane hands on the paraphernalia of her bed and began to throw back the bed covers and to lift the mattress, all of which would speedily have gone, of course, upon the floor."

The Supreme Court's opinion traced the principle that "one's home is one's castle" from early England clear up to 1901 on South Street.

Clark then observed that although Mrs. Goode "knew naught of legal lore," she had "an instinctive sense of her rights, and, by means of the wooden wand touched to the back of the (creditor's) head, she communicated electrically to his brain the same conception more effectually than if she had read to him the above citations."

Preacher Tom Jones may hold the distinction of being Raleigh's mass murderer, but the Lewis brothers hold a related title: they seem to be the only duo from town to be executed for a single crime.

As court records make it seem almost commonplace in 1824, Lemuel Lewis, Oliver Lewis and their friend Elizabeth Scott spent one Sunday afternoon getting drunk over a jug of whiskey. A stranger happened by and Lem challenged him to wrestle. When the stranger refused, the Lewises rushed him.

It was a one-fall match. The Lewises finished with knives what Elizabeth Scott had failed to accomplish with a tree limb to the back of the stranger's skull.

Lemuel Lewis was tried and convicted first, and despite some of his testimony against his own brother, he was hanged publicly. The execution was enough of a spectacle that it caused the *Register* to comment on it.

"It was with unpleasant feelings," editor Joseph Gales wrote, "that we saw the *hundreds* who had collected to view a fellow creature suffering the penalty of crime.

"Amongst the number collected, we regret to add that a vast proportion of *females* of every age and colour, in gay attire and with thoughtless levity, eagerly sought an opportunity to witness the separation of a soul from its earthly tabernacle....

"It is still more revolting," Gales continued, "to state the fact that many thoughtless men returned from the scene of misery in a state of complete intoxication."

Gales, who concluded that "drunkenness, swearing, sabbath-breaking and gaming" were the "strongest links in the chain which leads to destruction," argued that public executions were no deterrent to crime and that the state needed a penitentiary. (He had argued for one since 1803.)

After literally hearing the city's hurrahs over Lemuel's hanging, the other two defendants sought and won a change of venue to Franklin County.

A month later Elizabeth Scott was convicted there of felony manslaughter. When she successfully pleaded for the benefit of clergy, she was not hanged, but was branded with the ubiquitous "M" in her right palm.

Oliver Lewis, who was in the courtroom when Elizabeth was "burnt with the iron," decided that he liked his chances in Franklin County little better than in Wake. Again, he won a change of venue, this time to Warrenton.

Whatever else can be said about the quality of decision-making in 1824, there was no whining about drawn-out trials. Within the space of eight weeks, Ollie Lewis was convicted, appealed on technicalities to the Supreme Court, was turned down, and was hanged. The third venue was not the charm.

Petitioners on behalf of youthful offenders from Raleigh had every reason besides their age to try to spring them from the Work-House out on New Bern Avenue.

"Hanging up by the thumbs is the regular mode of punishment," one complaint about the Work-House read during the 1870s. (A subsequent inquiry by the Chamber of Commerce found that no inmate was suspended for longer than three hours, and that such measures were "customary.")

"He tied me up, bucked and gagged me, and put a bayonet in my mouth," read another complaint by a prisoner with reference to a Work-House guard. (The inmate had inadvertently set the jail on fire. In this instance, the Chamber's investigators found that the trauma to his mouth was inconsistent with a "deliberate" stabbing.)

When they were not tied up or skewered, the eight or so inmates at the Work-House made bricks. They averaged about 75,000 bricks each month during the 1870s. The record was 120,000 bricks fired in a month in which the Work-House contained only four inmates.

From the account books of the institution, the prisoners ate rations similar to those of Confederate soldiers towards the end of the war: bacon, corn meal, flour, molasses, and coffee, with occasional field peas to balance out the food groups.

(The Chamber of Commerce found these meals to be nutritious. It closed its report on conditions at the Work-House by saying that allegations of whippings could be dismissed because they had been "furnished by negroes.")

Up to the time of his departure, he was a teacher in the Sunday School... and was regarded as a thorough and conscientious Christian."

But then, one Saturday in 1888, the above-mentioned cashier of the State National Bank of Raleigh stuffed tens of thousands of dollars into a suitcase. Accompanied by the bank's president, he caught the train for Canada. It was not a holiday and the money was not their own.

The defalcation was enough to break SNBR, which locked its doors to all but bank examiners when the theft was detected three days later. What remained was a tangle of forged notes, bad checks, unsecured wire transfers, and missing currency.

Estimates varied as to just how much loot the pair had stolen. As speculation rose – from $40,000 in cash on up to $300,000 – rumors circulated about other banks being stung (several were, for as much as $10,000 each).

The bank's board of directors, in concert with a Federal receiver, first advised depositors that they would be paid in full, then at 75 cents on the dollar, and then at not less than 50 cents on the dollar. Many persons in Raleigh developed a keen interest in seeing the pair tracked down. (Oddly enough, they had left untouched all notes and valuables of their depositors.)

Few in Raleigh agreed as to motive. The bank president, Charles Cross, had bought "an expensive jewelry set" on Fayetteville Street the morning he absconded, announcing that he was going to marry a mystery woman from Greensboro.

Raleigh

Yet a bank porter, who toted the suitcase for the thieves until he became fearful in New York and caught a train home, said that there was no woman in sight. He volunteered that Cross and cashier Samuel White "were a'drinking all the way."

All that was certain was that Cross and White had fled only days before an audit.

Through swift work by Raleigh's police chief and mayor, descriptions of the fugitives were wired across the continent and they were immediately spotted in Toronto. Police arrested them on a single count of forgery – one of the few crimes for which they could be extradited. Cross and White had eluded the law for less than a week. Among the property checked in at police headquarters in Canada was nearly $25,000 in cash.

Back in Raleigh, Cross and White's lawyers tried to get them out of jail. (Edenton Street Methodist Church had a new Sunday School teacher.)

In an unsuccessful effort to move the trial into the Federal courts, their lawyers admitted to the defendants' forgery, but said it had been done solely for the purpose of deceiving a national bank examiner.

Once at trial, defense attorneys argued that the bank had been *in extremis* since before Cross and White got involved with it.

In his testimony, White said that "he found the bank was seriously crippled when he went into it.... He said the first statement he signed as cashier was a false one."

Cross recounted an early trip he had made to Washington to see the Comptroller of the Currency, "who informed me that a receiver ought to have been appointed many years ago to wind up the affairs of the bank."

The testimony took an ugly turn. One prisoner was the son-in-law, and the other a brother-in-law, of the deceased founder of the bank. Defense attorneys began to grill family members about their own knowledge of the bank's condition and alleged that Cross and White had been made patsies.

Simultaneously, Cross and White were testifying that they had cooked the books of the bank in an effort to preserve the reputation of the founder's family. They swore they had slipped their own money into the failing bank.

The jury was out for several days and then convicted Cross and White on two of five criminal counts. (While the jury was deliberating, the *N&O* published its numerical division, the names of the "hold outs," and speculation on venality by the uncertain members of the panel.)

The two received a "touching" presentencing hearing. White's wife and children were brought to the front row.

"In the densely crowded room," the *N&O* reported, "there were those who had befriended the defense and others who had bitterly denunciated them, but at this moment there was not a dry eye in the house."

Cross received six years and White five years of "hard labor on the county roads." (So much for coddling white-collar criminals back then.)

In a last statement, Cross maintained that "I came out of the bank without a dollar of the proceeds."

The State National Bank of Raleigh never reopened.

(Postscript: Governor T.M Holt commuted the sentences of Cross and White to the time they had served on January 22, 1891. The Governor wrote that "it was an attempt to save a sinking bank by unwarranted means.... In a fit of desperation and failure they succumbed to the temptation and fled carrying money with them belonging to others.... The former character of these men...show (sic) that they do not belong to the criminal class in the ordinary acceptance of the term.")

Occasionally, the residents of Raleigh received welcome messages from the Governor – commutations of criminal sentences.

A few from Governor Robert B. Glenn in 1907 are touching:

"The judge having recommended pardon," Glenn wrote about a thief, "and the Governor of South Carolina having written a letter as to his previous good character, sentence is commuted to 14 months and 21 days, provided (the) defendant leaves the State."

(Low-level radioactive waste has not been the State's only export to South Carolina.)

Or consider this commutation of a sentence for assault with intent to commit rape: "He is a very old man and the prosecutrix turns out to be a very bad woman."

Or this last commutation by Glenn of a prisoner who had been sentenced to two years on the Wake County roads for obtaining goods on false pretenses: "This was a little boy in knee trousers," the Governor wrote. "I bind him out to a good man."

Dead Horses Wheresoever They May Be

As of 1800, the residents of Raleigh had not yet been permitted to vote in a municipal election.

When the General Assembly chartered the city in 1795 and spelled out every detail of its laws, it also named the first officials. But unlike other new municipal charters, Raleigh's act gave the initial commissioners lifetime terms of office. So what was there to vote about?

(The Legislature felt that Raleigh was as much the seat of state government as it was a city and that the new residents, well, they might not be trustworthy for a while. Essentially, Raleigh and Washington City were in a paternalistic lockstep.)

But what if Raleigh *had* held an open, free election in 1800?

No; any election in that year would have been neither open nor free. White male landowners (meaning "Protestant"), whether they lived in the city or held long leases on property in the capital, could vote. Everyone else was disenfranchised. In fact, the major debate concerning elections in Raleigh was not whether more people should be enfranchised, but whether corporations should be allowed to vote proportionate to their taxes.

As for elections being free, a poll tax was extracted from the excruciatingly small class which was entitled to vote. (Students need to remember these facts the next time some would-be oligarch invokes the memory of the founding fathers.)

If the voting restrictions of 1800 applied in Raleigh today, fewer than 7 percent of the city's residents could choose their mayor. (Come to think of it, that is close to the percentage that *does* choose the mayor. Avery Upchurch might be in for life.)

Raleigh

Early Raleigh had no running water or fire brigades, only a mandate that every house which had a well be equipped with a wooden bucket. Citizens converged on a fire whenever the bell at the State-House sounded.

As a result, the city would periodically burn block by block.

The fires seemed to originate most often in privies, where homeowners liked to dump live coals from their fireplaces.

A fire in early Raleigh was free to spread until volunteers detonated a strategic house in its path in order to create a firebreak. (One house at Morgan and Wilmington streets was blown up, rebuilt, and blown up again in a subsequent fire. With that, the owner moved.) Occasionally firefighters would mix water with the city's dust and throw mud at a burning wall, or else use a proverbial wet blanket to try to stifle the flames.

What usually stopped a fire was coincidence: the wind happened to be blowing in a favorable direction.

Given the fact that the State-House and the octagonal floor of the first Market-House were the only structures in Raleigh containing brick other than chimneys, and they were wood-framed, it is a miracle that any early houses survived long enough to fall prey to developers.

Street maintenance – the task of opening new streets on Raleigh's original grid and trying to keep the existing ones in repair – was the city's chief governmental task for at least a century after its founding.

By 1800, only 19 blocks were largely developed. Purchasers of other lots out of the original 276 clamored for openings to their own property. (Some of them had a long wait; the last street laid out by surveyor William Christmas was not cut through until the 1930s.)

Many streets, starting at the State-House, were surfaced with a blend of mud, stump fragments and manure. The General Assembly seemed more amused than the residents of Jones Street when that right-of-way ignited and smoldered like compost before being extinguished.

Because many residents of early Raleigh resorted to finger-pointing when it came to paying for street maintenance, the city fell back on an old-fashioned, off-balance sheet financing technique: forced labor.

The average able-bodied male, including any who lived within a quarter-mile of the city limits, was required to work the streets unless he could hire a substitute or else assign slaves to do the work. (Joel Lane relied on both techniques.)

Men in Raleigh actually subsisted by acting as rotating substitutes for road work and other ungentlemanly duties. The Legislature had to redraw the first political wards to be laid off in the city because of a loophole which left the major north-to-south streets unmaintained.

Each evening at ten o'clock," an historian recalled about the early 1800s, "the bell was rung by the city watch, as ten was the curfew hour when honest people were expected to be abed."

Although all real property taxes in Raleigh in 1799 totalled only $42.04 for the year, 70 of the original lot owners were cited as delinquents. Not that the late-paying founders were charity cases; most of them were from out of town and received their mail late.

In 1799, the city received more revenue from tavern licenses and court costs than it did from *ad valorem* taxes. The average property tax bill in the capital was 6.3 cents per person.

City government may face legal hurdles today when it tries to cooperate with private enterprise on joint ventures, but such was not the case when the city was founded.

In 1802, for instance, the General Assembly authorized Raleigh's commissioners to cut and split into rails the pine trees which stood on state-owned land near the old race-ground. (Raleigh sponsored horse racing.)

The city commissioners were instructed to take the lumber and "enclose the race-ground with a good fence," and to lease the track for up to seven years to the highest private bidder. Revenues from the lease, as well as from the sale of excess firewood, were to go to improving the hazardous path to the track.

Over the generations, Raleigh's example of the race-ground – an ancestor of financing for facilities such as the Hubert H. Humphrey Metrodome in Minnesota – stands up well.

But after the collapse of bonds for Raleigh's first system of wooden water pipes in the 1820s and the railroad bond scandals which placed the City in default after the Civil War, legal barriers were created to prevent the city and other local governments in North Carolina from consorting too closely with private enterprise.

Those barriers, as State Treasurer Harlan Boyles can attest, stood far longer than the racetrack fence. They still delineate what the city can do today when it wants the private sector as a partner.

Our free-enterprising founding fathers did *what?*
At least once each year, the county government set prices for all rooming houses, meals, drinks, bottled liquor, corn, horse feed and even nails in the city. Those who deviated from the posted price were fined.

And citizens object to recent increases in city license tag fees.... In 1802, the yearly duty on a two-horse phaeton was $9 – an amount equal to $150 today.

(It appears to have been a tax-the-rich scheme by the founding fathers. The annual tax on a one-horse "chair", or buggy, was $2 per year, or just under $35 in today's currency.)

As early as 1813, the citizens of Raleigh had vociferous disagreements about how and where the city commissioners should intervene in personal affairs.

The *Star* urged the city to require that all wooden roofs be painted with black lead before the city burned down. Its editor claimed to speak for many in suggesting that "if our commissioners would take the subject under consideration we believe they would better promote the welfare of the community than by passing Ordinances regulating the deportment of Pigs."

The Raleigh Academy in 1818 decided it was time to insure its campus of two frame buildings, a preparatory schoolhouse, and a 22-foot-long chapel.

Its experience tells much about the value – even in the absence of fires – of the fire protection today provided by the city government.

The cost of insuring the Academy against Raleigh's periodic blazes was $27.50 per year, a premium which equaled one percent of the estimated value of the structures. (The Eagle Fire Company of New York billed the Academy an additional fifty cents for a copy of the policy.)

Consider for a moment the conditions which prevailed when the Eagle boys insured the premises: the Academy was built of untreated timber; it used fireplaces and stoves for heating and cooking, many of them under the charge of teenagers; there was no fire alarm other than the bell on the State-House; fireproofing materials and devices were generations away; and what with inadequate water and only a volunteer bucket brigade, Raleigh lacked effective fire protection. The sole positive factor was that Raleigh had none of the congested tenements of the North.

Raleigh

Now consider conditions in Raleigh today: the city has building and electrical codes; fire-retardant materials used in construction; smoke detectors and sprinklers; an emergency alarm and communications system; adequate water for its fire hydrants; and a full-blown fire department. Among municipalities, Raleigh's fire insurance rating is Class 3, about as good as one can expect. Many of the improvements are paid through the city budget.

So how do today's fire insurance premiums compare to those of 1818?

Under the approved schedule of the N.C. Rate Bureau, the cost of insuring a frame house in Raleigh, solely from a loss due to fire, is about 15.2 percent of what it was in 1818. (Put differently, if there had been any $100,000 houses in 1818, the cost of fire insurance would have been $1,000 per year; coverage of a $100,000 house in Raleigh today costs about $152 per year.)

Yet despite that $848 annual savings from one aspect of municipal services, it remains popular to complain about city taxes.

Candidates for today's city council may spend thousands of dollars in pursuit of their elections, but in early Raleigh, there was a policy of "serve or else".

Many commissioners who were elected under the city's 1821 charter were write-ins who had given no thought to running for office, much less campaigning.

The fine for any who declined to serve was $10, a penalty which was raised to $25 in 1857. Several men paid it rather than be city commissioners. Because of Raleigh's emerging regulations on conflict of interest, they felt that the small income to commissioners would not offset the money they would sacrifice when they were forced to stop selling materials to the city.

After a fire in 1824 which destroyed five buildings and could easily have taken half of downtown, Raleigh's commissioners decided to set aside a fire district.

In the downtown "combustible zone," as it was called, the commissioners ordered a halt of new construction of bakeries and forges. Existing ones were permitted to keep operating.

"Provisions were long since made for a Fire Company," the *Register* reported about the 1824 fire, "but nothing of the kind appeared." Nearly an hour after flames were reported at a blacksmith's shop – and Raleigh in 1824 was no more than eight blocks across in any direction – the city's fire engine arrived.

Raleigh

"It was found," the newspaper reported, "to be so much out of order as to be nearly useless, and had it been otherwise, no sufficient supply of water could be obtained, the water-works having been suffered to go out of repair and to remain in that state."

(The reference to water-works was to the wooden-pipe contraption which ran from Rocky Branch to Fayetteville Street.

Even on occasions when the pipes were intact, the quality of the unfiltered water was such that citizens called the output the "Yellow River of China." The device, built at considerable expense, broke down after less than a year and the city returned to relying on wells.)

For putting a Pump in the upper well on Fayetteville Street and making Platform... $62. For repairing bridge on Salisbury Street... 75 cents."

Weston Gales' report as treasurer to the city commissioners in 1833 gives an idea of how public works were proceeding 40 years after the city's founding.

"Nelson Andrews' 3d and 4th quarter's salary for lighting the Lamps in 1832... $85.25. Thomas Nelson for Work and Lime on public well... $1.50. F.H. Reeder for fire buckets... $25. Mrs. Wheaton's Alfred, 1 day's work... 30 cents."

Henry Clay may have lost the Presidency when he wrote the Texas Letter from Raleigh, but he must have had a hoot while viewing the city's militia which was detailed to protect him in 1844.

"A good many citizens had old cavalry pistols," wrote the Rev. R.H. Whitaker, "holsters of the flint and steel kind. And these were frequently used in the place of rifles and shotguns, to meet the requirements of the law.

"The pistol frequently had stuck into its muzzle a corn stalk, walking cane or umbrella, to give it length, and it was a sight to which a circus would be a tame show to see a company going through the manual of arms with such improvised weapons."

Whitaker wrote that the most common cadence from the militia was "hold on till I get my gun fixed."

To the command of "look to the right and dress," customary responses were either, "I dressed before I left home," or "can't dress here, too many women."

Raleigh

Mrs. Lucy D. Bryan wrote that "there was the greatest excitement in town" one night in 1851.

She heard repeated explosions and then "all the bells rang and I thought there was certainly something to pay with the negroes."

In fact, the excitement was so intense that Mrs. Bryan barricaded herself in her house with all of the oil lamps off until daybreak.

It had been no insurrection, only one of Raleigh's intermittent fires. The one in 1851 burned down 17 residences. As Mrs. Bryan clarified in her next letter, "it was the blowing up of houses that I took for the firing of cannons."

Two dollars was the price for such an indirect fling at our muddy streets."

The newspaper *We Know* was describing the fine paid by a man for public drunkenness in 1871. He had told the Mayor in court that he dreamed of being "swallowed by a monster cat-fish" which surfaced in one of Fayetteville Street's puddles, and was so unsettled when he awoke that he gravitated to the city's grog shops.

Hurricane Hazel may have knocked down abundant trees in 1954, but at least residents had notice that it was coming.

In 1877, downtown Raleigh was struck flush by a tornado. According to the *Observer*, "the memory of the oldest living resident furnishes nothing even approximately an equal to it."

The storm arrived at 2:30 p.m. on a Sunday. It blew out the windows of the Governor's Palace; the chimneys at the courthouse collapsed; a horse was lifted from a field and deposited in Walnut Creek; eleven large oaks on Capitol Square were either blown down or twisted in half; and the tin roof of Briggs Hardware store littered Fayetteville Street in pan-sized pieces.

There were no fatalities.

As the tornado veered through the city, it struck humble and grand structures alike.

It is safe to say that the trees at the Richard B. Haywood house on Edenton Street date no earlier than 1877, because on the afternoon of the tornado, the oaks, horse chestnuts and cedars in the yard were uprooted along with the garden fence. Oaks at the Mordecai estate went next.

Fifty convicts were detailed to clean Capitol Square. A controversy developed when Raleigh citizens, alert to a bargain, were stopped from entering the square by "guards armed with 16-shooting Winchester rifles."

Raleigh

The *Observer* wrote that the guards were too reminiscent of the recent occupation of the city by Federal troops. It asserted the right of Raleighites to cross the Capitol grounds whenever they chose. (Someone had forgotten why the city's newspapers had demanded a fence and gates 30 years earlier.)

Evangelists who passed through Raleigh and pronounced the city government to be corrupt were not engaging entirely in hyperbole.

Municipal politics in Raleigh became so tainted in the 1870s that the Legislature removed control over elections from the city and placed it in the hands of the county government.

Moreover, Raleigh's seventeen aldermen, who selected the mayor instead of the voters, were required to choose someone "not of their own number" for the position.

Sheriff John Baker might educate any complaining prisoners about what jail conditions were like in Raleigh 100 years ago.

Year after year, in report after report, the Raleigh chief of police and the city commissioners called for the demolition of the municipal guardhouse. Located in the basement of the deteriorating city market, the lockup must have been as acrid as its descriptions.

As early as 1875, the State Supreme Court upheld $2,000 in damages against the city on account of the jail. One John Godwin had been arrested that year, "found lying on the street," and tossed into the dungeon overnight. The next morning he was dead.

In its opinion, the Supreme Court said that Godwin's death "was accelerated by the noxious atmosphere" in the place; that the eight-by-fourteen foot common cell had "no opening connecting with the outer air or light" and "no ventilation even"; and that "the bad air would stay in indefinitely."

The Court, remarking about the "impure emanations" from the chicken and fish stalls at ground level, said that "a moment's reflection will teach that it will not do to have a prison underground."

"Nature teaches us," the Court continued, "that any person kept in such a place must soon die, and any person 'lodged' in such a place is injured by the first breath." (Speaking of being injured by a single breath, the author once shared a hotel in Grand Rapids with a cosmetics convention. At least Godwin didn't have to fumigate his clothes.)

"Not a chair," the Court concluded its description, "nor a bed, nor a blanket, nothing but the cold, hard floor in 'a hole like Calcutta's.'" The opinion was unanimous.

Raleigh

Yet ten years after the Supreme Court sent the city that message, the mayor was still pleading for a new guardhouse. In a report for 1885, he said the expense of moving it "would not exceed the costs and judgments in favor of plaintiffs suing for damages received during their confinement."

The condition of the jail might not have been as harmful to one's health as was its potpourri of inmates.

In 1888, the police chief wrote that "it is an injustice to compel the unfortunate victims of a vicious appetite (he was speaking of liquor) to be housed with criminals, or that youths arrested for bad behavior on the streets should spend hours, and it may be days, in company with thieves and murderers."

Finally the police department – whose own quarters were also in the basement – complained that its officers were getting sick from the "dark, damp, illy-ventilated" place, which they said was still "entirely defective in a sanitary view." About eight years later the city moved the lockup.

The evolution of Raleigh can almost be deduced by leafing through its old charter amendments and ordinances.

When the city in the 1800s made it a crime to turn in false fire alarms, for example, it is certain that the city's alarm system had finally been installed.

When Raleigh obtained its first telephone service, an ordinance soon followed to punish obscene callers.

With trains came provisions to discourage train-jumping. With the end of individual wells came an ordinance on tampering with the municipal water pump.

Automobiles quickly led to ordinances on parking, drunk driving and speeding (although the city had placed speeding laws in force in the era of horses and buggies).

Pullen Park got a menagerie and the city aldermen soon passed ordinances against tormenting the animals. The advent of moving pictures led to laws regulating theater projection booths.

The lag in each instance seems to have been about six months before the inhabitants of Raleigh so abused each innovation that it was necessary to adopt penalties.

The ordinances you are about to read are real. It is somehow illuminating to browse through what city hall has chosen in the past to worry about.

Raleigh

A word of explanation: despite periodic revisions of Raleigh's city charter and its ordinance books, new versions never make a clean break with the old. Each new version does proclaim that all prior laws in conflict with the new ones are repealed, or in any case, that the new laws control over the old if a conflict exists.

But that is different from a blanket repeal of all old laws or a statement that the new version is the sole and self-contained law.

The practice is as it should be. But what that gibberish means is that some of the old provisions are still in effect, although in a kind of remission, just waiting to be slapped on some latter-day miscreant.

Now for some old-fashioned law and order, Raleigh style:

• The fine for talking to a St. Mary's student on the sidewalk without the permission of her teacher: $10.

• "Wantonly cracks his whip to the annoyance of others": $10. (This clearly is the origin of the term "whippersnapper".)

• For allowing a "bull dog, bull terrier, or any other fierce, dangerous or vicious dog" to "go upon the streets of the city without being securely muzzled": a penalty of death (to the dog, not to the remiss owner).

• Drives a herd of cattle through the streets of Raleigh without an attendant: $10.

• For showing a motion picture of an interracial prize fight: $50 per day. (Heavyweight fighter Jack Johnson apparently did frighten the white folks.)

• Calling someone any epithet which would "insult, offend, worry or annoy" that person, whether in public, by mail, or over the telephone: $50 or 30 days in jail. (If the phrase "tax and spend liberal" qualifies under this ordinance, G.O.P. Chairman Jack Hawke may be in trouble.)

• For selling gasoline to any person who is under the influence of liquor or drugs: $50 or 30 days in jail.

• Dumping a cuspidor into one of the city's lined trash cans: $10.

• For failing to cut down any ailanthus tree or paradise tree in the city, $25; for cutting down any tree in the city without permission of the aldermen, $30. (This is called a conflict of laws.)

• Failing to remove political or other advertising fliers within 24 hours after an event: $50 or 30 days in jail or both.

• For allowing someone to use a car for immoral purposes: $500. (This applied equally to alcohol, drugs and sex.)

• Heaving trash onto a sidewalk from a second-story window or above: $5.

• For selling bolo bouncers: $200. But any or all of the bolo-bouncer fine could be remitted by the police justice. Until the various forms of city

Raleigh

courts were replaced, Raleigh's mayors and justices held enormous power in their ability to waive fines. And the level of fines, particularly in the early decades of the city, were so high that most residents could not afford to pay them even for minor offenses.

Essentially, a bolo-bouncer salesman who was on the wrong side of the city administration stood to lose. Out-of-towners were routinely fleeced by city hall for offenses which were committed on the cheap by Raleigh's homegrown misdemeanants.

• For constant and systematic begging without written permission of the mayor: $5 per offense.

• Permitting animals to mate in public: $10 per offense.

• For throwing a banana peel onto the sidewalk: $5.

• Failing to remove manure from stables weekly from April through September, and monthly from October through March: $10.

• Letting hogs or pigs break into your privy: $10.

• For staging a fox and rabbit race in the streets: $10.

• Giving a haircut on a Sunday unless the patron is dead or near to death: $25.

• For using a beanshooter on the sidewalk: $5.

• Refusing to open a brothel when the police knock at the door: $10; keeping a brothel in the city: $10 per day of operation.

• For an unlicensed pilot to fly over the city unless the airplane had been inspected by a licensed pilot: $25.

• Selling fruits and vegetables in the city market other than by dry measure: $2 per violation and seizure of the produce.

• For performing any "indecent, immoral or lewd play or dance," or for singing "to a public audience... any sacrilegious, vulgar or lewd song," or for exhibiting or selling "any obscene, vulgar or licentious book": $25 per offense.

• Acting as a "capper, booster or shiller" at any auction: $25.

• For placing a flier under the windshield wipers of someone else's car: $25 or 30 days or both.

• Driving while impaired, first offense in 1929: immediate revocation of license for as long as the court deemed advisable.

• For holding a marathon dance: A fine of up to $50 for each eight hours.

• Washing an automobile on the streets: $20.

• For permitting a dog to enter the city market: $1. (This last ordinance from the 1940s represented a great improvement for dogs; prior to its passage, the keeper of the market was required to see that they were "whipped out" of the premises.

Raleigh

Motorists who curse city hall if they encounter a pothole today ought to consider the condition of even Fayetteville Street in the last century.

In an editorial in 1882 entitled "Not True," the *Spirit of the Age* newspaper sought to reassure its rural readers that Raleigh was a safe place to visit and trade in despite its streets.

"The report to the effect that a man fell from the crossing near Pescud's Drug store and was drowned, is not true," the newspaper related. "He was rescued."

"Nor is it true," the *Spirit* continued, "that a drove of beef cattle got into a quagmire coming down Fayetteville Street and were all lost in the mud. Nor is it true that mud turtles, the size of wheel barrows, crawl up on the sidewalks, occasionally, out of the mud and swallow half-grown boys.... Nor is it true that a line of ferry boats is running from the Capitol to the Graded school along Fayetteville Street."

The *Spirit* noted that "there are many more things said about our streets and our mud and they are having a damaging effect upon business."

The newspaper counseled that "if a man is sober, and careful how he walks, he may cross our streets very easily (if he is well acquainted with crossings) without getting into mud that is more than a foot deep. But should he miss the crossing, we don't know how deep he might find it."

The policeman's lot in Raleigh in 1882 may not have been happy, but it certainly was preoccupying.

Officers were on call at all hours of the day and night and were ordered to wear their uniforms even when off-duty.

When walking their beats, they were required to check all doors, rear gates and low windows at houses and stores to see that they were locked "at least two times each six hours" each night. Patrolmen also were required to know residents of their beat by sight, to keep track of "questionable" persons, and to be on the alert for sanitation offenses.

"If offenses against persons or property become frequent occurrences on any beat," the Police Force rules stated, "they will be deemed sufficient proof of negligence" and the officer could be dismissed. (There was no civil service or grievance system until well into the 1900s.)

Patrolmen were ordered to arrest persons in "as easy and as quiet a manner as possible" and to use their nightsticks "only in self-defence." The officers did carry revolvers, but from department inventories, it appears that the men paid for both their guns and their uniforms themselves.

Here again, the subject of dust in Raleigh's olden streets: "The life of the poor pedestrian," an observer wrote, "has become reduced to little less than a succession of pains and penalties." Speaking of the new trend of taking carriages out after dark, he complained that "Fayetteville Street is lost in a cloud of dust from noon until night."

Fighting city hall.... J.D. Riggan went before the city commissioners in the 1880s seeking justice on a deal he had struck with the fire department.

"In a 'hoss trade'," a report read, "the fire chief had palmed off a 'stump sucker' horse on him." (A stump sucker is a horse which dines on stumps, fences, troughs and other wooden objects of low nutritional value. In addition to destroying property, such a horse loses weight and strength.)

Riggan calculated that he had $80 of value in the animal and said that in a matter of weeks the horse had become so emaciated that he couldn't sell it for $15.

He told the commissioners that firemen had failed to inform him that they kept "an electric wire in the feed trough to keep the horse from eating it." The city settled the case.

Good fences make good neighbors".... The city in the 1880s ordained that "no privy shall be suffered to remain in such a manner that a hog or pig can enter...."

Another ordinance required that new privies be located as far from other people's houses or lots as from the privy owner's home.

The city itself has discussed its shortcomings in annual reports.

In 1884, the city's street commissioner threw up his hands at the progress of improvements.

"From the condition of the streets and the character of the work done on them, I find it impracticable to give a detailed statement of the work done," he wrote.

(The city was laboriously paving Fayetteville Street, one block per year, and intermittently ripping out its work in order to accommodate the streetcar construction.)

A commissioner also described Raleigh's streets as "almost impassable" and said that they were "lower in the middle than on the sides and beds of the gutters, ravines and washes."

Raleigh

By 1889, the mayor reported that Raleigh was "using some of the low grounds... (and) old ravines for dumping ashes, cinders and such refuse." He said that because citizens sneaked out at night to add in garbage, the city was getting complaints about "unpleasant odors arising from these dumps."

The slog of progress... In 1885, Mayor H.V. Dodd impounded money which had been earmarked for paving and repairing streets because he thought that having surplus funds would bolster the city's credit rating.

(At the time, the city was not borrowing any money, primarily because the voters had gotten into the habit of rejecting bond referendums. Most of what the city did owe was in default.)

The earthquake which devastated Charleston, South Carolina, on August 31, 1886 may have run out of power when it resonated through Raleigh, but it caused ample consternation in the capital.

"It is safe to say," a newspaper reported, "that Raleigh people last evening had the greatest scare in all the city's history. Neither battle, murder nor sudden death had ought to compare to it in town.... It was the sensation of the century."

At 9:50 p.m., "the earth began to shake, at first slightly, then more vigorously, and the agitation speedily became astonishingly regular," reported the *N&O*. "People looked at were seen to stagger" and "buildings swayed or oscillated with regular motion."

Caught standing on the steps of the Governor's Palace when the shaking began, Governor Alfred M. Scales recalled that "never before have I had such a sense of helplessness."

Convicts were reported to have been particularly fearful. The *N&O* had to use the inducement of liquor to keep its pressmen at work. Residents had recurring nightmares or nausea for weeks afterward.

What Raleigh in fact suffered was later described as "freak damage": falling chimneys, cracked windows, ringing bells and shattered porcelain.

And some bon vivants, according to the *Biblical Recorder,* acted as if nothing had happened. They "claimed to have continued dancing through the earthquake" at a cotillion which had been in progress.

"Their friends regarded them with amazement," the *Recorder* wrote, "especially those who saw them with white cheeks and shaking knees during the shocks."

Raleigh

Before the appearance of electric lights in 1886, Raleigh was illuminated by 180 gas lamps on iron posts, which were "lighted for 21 nights each month (this was when the moon was not scheduled)."

Once electricity was installed, the city immediately fell into arbitration with the Raleigh Lighting, Heating and Power Co. because its fixtures delivered only 775 candlepower apiece instead of the 1200 candlepower guaranteed in the contract. The arbitrator decreed that the city should pay only 775/1200 of the $80 annual charge for each light, or $57.666 each.

It perhaps defies all odds that any historic structures survive downtown.

Consider a fire in 1887 which wiped out the Raleigh Oil and Fertilizer Co. At the time, the city had cisterns as well as buckets, had replaced wooden shingles, and had a fire company that was organized enough to have pump wagons and to make a healthy claim on the city budget.

On the other hand, even though brick and frame had replaced all-frame construction, the seasoned wood in brick buildings and their spaces for updrafts made them ripe for incineration.

According to spectators, the heat from the factory fire bent steel rails at the company's loading spur and "was sufficiently great to draw rosin from fences 100 yards distant."

In the *N&O*'s account, "at times the force of the flames in the large buildings would rip up a piece of the tin roof, double it over and over into a roll, and send it hissing full of flame away up into the air and over upon other buildings."

Losses were estimated at $100,000. (Interestingly, news reports and city records used to differentiate between a "loss" and a "loss covered by insurance," and also distinguished fires depending on whether they were covered by local or out-of-town insurance companies. "None of our home companies are involved," was one statement.)

Through heroic effort, the one building to be saved was the guano house.

A Raleigh newspaper reported in 1888 that police officers "will be instructed in a day or two to take up all dogs which do not wear medals, and a sausage factory will be started shortly."

Raleigh

What Raleigh firemen faced in the 19th century is typified by the destruction in 1890 of the roundhouse and 17 locomotives of the Raleigh and Gaston Railroad.

Although firemen arrived within three minutes of the initial alarm, they had to pull hoses 2,800 feet to the nearest cistern and then contend with inadequate water.

By the time firemen were able to produce the first stream of water, the question was not whether the roundhouse could be saved, but how the fire could be prevented from spreading.

Pierce firetrucks might cost $3 million a dozen, but a good fire horse....

Henry, the Raleigh fire department's favorite old gray horse in 1890, deserved all the apples and candy which local children left him each Christmas in his embroidered stocking outside the city stables.

In winning a state competition that summer, the fire crew hitched Henry to the "Old Hickory" pumping wagon, sped 331 yards and produced a steady stream of water, all in a reported total of 55 seconds. Today's trucks would have trouble improving on Henry's time.

Upon every lawyer... or street huckster... a license tax not exceeding ten dollars a year."

Raleigh's aldermen not only set out to raise revenue in the city's 1891 charter revision, but by placing those two esteemed occupations in the same section, they did so with sarcasm. (The humor was not lost on the lawyers; they managed to get themselves exempted from the tax a few years later.)

City licenses are as old as the founding of the capital. The first appointed commissioners charged for permits to retail liquor in Raleigh's proliferating saloons.

Over the generations, Raleigh's license taxes were usually designed to collect a kind of toll from successful businesses in the city. Depending on who was in office, taxes on particular activities could rise or fall radically or be eliminated altogether. And for the most part, at least until recently, the commissioners and aldermen in Raleigh did not levy taxes to the maximum levels which were authorized by the General Assembly.

But if some taxes were simply tolls, others were intended to send messages: they might be set so high as to keep unwelcome enterprises out of town, or drafted so as to halt the evasion of other municipal levies. One license provision in fact amounted to a license to steal.

Raleigh

Following are some of city hall's more noteworthy license taxes since 1795:

• On every hog "kept running at large in the streets" in 1851: $3. (Rural farmers kept their hogs in pens, but the pork producers in the capital simply branded their stock and let them loose to eat whatever they could find. And Johnston County residents today think they have a problem with hog farms.)

• On every "billiard table, nine or ten pin alley, victuallizing house or restaurateur" or saloon: $25. (Unless Raleigh's pool tables had slots for Liberty Seated quarters, the city fathers were discouraging billiards.)

• On any merchant in the city who was in the wholesaling business: ten cents on the dollar of gross sales. (This exorbitant tax dropped after the Civil War to twenty-five cents per $100 of sales, except for liquor. It is unclear what happened to merchants who claimed an exemption from the tax on the grounds that the word "wholesale" was just a gimmick.)

• On "itinerant merchants and peddlers" in 1857 who sold anything other than books, charts, maps and North Carolina products: $5.

• On circus riders and other performers within a mile of the city limits: $15 per performance if paid in advance, or $30 after the show.

• On the retailing of liquor by the drink in 1886 within a mile of Raleigh: $500. (A license today, at equivalent rates, would cost in excess of $10,000 per year. By 1908, such a license tax had risen to more than $12,000 in today's dollars.) Beer and wine permits were $100.

• On every "stock and bond broker, junk dealer..." the tax in 1891 was $25 per year. (Some modern bankers could justifiably claim that they were being taxed twice.)

• On non-resident organ grinders, street dancers and musicians: $10.

• On every share of common stock owned in the city: one percent of book value.

• On any "portrait painter, photographer or daguereau artist... taking or enlarging likenesses of the human face": $10. (Photos of other parts of the anatomy were covered by other laws. See *Helms v. Mapplethorpe, et al.*)

• On any trading stamp company: $100.

• On any druggist who sold liquor by prescription: $125.

• On "every person, firm or corporation engaged in the business of pressing or cleaning clothes, commonly called a 'pressing club', $25, provided that disorderly conduct of any persons in and around the place where such is carried on shall ipso facto revoke the said license." (What sorts of activities were going on at the forerunners of Medlin Davis Cleaners?)

The city decided one year that not enough businesses were coming forward to pay their license taxes and that it lacked the resources for a door-to-

Raleigh

door search. Who should come to the city's aid but the General Assembly, which enacted a short-lived law. It provided that "every other occupation... not mentioned" in Raleigh's license list would pay $1,000 per year in fees. City hall was swamped by businessmen who came out of the woodwork to qualify themselves as one of the $10 or $25 occupations.

By 1940, the city commissioners had apparently decided that all money was green.

Fortune tellers were licensed for $200. For $500 a person could be a licensed "clairvoyant." A phrenologist gained a seal of legitimacy for $1,000. "Emigration agents employing persons to perform work outside of the state" – the migrant labor trade – could operate for a $500 fee.

Then there was a certain license fee of $500: it applied to "every band" of persons "practicing any of the artifices usually carried on by gypsies."

So much for heterosexual singles bars.... In 1891, the Raleigh code punished with a $5 fine any "woman whose general reputation for chastity is bad" or who conducted herself "in a forward or improper manner." (No comparable penalty existed for men, but the era *was* called the Gay Nineties.)

And Milton Berle better beware.... The same 1891 version of the code levied a fine of up to $25 not merely on women, but on "any person who shall, in the City of Raleigh, appear in any public place in an indecent or lewd dress."

For reasons which will remain murky, the mayor in 1890 not only took down the occupations of persons arrested in the city during the preceding year, but he included the information in his annual report.

In descending order, the accuseds' occupations were: laborers, 330; farmers, 105; washwomen, 46; porters, 29; hackmen and clerks, 28 each; carpenters, 24; schoolboys, cooks and printers, 23 each; drivers, 21; prostitutes, 18; lawyers, 8; physicians, 3; and editors, 2.

These 739 individuals accounted for 1,196 collars by the police department. Forms of drunkenness led all offenses with 426, followed by assault and battery, robbery, breaking and entering and receiving stolen goods. Eighteen persons were arrested for "fast driving" in their buggies, nine for indecent exposure and eight for "keeping a disorderly house."

The possible permutations in this accounting by the mayor are some-

Raleigh

thing to behold. Who did what, with, or to whom? It made for a wonderful parlor game in 1890.

Who says that the tax revolt started in California. In 1893, the Legislature passed a revealing local law concerning Raleigh.

It seems that in the years 1887, 1888, 1889, 1890, 1891 and 1892, no one stepped forward "to purchase lands exposed to sale by the sheriff" and "there was due to the county and the state of North Carolina a large amount of back taxes from persons who failed to pay the same during said years."

The law required the county commissioners to buy in the lands and auction them or else be subject to arrest.

Dead horses wheresoever they may be have no effect on my soda and mineral waters."

Using that advertisement in 1895, druggist John MacRae tried to comfort his patrons that the products at his fountain had nothing in common with Raleigh's water supply. (The Perrier people were spared his ingenuity a few years back.)

Several weeks earlier, the city waterworks staff had helped a farmer by burying a horse. They planted it in a shallow grave which lay uphill from the city's sole water intake on Rocky Branch.

After the overripe presence of the horse was noticed following a rainstorm, the city took four days to improve the grave, then did so at night and without notice, and then lied about it.

In an uproar, Raleigh citizens turned off their water taps and the *N&O* reported that "drug stores did a big business in mineral water." So did a Mr. Wooten, who had the good timing to be in town trying to sell a newfangled water filter when the horse surfaced, so to speak. "It takes out all the horse," he said of his device.

Among other things, the incident prompted the city to consider purifying its water. (But chlorination was still nonexistent 20 years later.) And druggist MacRae was able to print the rest of his memorable advertisement:

"'A Horse! A Horse!! My Kingdom for a Horse' Says Richard III. I wonder how a dead horse on the water shed WOULD HAVE SUITED HIM..."

Mayor William Russ opposed a bill in the legislature which would have created a reform school for juvenile offenders in 1896.

The mayor took the position that "companionship, moral instruction and a hickory stick" were adequate measures for discipline until children reached the age of 14, when he believed they were old enough for regular jail or prison.

Raleigh's fire personnel were not paid until 1913. It was only in 1897 that the city's fire chief reluctantly agreed to pay a $50 annual premium for accident insurance to cover the volunteers.

The slog of progress.... The city board *almost* directed a criticism at the Raleigh Water Co. in 1897 for "using one inch pipe rather than four-inch pipe" under downtown streets, causing new pavement that was being put down to be immediately torn up to serve adequate water to the city.

But the city board rethought the matter when someone pointed out that "in the company's defense, the city repeatedly rejected its requests and recommendations" for using larger pipe at the outset.

The more things change.... After complaining without effect about utility service at the turn of the century, a citizen wrote about the streetcar company: they said "If you don't like it, you don't have to ride."

He reported a similar response to a price inquiry from Raleigh's sole ice distributor: "Well, if you don't like it, you don't have to buy ice. Giddap, Bill."

(The writer won out on streetcar service after the board of aldermen threatened not to renew the franchise unless more cars were allotted to the Hillsborough Street line.)

> What is the news comes in from Chavis?
> What do you hear from Lonnie Davis?
> They're voting alley cats and fices
> From the Rabbit Gum to Louise Price's."

The organizers of Raleigh's predominantly black precincts were not quite as efficient as the above rhymes suggest, but in the early 1900s – as today – they could run up staggering margins for favored candidates and issues.

(To explicate the poem, written by a city official: Lonnie Davis was popularly known as "The Boss of Chavis Heights;" the Rabbit Gum was "one of the lower resorts" in the eastern part of the city; and Louise Price was the madam of "a famous or infamous abode" near the old Garfield-Hunter schools.)

Close elections often depended on the returns from East Raleigh. Those returns were consistently reported last.

Rumor had it that the proprietors of illegal bars, vice traps and policy rackets would trade votes in return for the city commission looking the other way as they pursued their business.

Distressed at garbage in the streets, the Woman's Club in 1905 recommended that city aldermen adopt a kind of punishment by community service.

"The board should be requested to place some slight penalty upon the careless city urchins who in search of a 'find' throw the contents of garbage cans in the street," the Club announced. It proposed that each offender "be required to sweep 25 feet of sidewalk."

Raleigh may never have had a municipal poet laureate, but city clerk Joe Sawyer could have been a contender in the early part of the century.

Addressing the aftermath of one of the city's first annexations, Sawyer wrote that:

"You're in the city now,
You cannot keep a cow.
R.N. Simms is keeping two
But don't you think that they'll let you
You're in the city now."

So what if it was a derivation of "You're in the Army Now"? The doggerel had a mordant second verse:

"They've left you in the mire
And so in case of fire
They'll ring the bell
And wish you well
And raise your paving taxes higher."

On another occasion, Sawyer's new car caught fire and his insurance carrier refused to pay until he mailed them this opus:

*"It burned the speedometer and smoked its face.
It burned out the plates in the battery case.
It burned out the lights and burned up the wires.
It was mighty damn hot if it weren't no fire."*

According to Charlie Johnson's version of the story, Sawyer never knew for certain whether the insurer paid him $100 for the loss or the poem.

An umbrella is not the first necessity that comes to mind when packing for a train trip, but in Raleigh in 1907, the Southern Railway offered the unexpected.

"A veritable death trap," wrote the *N&O* about the bridge spanning Walnut Creek. "It has vast numbers of rotten ties."

(A train had derailed on the bridge, sending six freight cars end-over-end down the creek embankment. Somehow, no one was seriously injured.)

"The wrecks there caused the putting in of some new ties," the newspaper noted, "but even after the wreck yesterday about 15 rotten ties were found on the embankment while remnants and pieces of others could be seen in the wreckage." One spectator strolled around the smash-up, poking his umbrella tip into rotten ties as he dramatized the problem.

Umbrellas had another use on the Southern, however. It seems that the "first class cars for whites leaked like sieves," and that passengers had to ride with open umbrellas over their seats.

Raleigh's most recent municipal election may have drawn fewer than 20 percent of the city's registered voters, but such apathy was unknown in elections in the early 1900s. Turnouts averaged more than 80 percent.

Of course, under the commission system, the feeling was stronger that if a person did not participate, he (and later she) was going to get the dirty end of the stick.

"They'll never enjoy the fruits of this election," one malcontent wrote in 1915 about the commissioners, "and some of them will sleep behind bars when it is over." What disturbed the writer had been the presence of city employees and uniformed policemen "inside the ropes about the ballot boxes" on election day.

No one went to jail. And in those days of voter intimidation, fistfights at the polls, buying drinks in return for ballots, bloc voting *en masse,* and even Federal observers at Raleigh polling places, few residents were secure enough to be apathetic.

Writing about the introduction of automobiles in Raleigh and the resulting increase in police work, Fred A. Olds recalled this:

Accidents "happen quickly, all over in the twinkling of an eye, (and) hence fail to furnish the prolonged thrill, the cumulative collisions and successive wrecks, supplied by a pair of horses or mules or a yoke of oxen on a mad rampage down Fayetteville Street on a crowded Saturday afternoon while the terrified spectators scudded for safety or struggled to restrain their own panicky steeds."

The arrival of automobiles in Raleigh had a dramatic and adverse effect on law enforcement.

By 1916, the police department reported, "every man or woman with an automobile became a potential perpetrator of manslaughter to the man on the beat. Almost anyone could outrun the law." The city fathers purchased two Fords for the officers.

Until the creation of a civil service apparatus, personnel matters at city hall were often public.

A policeman who was discharged "for inebriety and neglect of duty," for instance, or a clerk who was sacked for "deception as to sickness and drunkenness," could read all about it in the newspapers.

Uncontrolled development prior to 1923 was not the only issue in Raleigh to concern Mayor T.B. Eldridge.

In 1921, the mayor became disturbed that food prices seemed vastly higher in Raleigh than in neighboring cities. The situation seemed to have occurred about the time of the demise of a food cooperative in the capital.

In typical fashion, Eldridge set out to learn whether the city's grocers were gouging the public. He rounded up enough pocket money for a shopping trip to the A&P store in Durham, where he bought basic commodities such as flour, potatoes, chickens and pork chops. Then he returned to Raleigh for a little comparison-shopping.

Raleigh

The next morning, the mayor called a press conference in his office. Displaying the groceries from Durham, he revealed that the price of the same provisions was 44 percent higher in Raleigh. Eldridge announced that he would chair a public meeting the next week so that the city's grocers could explain the differential. He gave the Durham foodstuffs to the needy.

A few days later, before a packed commission chamber, the grocers' association attacked the mayor's conclusion about higher prices in Raleigh. First, they said Eldridge's study was unrepresentative and unscientific. Next, they complained that Raleigh's residents demanded nothing but the best in groceries and that the capital's pork chops and potatoes were superior to those eaten by the plebeians in Durham. Last, they said the higher prices in Raleigh were caused by greater overheads and taxes than elsewhere.

Mayor Eldridge responded that all he knew was that grocery prices had dropped in Raleigh in recent days and he hoped it was the start of a trend.

Former Senator Willis Smith's advertisements were decades in the future when F.H. Hunnicutt ran in 1917 for commissioner of public safety and was accused of negative campaigning.

Hunnicutt distributed a booklet entitled "Hot-Shot Truths About Raleigh City Affairs." In it, he pledged to slash what he termed a "padded" city payroll in an era when that adjective implied corruption.

"There are three (count 'em, 1-2-3) 'janitors' detailed to 'keep' our more or less ornate and not one-half occupied 'city market house'", he fumed, "and lasso it if it tries to run away." He had similar misgivings about the city auditor's staff, the "75-a-month stable inspector," and the clerk in charge of licenses for horses and buggies.

As for these last two areas, Hunnicutt not only recognized the advent of the car, but he seamlessly tied that development in with the city administration he despised.

"The city employees," he wrote with reference to those who drove city-owned cars, "seem to think it necessary to use part of their working hours speeding in these machines.... (They) should at least pay for the gasoline consumed."

Negative advertising or not, Hunnicutt lost. His spiel might have gone over better on television.

A camp full of tanks or not, Raleigh knew comparative quiet once each week during the last months of World War I.

In an effort to save gasoline, the Fuel Administration ordered what became known as "Gasless Sunday," when all but essential trips were banned.

Raleigh

The ban annoyed some who had to work indoors all week and relished a Sunday spin. "The family car," wrote the *Raleigh Times* in support of prudent Sunday outings, "does not glide up and down Fayetteville Street, scorch past St. Mary's and the State College, or dip the dip on Person Street."

Moreover, every time there was a rumored armistice, hundreds of motorists would emerge on Sundays, riding around hollering and waving flags. "One of the most gas-indulgent days since the Fuel Administration made its requirement," the *Times* sniffed about one Sabbath.

Mayor Eldridge rides again.... In 1920, the mayor deputized ten automobile dealers as "special speed cops."

The car dealers, who had offered to help slow down Raleigh motorists through their Raleigh Automotive Association, carried badges, had the power to make arrests, and were anonymous.

(Well, life was simpler in 1920. If nothing else, liability law alone would deter any such joint venture today between city hall and the private sector, not that anyone would want to be nabbed by a Yugo salesman.)

The slog of progress.... Although Charlotte instituted a parks commission in 1905, Raleigh did not ask for and receive one in its charter until 1929.

For that matter, the city was out of step with its urban brethren on other civic activities. People in Raleigh were still complaining about weeds growing in New Bern Avenue, for instance, more than 20 years after the City of Asheville began an aggressive paving program.

A waterworks system? Raleigh was generations behind. Electric lights? Two years behind. Urban renewal and public housing? A decade behind. Schools? Decades behind. Council-manager government? Who knows, but by 1930, fourteen cities in the State had adopted it; Raleigh got around to embracing the system in the late 1940s.

At times, it appeared that an observer in 1888 had accurately captured the mood of the city: "Raleigh never takes a step backwards," he wrote, "but its forward movements are indetectable."

He ascribed this tendency to a belief by the city's establishment that merely because state government was there, good things would happen to the city without any effort on the part of the citizenry.

(It is an interesting idea for people who so enjoy denigrating state government.)

It has been true in Raleigh for decades that, as the saying might go locally, a decent prosecutor can win an indictment of a barbecue sandwich.

A review of available grand jury records from this century reveals that the prosecutor gets an indictment an average of 95 percent of the time. When a grand jury fails to return a true bill, two factors are usually afoot: witnesses have failed to appear, or the indictment most likely will be forthcoming the next time that the grand jury convenes.

Some of the most interesting grand jury work in Raleigh did not involve indictments, but related to investigations of the police department in the 1930s and 1940s under the old commission system. (It was bandied back then that "the way to get on the police force is first to get some experience as a taxicab driver.")

In 1933, a grand jury recommended that a "non-partisan policy" be adopted for the Raleigh police department so that officers could serve "without having to account to any political dictator." Another recommendation asked that the courts step in to protect Raleigh officers "from the demoralizing influence of selfish politicians."

Matters became worse. In 1934, a grand jury investigated charges of collusion between members of the police force and what by then was called "highly organized and well financed crime."

Although it did not find a systemic corruption, the grand jury reported that "there are indications that this condition may exist in some cases."

Evidence was difficult to gather. For years, prosecutors were unable to confiscate slot machines in the city because, according to the grand jury investigation, police sources tipped off establishments before the raids.

So the grand jury determined on occasion to bypass the police.

In a report to a judge in 1938, a panel said: "in a number of Soda Shops which the committee visited from time to time we find indications which point to the fact that these places are being continuously used and the proprietors or clerks continuously engaged in the tip-book racket, the numbers or policy racket, the baseball pool racket, and other gambling rackets which are highly deleterious to the moral health of this community."

In 1948, another grand jury confronted an unchanged situation.

"Several places are open primarily" for gambling, foreman Earl Hostetler wrote, "and it is impossible to effect further control" without additional funds and personnel. Ministers took to appearing before the grand jury with detailed accounts of vice in the city. Another grand jury foreman was advised that he could become a wealthy man if the panel failed to return a true bill on a policy-racket case. He replied that he had done quite well by playing life straight and intended to continue to do so.

(Note: In the present debate over a State lottery, both proponents and opponents refer to North Carolinians who bet on Virginia's legalized games; little is said of the illegal gaming already here in the State.)

The grand jury's menu went beyond payoffs from gambling, bootlegging and prostitution.

One panel found that although there was "no evidence of coercion," it was desirable for members of the police department to halt their political contributions to the city commissioners who hired and fired them.

Another jury, investigating "vote buying, fraud and other irregularities in the recent city primary and election," recommended purging the voter registration books and dismissing the registrars. "The new registrars should be specifically instructed to see that only definitely qualified voters are permitted to register," it wrote. Two workers connected with the city commission went to jail.

Addressing the subject of corruption in a forthcoming city election in 1935, Dr. L.B. Capehart had this to say:

"The herder is no better than the herded. The buyer is no better than the seller. Negroes should know that he who would buy him for a dime would sell him for a dollar."

Lest anyone get the idea that there ever was unanimity on setting priorities for the Raleigh police department, consider this editorial in the *Raleigh Times* welcoming a new chief in 1935:

"If he can bring his detective forces to the point of showing the same efficiency in sending this murderer to the chair," the newspaper wrote about an unsolved murder, "that they display in uncovering caches of whiskey hid behind the panels of soft drink stands or in swooping down upon the Sunday gambling games of bored negroes," the new chief might merit support.

By 1936, the *Raleigh Times* could boast of the city's "thundering new V-12 pumping engine," which it said was "the latest word in fire-fighting equipment."

The fire department had seven vehicles and according to the Times, "the firemen, it seems, aren't the enthusiastic motorists average Raleighites are... last month, all the trucks were in service only an aggregate of one and a third hours."

Half of the department's calls in 1936 were false alarms.

Raleigh

As much hilarity as the news media has had over the years with the Jaycees and their boffo conventions, that organization deserves more credit than any for Raleigh's present form of municipal government.

The transition from a commission government to the council-manager form was anything but agreeable.

When the Jaycees first pressed for a change in 1935, they not only were skunked in a referendum, but the election was marred by irregularities and outright violence.

"One of the commissioners' ward heelers, a former murderer, assaulted the Jaycees' campaign manager at a Negro precinct," a report read. The incident ended with the attacker in jail but with the three commissioners still running the city.

Nor did the Jaycees triumph in a second referendum which they stirred up in 1940. Then, in 1946, the Jaycees tried again, hoping to capitalize on post-war spirit and optimism.

In soft, non-partisan terms, the Jaycees opened their campaign by calling the incumbent commissioners "parasites of the city, drawing their salaries and doing nothing to earn them."

The Jaycees rented a suite at the Sir Walter Hotel, mailing literature, writing speeches, and organizing voter transportation.

The commissioners hunkered down at the Hotel Andrew Johnson and commenced to try to frighten the bejesus out of Raleigh voters.

First, the commissioners spread a rumor that an unpopular out-of-towner – in fact, the man who had enforced wartime price controls in Raleigh – had been handpicked by the Jaycees to be the new city manager. The commissioners next claimed that a change to council-manager government would mean the end of backyard garbage collection and that the new manager would order curbside pickups.

(Well, the old buzzards did have some limited insight.)

Worst of all, the commissioners circulated a report which showed that tax rates were substantially higher in those North Carolina cities which had adopted the council-manager form of government.

Here the commissioners made their mistake. Their tax comparison sheet contained fraudulently inflated tax rates for the other cities.

Attorney William Lassiter exposed the sham in a public meeting, and after it had ended, he asked one of the red-faced commissioners "why he altered the tax rates upwards when he could have murdered (us) by using the correct rates. (He) replied that he wanted to make it worse."

By the end of the campaign, when the commissioners tried to exploit fear of the unknown (historically an effective tactic in Raleigh), the voters no longer believed them.

Raleigh

The commissioners warned of a "city run in an unknown fashion by an unknown non-resident." They predicted that the new city manager would "always have his eyes open for another job and as soon as that happens he'll drop Raleigh like a hot potato." They asked voters to keep them on for "one more term," until the post-war turmoil was under control.

Raleigh's voters approved the council-manager form of government by more than 1,200 votes, losing ten of the city's 18 precincts but carrying northwest Raleigh by large majorities.

But all was not paradise. At the ensuing city council election, Miss Ruth Wilson won the most votes but was passed over for Mayor in favor of P.D. Snipes. The new council had cut a deal reminiscent of the old commissioners.

In all, five of the new councilmen came from the same precinct – Hayes Barton. The development train was on the tracks.

And neither had the old commissioners given up.

Ask residents to list Raleigh's city managers, and if they have lived here long enough, a few might name William Carper, L.P. Zachary, and Dempsey Benton.

But how many remember the first city manager, Roy S. Braden?

Braden arrived while the defeated city commissioners still nursed hopes of reviving the old system, either through a new referendum or a legislative charter amendment. His conduct soon became intertwined with the survival of the council-manager arrangement. Depending on one's viewpoint, what happened to Braden was either his own fault or he didn't stand a chicken's chance of survival from the day he accepted the manager's job.

Braden was described by some as an excellent manager, a friendly administrator, and a man who had "dynamic energy." Others characterized him as an "old reprobate" who had "questionable morals."

When Braden promptly got himself involved in a libel suit, the city fathers watched with apprehension.

The new manager had been in the municipal employees' parking lot one afternoon, admired a new car, and was told that it belonged to a police officer. "If a policeman drives a car like that he must not be living right," snapped Braden, who happened to be standing within earshot of the officer.

When the officer retorted that "all of the crooks are not in the Police Department," the suit and countersuit were on. (Both actions were dismissed on the grounds of equal damage to the parties.)

Next, Braden was beaten up by a painting contractor who claimed that Braden had alienated the affections of his ladyfriend of 11 years' standing.

Raleigh

The painter received a $30 fine and a 30-day suspended jail term.

With every available tongue wagging in town, Braden tendered his resignation to the city council. But he withdrew it after 558 city employees signed a petition which said that they "resent and abhor... the scurrilous rumors... which have been made to degrade his character."

Braden scarcely paused before he attracted attention again.

He sponsored a $6,000 appropriation in the city budget for a new Director of Public Safety who, it became known, was a pal of Braden's who had little police or fire experience.

Next, Braden attempted to throw out the low bid for city parking meters in favor of a higher bidder who, it was alleged under oath, had attempted to bribe the City Attorney. (The City Attorney believed that Braden had been approached as well; in any event, the low bidder prevailed in court.)

Last, despite a new $33,000 contract for traffic signal and synchronization equipment, Raleigh's stoplights were still out of kilter. Investigators proved that the new hardware had not been hooked up and was stacked on the floor of a city building.

Amid quiet inquiries by council members about the circumstances of this contract, Braden tendered a second resignation. It was accepted. The ousted city commissioners must have loved it.

What crime rate?... Not until 1950 did the Raleigh police department have a filing system. Prior to then, "officers had to keep their own records in their pockets and desk drawers."

Just say "perp".... In 1952, city manager Carper conducted a meticulous – some would say nitpicking – study of the costs of annexing fringe areas into the corporate limits.

Carper concluded that one additional police officer was needed for each 1,000 increase in Raleigh's population. (And to place his study into context, Carper at the time was seeking to identify every conceivable cost of annexation because he worried that the city had no idea how much its expansion boom was really costing.)

By 1977, Raleigh's chief of police reported in his 18-year plan that the city had 2.1 officers per 1,000 population. His target for 1983 was 2.3 officers per 1,000. By 1995, he thought, the city should have 2.9 officers per 1,000 residents. The city council concurred that these levels of law enforcement were vital to the safety of the city.

How does police strength stand today? Raleigh has 2.1 sworn officers who are authorized – not necessarily hired – for each 1,000 citizens. The council fell behind its targets even as drug trafficking expanded in town.

(Of course, the majority of people who are getting shot in Raleigh do not yet contribute their per capita share of taxes. And many persons now believe that law enforcement is not so much of a solution as are education and treatment.)

If the experience of the mid-1950s is remembered, Raleigh's municipal headquarters will stay where it is for generations to come.

By 1954, the old city hall on Fayetteville Street had for some years been unfit for any offices, much less those of the state's capital city. As the *Raleigh Times* described it, "there have been additions, alterations and repairs until the structure built in 1909 is a maze where even the rats must get lost."

But how to pay for a new municipal building, and more important, where to locate it, absorbed much of the city's attention for years.

Without giving an exhaustive litany of the debate – three bond referendums were rejected by the voters, each for different reasons – it seems that every faction in the city had at least one favorite site. Each faction was also willing to accuse the others of being self-serving and manipulative, at best.

Further, the alliances kept changing. And there was the extracurricular effort of former Mayor James Briggs, who could oppose a bond issue either on principle or on whim. (He confessed that he worked against the second proposed bond issue simply to see whether he could kill it.)

One option was to rebuild on the old site. But many lobbied for property in the 200 block of Hillsborough Street. City Manager Carper favored a plot on New Bern Avenue.

For a time, the site of the present State Legislative Building was in the lead, until the State recognized a bargain under its nose and asked the city to keep its hands off the property.

Some people favored the south side of Moore Square, which would have involved flattening the city market. A fellow named Jesse Helms wanted to tack the new city hall onto the recessed front of the old Wake County courthouse, bringing the fronts on Fayetteville Street into alignment.

Options were fought out in the newspapers and before civic clubs. Some of the choicest commentary came from soon-to-be Mayor William Enloe. When one group suggested putting the new city hall on the site of what was then the Devereux Meadow ballpark, Enloe cracked that "every time a train comes by you'll have to say 'Hold the phone.'"

Then, when Enloe threw his support to those who advocated New Bern Avenue, he pronounced that "we have such a group that we could put whorehouses in Raleigh." (Not that the city lacked brothels in the 1950s.)

Councilmen Charles Bradshaw and Frank Jolly suggested a way to get around the repeated voter disapprovals of bonds: to sell "surplus" city property, rent temporary quarters, and build the new facility without a bond issue. The old city hall, the ballpark, the city farm, acreage along Downtown Boulevard and the city incinerator were on their disposal list.

The Planning Commission approved their concept unanimously, especially since it did not specify a site. But after the City Council rejected it by 4 to 2, Jolly rose to rebuke them. "We are elected to think," he said. "But all you have to say is, 'You can't do it. Hell, no, you can't do it. Not unless you try."

Finally, the city approved a variant of the Bradshaw-Jolly plan. The city sold certain properties and then issued just enough bonds to fall short of the requirement for a vote of the people. It acquired the location of the present Police Department, which had been at the top of no one's public list.

The city then stood back and took criticism that the choice had lined everyone's pockets from those of Frank Daniels, whose newspaper was nearby, to those of a gas station owner, to those of council members themselves.

The city had hoped to realize $400,000 from the sale of the old city hall. But after an initial attempt at auction (as the sale opened, the chimes in the former Durham Life Insurance Building played, "Shall We Gather at the River"), the building was sold for a disappointing $350,000.

Immediately after the sale, it was disclosed that the buyer had been acting as a "blind" for a major local bank and a retailer.

Another landmark was gone.

Take Two With Meals (And Get Right With God)

> *"Last year I asked twenty women what they meant by their daughters having a good time. You would be astonished at the answers I received, if I should tell you. Usually, though, it meant doing something very unhealthy."*
>
> – Dr. Hubert Royster, 1916.

In a promotion which would get the pack of them arrested today, the N.C. Medical Society offered a $25 prize in 1800 to the North Carolinian who could grow the most opium.

Five pounds of production was the minimum, and the new Society pledged to buy the winner's total output for 112.5 percent of the usual price on the New York and Philadelphia opium exchanges.

The chosen place for purchase and exhibition of the winning entry? The State-House, of course, where the Society held its annual convention.

The Society's stated objective was to reduce North Carolina's dependence on foreign drugs, whose delivery was subject to delays and price increases. (Somehow this sounds familiar. Opium and whiskey were the two prevalent anaesthetics of the age, and societies had already been formed to eradicate the latter.)

No archives reveal whether this competition was the inspiration for Raleigh's garden clubs.

Raleigh

Early Raleigh had little medical care and what existed cannot be called comforting.

The *Raleigh Register,* when the N.C. Medical Society convened in 1800, hailed the organization for "enabling the community to distinguish the true Physician from the ignorant Pretender" and predicted that it would put an end to the "fatal and criminal practices of Quacks and Empyrics." But a reading of the newspaper nudges Raleigh's health problems into the open.

Ignore the fact that the *Register* trumpeted the virtues of the same nostrums that it hawked over the counter of its editorial office. ("Ching's Celebrated Worm-Destroying Lozenges" and "Daffy's Cordial Elixir" were popular cures for everything from convulsions to leprosy to "evil".) The newspaper also dispensed its own brand of medical advice.

After pontificating on whether George Washington was killed by medical malpractice, the newspaper reminded readers that "an ounce of blood drawn at the temple relieves an inflamed eye more than a quart drawn at the arm." (The *Register* may have been right, but of no help to poor George, whose true physicians relieved him of two quarts, eight ounces before he posed for that great dollar bill in the sky.)

The *Register* comforted subscribers in 1800 with advice from a local physician that vinegar was "a certain and inevitable cure for that destructive and frequent evil, THE BITE OF A MAD DOG." (On the non-medicinal front, the newspaper endorsed the use of mashed Irish potatoes, chalk and water to whitewash ceilings.)

To judge by the measures which were deemed essential a few years later, public sanitation in early Raleigh was deplorable.

The city lived in dread of epidemics. Each week, Raleigh's newspapers reprinted reports of the decimations of smallpox, typhoid and yellow fever in the Northern cities. Any sudden or unexplained death in Raleigh could cause a panic.

(One local man died and created "great alarm" in 1800 until it was determined that he had died not from typhoid, but from cholera. Physicians attributed his infection to being out in the rain on a trip.)

Although it would not be identified for decades, many in Raleigh had contracted malaria by 1800 because the city had stagnant water in its cellars and was bordered by undrained swamps.

From the very first, Raleigh's government had a running battle with animals. It was a losing proposition. Based on the amount of ink it received in the ordinance book, the pig was the hands-down ringleader of an animal population which outnumbered and outflanked humans in the capital.

Raleigh

Although pigs did chip in to help clean the streets, they had the custom of breaking into privies. Citizens became polarized into pro and anti-hog factions. (City Manager Benton might attest even today about the controversial nature of animal control laws.)

Loose dogs, sheep, goats and cattle – the latter herded through the streets until the 1930s – all contributed to the sanitation problem. Their owners were not much neater, given their tendencies to throw refuse of all kinds off their property, and to bury family members on it.

Confronted with a town whose slogan could have become the "City of Odors," Raleigh's commissioners in 1800 instituted what would have amounted to curbside pickup of garbage if there had been any curbs in the city. The public went along without recorded complaint, except for those who were forced to collect it as part of their street labor.

Raleigh's earliest practitioners made house calls which are documented in private account books.

Dr. John Streater charged $2.25 for each four-mile visit to counsel a patient's dyspeptic mother; he had to sue to collect his fee. On the other hand, office visits cost between 75 cents and $1.50, and one could have a tooth extracted for $1.00 by the same man who sold boots and fodder.

In the early 1800s, one Calvin Jones advertised that he would inoculate Raleigh residents for smallpox if enough came forward to make it profitable, but that he would do so only in April.

"I have not such confidence in my own skill as to be willing to undertake the management and safe conduct of this Disease" in the summer months, Jones wrote – a refreshing case of truth in advertising.

He charged eight dollars "for white persons and a guinea for mulattoes and negroes."

One of Raleigh's earliest doctors was Sterling Wheaton, whose treatments are preserved in an invoice to Treasurer Haywood.

"Extracting Tooth, and the stump of another": seven shillings sixpence. (It hurts just to contemplate.)

"Curing Negro Boy of Gonorhea": five pounds.

Wheaton's methods give proof to the saying that in order to live a long life in the early 19th century, it was prudent to stay as far away from doctors as possible.

Raleigh

Among the prescriptions he administered were "sugar of lead for negro wench"; a "bottle of oil to Boy Drunk at Peter Casso's Kitchen"; and of course the ubiquitous "bleeding."

In a new place like this, where institutions and habits are forming, it is all-important to begin right."

With those words, the city commissioners tried in 1806 to get Raleigh residents to use the new Public Burial Ground rather than to continue to bury their loved ones in their individual lawns.

Noting that random burials could ruin the city's supply of spring water, the commissioners said that the public cemetery was "remote" from residents. (It is a few blocks east of the Capitol on New Bern Avenue.) Inhabitants of the city and their family and friends were to be interred in the cemetery's two northern squares, strangers in the southwest square, and negroes and mulattoes in the southeast quadrant.

The commissioners also noted in their ordinance that "in this city, we have no religious prejudices in favor of interments in Church-yards to combat." (But in 1806 the city had no churchyards at all.)

If Raleigh citizens were feeling puny – if they craved a sea change in the old metabolism – if they couldn't find the right pill in the 1811 version of the *Physician's Desk Reference* – they could resort to these remedies proposed by a local doctor in a letter to the *Star:*

For sore eyes: "Open the eyes over the steam of boiling spirit of Turpentine."

In case of the "Bite of a Mad Dog: take an ounce of Calomel and a certain quantity of dog's jaw-bone powdered, to be given at one dose." (Presumably this was administered to the bitee.)

The physician also told Raleigh citizens what to do for the "Bite of the Rattle Snake." They were advised to swallow, every ten or fifteen minutes, "strong spirits of Hartshorn, a volatile alkali," but that in case that concoction was sold out at the apothecary shop, the doctor said that snakebite victims could also choke down half-tablespoonfuls of wood ashes.

For "habitual headach," the physician recommended "half a pint or a pint of sound hard cider in the morning daily before breakfast." That eye-opener was to be accompanied by cold water applied to the head. It probably worked.

Raleigh

In early Raleigh, as today, women outlived the menfolk.

An historian in 1812 explained that "by living chiefly within doors they escaped the diseases that are caused by a sudden change of weather or obstructed perspiration."

(Creative explanations for the age differential still abound: in 1968, an N.C. State Professor told his class that women live longer "because they worry us to death," an equally plausible but at least facetious reason.)

What was the prescription? In the early 19th century, physician Richard B. Haywood instructed one of his patients as follows:

"I have prepared the medicine to be taken instead of liquor... whenever you feel a weakness of stomach and a strong inclination to drink to excess, drop 30 drops of this medicine in a glass half full of water and drink it.

"If this does not allay the thirst," Dr. Haywood continued, "repeat the dose and you may continue to repeat it until the inclination is done away – if you prefer it, you can sweeten it as you would Toddy."

After the *Star* included a medical advice section in its 1810 Almanack, a Raleigh physician wrote in to commend it.

He was less complimentary, however, about other publications, which he said promoted treatments which were "ridiculous or worse" and were the "occasion for the annual loss of many lives."

The anonymous physician urged Raleigh residents to avoid patent medicines, especially the "infallibly tasteless Ague Drops," which he disclosed were composed of a "solution of Arsenick or Rats-bone." (The *Raleigh Register* stocked them, which helps explain why the *Star* devoted so much space to the doctor's letter.)

If a Raleigh patient "escapes by the narrow road which lies between inert medicines and poisons," the physician concluded, "he should cry out 'a miracle'!"

The wistful vision of a millpond never included what occurred in Raleigh in 1821 and resulted in the case of *The Attorney-General upon the relation of sundry citizens of Raleigh v. Theophilus Hunter.*

It seems that Hunter, who was as well-connected as anyone in early Raleigh, decided to divert Rocky Branch creek near to the present-day Dorothea Drive. (Now who would want to divert that nice creek?) Hunter installed a dam and created a 10-acre millpond.

Unfortunately, several drains from the city emptied into the creek above the dam. The waste, "filth," vegetable matter and stagnant water, when acted upon by the sun, produced a condition which the "sundry citizens" said in their lawsuit was a threat to the city. In particular, they complained of foul odors, a loss of property values, and disease.

Although the name "malaria" had not yet been put to the disease and the role of the mosquito in transmitting it was unknown, the Raleigh petitioners knew that more and more citizens were coming down with what they called "intermittent fever." The source, they were convinced, was Hunter's Pond.

The citizens – Willie Jones, Thomas Devereux, Charles Manly and Joseph Gales among them – used many expressions to describe Hunter's Pond when they filed for an injunction against it, but the term "idyllic" was not in their vocabulary. Their words were "putrefaction" and "noxious" and "epidemic."

Using local physicians as expert witnesses, the plaintiffs traced the spread of malaria which had begun in Raleigh once Hunter dammed up the creek. The first summer, fever touched most of the households south of Cabarrus Street; the second summer, it progressed halfway to Hillsborough Street; the third summer, families on Hillsborough Street were getting sick. That was when they filed the class-action lawsuit.

But in addition to illness, the plaintiffs swore that Hunter's creation would harm the city in another way that it understood best: loss of money.

"Your orators show," their lawyers told the Superior Court, "that one great inducement to their becoming citizens of (Raleigh) and investing such large sums of money in the purchase of real property there, was a belief, grounded on their own observations, and on the experience of the oldest inhabitants for a number of years, that they and their families would continue in the enjoyment of good health."

They said that until Hunter rerouted Rocky Branch, they had had "no cause to regret the investment." They intimated that until the appearance of the pond, Raleigh had experienced "no depreciation in the price of property in it."

(The latter statement was technically true, since real estate prices in 1825 were on a par with those of 1792. But either the petitioners had no grasp of inflation and carrying costs or they chose not to mention them in their pleadings. In real dollars, property values were as much under water as Hunter's former meadow.)

The plaintiffs asked the court to declare the pond a public nuisance.

As for Hunter, any member of a family which could get its tavern mentioned favorably in a state law was not going to give up without a fight.

Hunter's lawyers tried to introduce reasonable doubt into the evidence.

Why were Raleigh citizens *really* getting sick, they asked. Had not all of the pines and nearly all of the oaks been cut down between the stream and the Governor's Palace, they asked. Had the introduction of cotton-growing into the city occasioned the disease? Didn't those heaps of cotton seeds used for fertilizer smell to high heaven after a few rainstorms?

Hadn't the pond area been a "quagmire" long before Hunter developed it, the lawyers asked. Hadn't Hunter really *improved* the area? Hadn't people been similarly sick before the pond appeared? Couldn't the victims have fallen ill elsewhere? They traveled a lot, didn't they? How about those new immigrants who could have brought the disease into the city?

Weren't there some people living in good health near the pond, the lawyers asked. What disease, they concluded. The arguments make textbook reading.

Inconveniently for Hunter, however, members of the judiciary not only had viewed and smelled his pond, but one of them suffered from an ailment which seemed suspiciously like intermittent fever.

Hunter was enjoined into perpetuity from tampering with the flow of Rocky Branch.

In its opinion upholding the injunction, the State Supreme Court used few words to balance the rights of private enterprise against those of the common good. The state capital, the court held, is special. In sentiments which may live again someday, the justices wrote:

"The injury is irreparable; the place is the seat of government, where its officers are compelled to reside. These things make a difference between this case and that of a common nuisance.

"This is something like the interest of the many (against the few)," the Court concluded, "for every individual is in some way or other interested in the welfare of the capital."

Fifteen leeches – $1. Extracting tooth – $1. Bleeding – $1." Malpractice premium – no, there was no such insurance in 1838. At least the Raleigh physician who submitted the above bills was consistent in his fee schedule.

The doctor will remain anonymous; but his handwritten, personal treatment guide is in the State Archives. What is horrifying is the thought that 150 years from now, physicians may regard today's cures with as much amusement as we do those of 1838. (Or worse, they will conclude that the Raleigh physician in 1838 was in many cases on target.) A selection of his remedies:

"For the Bite of a Mad Dog" (How, in view of Raleigh's problems with hydrophobia, did the dogs come to be man's best friend? Who did they hire for their press agent?): "Do not close the wound; burn it with a hot iron or coal... produce a running sore and keep it open and running, and the blood will throw off the poison. If it is kept open like an issue for months so much the better; the poison ceases before the nerves are affected."

For a dog bite: "take the yellow of an egg, sugar and the dog's hair and mix them together" and make the victim drink it.

"To stop bleeding at the nose: inhale snuff pounded together with sugar of lead."

For shortness of breath: take an iron pot, pour vinegar into it, add snake root and 120 eight-penny nails, and simmer overnight.

The patient was supposed to swallow one tablespoonful of this specialty of the house with every meal.

"Cure for a rising on a woman's breast": use "equal parts of camphor and Rabbit's grease" and anoint the area.

And "for an old stubborn pain: Make a hoe cake of corn Bred with salt and red pepper in it, split it open (and) put one half of it to the pain." (The other half was for dinner.)

Nor were animals safe from the doctor's advice. For a horse's eyes, he prescribed, "take vinegar, dissolve salt in it as long as it will, then put it in the eye, or soap suds and salt is very good, or take molasses in your mouth and you spurt it through a quill in the eye." (Small wonder that nearly every issue of Raleigh's newspapers had advertisements for missing horses.)

The doctor also knew about houses. In an afternote, he reminded himself to "heat lime, brown sugar and fine salt" as a preparation to coat and fireproof his roof.

Tell it to the Southern Californians.... A Raleigh physician, advising citizens on how to view the coming solar eclipse on February 12, 1831, wrote that "the safest method of witnessing an eclipse is in a tub of water," looking from beneath the surface.

As perceptive as the *Microcosm* was about the connection between smoking and poor health (see the section on vice), the newspaper operated with less sound instincts in giving advice on how to remove skin cancers. Or did it?

For a cancer on the nose, Raleigh readers were advised to cook up "a potash of red oak bark boiled down to the consistency of molasses." The next step was to lard the steaming mixture over the carcinoma. Then, after an hour, a plaster of tar was to be placed over the spot. The *Microcosm* said that the entire procedure should be repeated "every few days" until the cancer disappeared.

(It is fortunate that North Carolinians were not known as Tar Noses, or worse, instead of Tar Heels. But aside from the lack of a microscope, how much more primitive was this technique than is today's use of a scalpel and cauterization?)

John Rex is remembered for the hospital which bears his name, but that charitable bequest was only a secondary consideration in his will in 1839.

Foremost in Rex's mind was how to dispose of his 17 slaves, in view of the fact that his immediate survivors were old and financially well off.

Rex instructed his executors "to remove... said negroes from the state to Africa in some colony there under the patronage and control of the American Colonization Society."

Although Rex provided that the deportation of the slaves was voluntary and would make them free, he added a further incentive: any slave unwilling to go would be auctioned at public sale, with the proceeds to be shared by those blacks who caught the ship out of Norfolk.

(Only one slave, Winney, refused to go to Liberia. Since Rex had recently acquired her on the installment plan, she was returned to her owner and Rex's promissory note was retrieved.)

But if the sixteen who went to Liberia managed to prosper, it was without the assistance of the trustees of the Rex Hospital fund. They were indignant that the slaves were to receive more money than the hospital.

In 1841, the trustees sued to prevent the former slaves from receiving $1,182.41 from the sale of hides which had been in the Rex tannery's inventory when he died. (Rex had ordered that the proceeds from certain property sales be used to give the blacks capital with which to begin their new lives.)

"A slave is considered as a chattel and not as a person," the hospital board argued, and following that logic, they were "incapable of taking property" and the Rex will was "illegal."

As a matter of fact, the trustees told the North Carolina Supreme Court, all monies sent to the blacks in Liberia since their embarkation had been "ill disposed of" and were a "lapse" by Rex's executors. The trustees hinted that they wanted all the money back, along with the note for Winney.

The Supreme Court agreed that the slaves were non-persons, but it found a way to uphold Rex's will on separate grounds: that the will had a "charitable purpose" because the exile of free negroes from the state furthered "public policy." Rex's executors, Duncan Cameron and George Mordecai, were free from the threat of having to fork over more than $12,000.

The former slaves did not see the remainder of their inheritance for 14 more years. The state held the money, earning interest, while it devised tests for the blacks to pass to prove that they had in fact gone to Africa and were the same negroes who had been the property of John Rex.

An agent of the blacks wrote in 1848 that "their hope has been so long deferred that their hearts are quite sick." But not until they retained Washington counsel in the 1850s were the blacks paid. By then several had died or could not be located, and their unpaid shares went to the Rex Hospital trustees.

Except for its effect on Raleigh, what happened to those trustees next would be sweet irony. In 1861, the trustees took most of the money and interest they had amassed since 1839 and invested it in Confederate bonds. By 1866, the $50,227 in assets had dwindled to $5,000, less than when the bequest was made.

Raleigh would not have a permanent hospital for about 50 years after the death of John Rex.

I do not feel very bright this afternoon," a Raleigh woman wrote in 1849, "after having a Dentist to operate on my teeth this morning."

Mrs. Lucy Bryan wrote that "my nerves are completely unstrung – he came at half past nine – and I asked him what he wanted.

"There was a servant to get it for him," she continued, "and the first thing he ordered was the coarsest table to be brought in – large enough to lay me out on – this he wanted to put his instruments of torture on."

Mrs. Bryan said that "I told him the preparations looked much more like I was to be beheaded than to have my tooth extracted."

She wrote that instead of yanking her tooth, "he done a great deal of filing – it is all over and I feel very much relieved."

The Independent (no connection with the present-day weekly newspaper) reported in 1845 that "disease is prevailing in the city," causing several deaths and a minor epidemic.

The malady, called "black tongue" or "Swelled head," was thought to be "generated by the atmosphere."

The *Independent* advised Raleigh's fearful rural neighbors that they might as well venture into town since they could catch the disease as easily on their farms.

"Though called black tongue," the newspaper reassured, "the tongue is not black" but was a "dirty looking grey color with red edges and other varying colors." It recommended a cure "by drinking Red Pepper Tea."

When a slave was badly burned (not at the stake) in 1849, Dr. Richard B. Haywood offered advice which seems ingenious.

Haywood recommended that a liniment be applied constantly to the burn, composed of "equal parts of lime, water and sweet oil or hog's foot oil (if more convenient)."

After suggesting that "the limbs be kept straight to prevent deformity," he told the attendants to keep germs out of the wound but to keep the bedclothes off of the patient. Haywood advised that they disassemble a barrel, saw the hoops in half, and make arches out of them under the sheets. The procedure worked.

Where are they now and in what condition? Raleigh in 1860 was the home of three curative springs.

The Ingleside, owned by Governor Charles Manly, offered baths in "chalybeate water with several minerals." It was located just northwest of the original street grid.

The Suzie Spring, near to Nash Square, was less forthcoming about the contents of its water but made great efforts to warm it. (The *N&O* probably hit this spring several decades ago when it was digging to expand its press operations.)

And a few paces from South Street, nearly opposite Bloodworth, was the Dodd Sulphur Spring, whose name tells it all.

Great moments in Raleigh medicine.... E. Burke Haywood, who spent much of the Civil War as chief surgeon of the Pettigrew field hospital in the city, was ordered by the Confederacy to try a substitute for scarce and expensive quinine.

To relieve what today is called malaria, the Confederate command told Haywood to slather turpentine over the torsos of his patients. Haywood was to anticipate when the next fever and chills were due in a soldier and then have his staff apply rollers much like painting a wall.

Whether he was smiling or not when he filled out his report, Haywood told the officers in Richmond that the turpentine not only prevented malaria attacks from recurring, but that it "cured" the men so that they could return to the front lines.

(One hopes that Dr. Haywood, cognizant of the need for after-care, warned his patients to approach the Union troops from downwind.)

If the Civil War had been a contest of paperwork in hospitals rather than bullets in the field, the South could have won in a walk.

Even as the war was being lost in August, 1864, surgeon Burke Haywood had to write at least 176 official letters in addition to his monthly reports and forms. In all, Haywood's archives contain 27 separate and overlapping forms to be sent to the Confederacy, all of them requiring at least one duplicate.

Haywood occasionally was rebuked by the brass in Richmond concerning the quality of his paperwork.

Once, while filling out one of the endless forms, he arranged the conditions of his patients into these whimsical categories: "not very good; good; pretty good; tolerable; bad; and very good."

The bureaucracy wanted more detailed diagnoses. Haywood, trying to keep his hospital together, was fortunate even to report.

On another occasion, Richmond assailed Dr. Haywood again, asking for new duplicate invoices for everything that Pettigrew Hospital had purchased in the prior three months. (The war appears to have ended before he could reply.)

Haywood's reports tell a great deal about Pettigrew, which together with Hospital No. 7 and the building which later became Peace College were Raleigh's first hospitals.

The physician not only performed surgery, but he managed a staff which averaged 40 and included free Negroes and slaves. Their official job descriptions ranged from the conventional "nurse" or "matron" to "scavenger." Three of Haywood's own slaves worked at Pettigrew for $20 per month each, paid by the Confederacy to the surgeon in addition to his own salary.

The three hospitals in Raleigh contained 588 bedsteads; 239 mattresses; 376 strawsacks; 228 hospital shirts; 848 pillow cases; 1,605 sheets; 365 chamber pots; 377 mugs; 198 spit boxes; 190 spit cups; 138 spittoons; and 48 stoves, some of which were without fixtures. (One can infer that if a stove fire got out of control, the hospitals had an ample quantity of spittle on hand to extinguish it.)

Raleigh

In the Confederate system, every 100 rations of bacon and corn meal – that was the patients' diet – entitled the hospital to 10 pounds of rice, one gallon of vinegar, 24 ounces of candles, four pounds of soap, and three pounds of salt. (The calculation works out to .64 ounces of soap per patient each week. Raleigh citizens were constantly supplementing the supplies at the hospitals.)

Every so often, Dr. Haywood was ordered to scrape the crust off the arm of a youthful victim of smallpox, seal and date the specimen, and put it on a train to Richmond so that the Confederacy could make more vaccine.)

Haywood also described the ailments of patients in the hospitals who were incapacitated by causes other than combat: mania, nostalgia, syphilis, herpes and two kinds of gonorrhea.

Writing about a colleague who suddenly died in 1866, State Sen. Leander Gash compared him to a child he had once seen who died from a reaction to the wrong medication.

"For ought I know," Gash wrote, "Mr. Sanders might have yet been in his seat if there had been no physicians in Raleigh."

No inspector at the City Market could have prevented an incident such as one reported by the *Daily News* in 1872:

"An old citizen was gratified to find at the market last Saturday a nice lot of partridge eggs," the account read, "which he bought for his breakfast.

"Before cooking it was necessary to test the condition of the lot by opening one. The shell broke easily and out came a young snake that doubtless would have been hatched in a few hours had it remained in the nest."

To see ourselves as others see us.... The following reports on Raleigh appeared in a newspaper in Binghamton, New York in 1872 and were pronounced to be "very fair and truthful descriptions" by the *Daily News*, even as to their accounts of loathsome health habits.

"It is called the 'City of Oaks,' Professor F.B. Fairchild wrote about Raleigh, "but I have named it the 'City of Dogs.' We have dogs of every size, color and bark – At night you would think, by the howling, that a pack of wolves had taken possession of the city."

The professor next turned his attention to Raleigh's steer-drawn carts, or "keerts" as the locals pronounced it. (Most of the city's horses and mules were requisitioned in the Civil War and had not been replaced. Steers or oxen were attached to two-wheel, poled carts by "rope lines or chains fastened to their horns.")

Many of the animals appeared "stunted" or overworked. "I have often seen them no higher than the hubs of the carts to which they were attached," Fairchild wrote.

"Someone remarked the other day," he informed his Northern audience, "that when niggers went out of slavery, steers went in."

Fairchild also related an anecdote to show that the steers were so important in post-war Raleigh that they were regarded as family members. Asked how his family was, one weathered local was said to have remarked, "Oh, the steers is quite pert, but the old woman has got misery in the back."

The "old woman" may also have had misery in the gums, from the description Fairchild gave of snuff-dipping.

Dipping was "indulged in, more or less, by the women of all classes," he wrote. "The process is too disgusting to describe."

He then proceeded to describe it.

"It is a common thing," he explained, "when they meet for a social dip, to use each other's brushes. These brushes are made from small branches of the black-gum or birch, about half as long as a lead pencil, with one end splintered up to form a sort of swab."

Fairchild reported that in Raleigh, "the venders of these brushes are usually country people, who bring them in and advertise them as they pass along the street in this way: 'Tooth brushes by the bunch; ten cents chawed; five cents not chawed.'"

With details such as those being disseminated in the North, how could the city have failed to attract a host of eager settlers?

The Rex trustees were still recovering from their venture in Confederate bonds when Raleigh at last got its first hospital from the Guild of St. John's in 1878.

Begun on Wilmington Street as a hospital for the destitute, St. John's moved in 1882 to the residence of former Governor Charles Manly. With citizens making donations to buy the property and the city contributing a well, two wards opened which could accommodate eight patients each.

Bless the *Observer*'s heart.... In 1878, the newspaper published an environmentally-correct answer to the torment of mosquito bites:

"The only safe and Christian way to keep from being devoured... is to get a real good live fresh baby to sleep with.

"The mosquito is an epicure and will desert (your) hardened countenance... and caress the soft cheeks of the helpless infant with the accomplished taste and judgment of a cannibal bon vivant."

Physicians' fees and insurance costs – two topics of conversation today – burst into the open in Raleigh in the 1880s with the case of Dr. R.B. Ellis.

At the time, life insurance was only "beginning to be recognized as a necessity" in the city. (As Dr. Ellis put it, "in times like the present, fortunes are lost in a day," and survivors left penniless.)

But what Ellis called the "Old Line" insurance companies charged high premiums. So the city's secret societies – the Masons, Odd Fellows, and others – began to insure their own members and were able to qualify as non-profit charities thanks to some lobbying at the Legislature.

Enter Dr. Ellis, who got into trouble as soon as he became the medical examiner for the societies. He negotiated a fee of two dollars for each pre-insurance physical examination he performed under his contract.

The Raleigh Academy of Medicine, however, imposed on each of its members a fixed fee schedule. In the case of pre-insurance physicals, the fixed fee was $5, or $10 if the checkup included a urinalysis. The Academy ordered Dr. Ellis to jack up his fees to the posted level or be expelled. To put some teeth in its order, the Academy added that if Dr. Ellis were expelled, no Academy member would thereafter be permitted to consult with him.

Dr. Ellis's appeal took months. He pointed out that the Academy's fee schedule applied only to insurance companies, and that the secret societies were specifically exempted from that status.

He cited ongoing deviations from the Academy's fee schedules, including the custom of providing free service in "charity hospitals and in the families of ministers of the gospel." He printed circulars. He named several prominent Raleigh doctors who were helping out gratis at Shaw University. He even quoted Dr. R.B. Haywood, who had said it was "scandalous" that the State paid him only 52 cents per head for treating convicts "and require(d) him to furnish his own conveyance and driver."

None of this evidence exactly benefited the newcomer Ellis. The Academy ruled that he must charge the societies five dollars per examination. But it added, magnanimously, that if Dr. Ellis felt like it, he could "donate back" whatever portion of his fee he chose.

In his last pamphlet before he moved his practice to another city, Dr. Ellis observed that "action must be taken and there must be a victim."

Consider a report from the *News and Observer,* circa 1885:

"There is a young man going around in this city, physicians say, teaching his companions the morphine habit. He carries with him a small syringe and administers... hypodermic injections."

Yet how innocent some areas of Raleigh appeared to be as late as 1958. That year, a leading medical supplier sold hypodermic kits to eighth-graders from Daniels Junior High School. The students, who had not been to the supplier before, claimed that they needed the syringes for a science project.

(It was true; but as a participant recalled it, they wanted to see what would happen when they injected concentrate of Texize detergent into a neighbor's okra pods the night before they would be harvested and cooked. Bubble, bubble, toil and trouble.)

Right next to the patent medicine advertisements, the *Democratic Banner* in 1892 published this little poem:

*"One dose, said the quack, will be quite enough;
It will quickly banish your pain.
The victim took one dose of the stuff
And never complained again."*

It is an uncomfortable feeling for one to think he is drinking water daily that causes fish to turn over and die without a struggle."
Josephus Daniels had a point.

In 1895, a researcher at N.C. State had decided to test the city's drinking water. He filled a pool, placed some of the Experiment Station's fish in it, and cringed as they promptly went belly up. Concerned that some outside substance might have contaminated the pool, he went inside to a sink, filled it, and dipped a strip of blue litmus paper into the tap water. The strip turned a brilliant red.

The culprit was sulfuric acid. Three years earlier, when the Caraleigh Phosphate Mill burned to the ground, acid had soaked into the water table at a point above the city's tile water pipes. Although the company and the city pledged to repair the damage, neither had taken action by 1895. Nor was there any practical method of getting the acid out of the ground.

Whenever it rained, sulfuric acid leached into the city's water, producing "enough acid to kill fish. Whether it will hurt the populace that drinks the water is an open question."

Raleigh

As for the N.C. State researcher who discovered the problem, the *N&O* reported that "to say that Mr. Burner was surprised when he saw what he had been drinking would be putting it mildly." The city had another run on bottled water.

Great moments in Raleigh medicine.... During the 1896 Presidential campaign, William Jennings Bryan addressed a crowd in Nash Square.

During the course of his speech, "a large bug flew into his mouth, lodging in his throat, causing much pain." Bryan was rushed to the Park Hotel where Dr. Hubert Royster removed the insect.

(Royster did not report whether or not it was a "gold bug" which afflicted the orator.)

Apart from a few beds at the Leonard Medical School at Shaw University, Raleigh's first and last hospital for blacks was the St. Agnes Hospital which opened in 1896.

Converted for $1,600 from a house on the grounds of St. Augustine's College, when the hospital opened it had "no water in the house except for one faucet in the kitchen."

In fact, reading over the conditions at St. Agnes when it opened – written by a physician who attended there for many years – would make one prefer to be ill at home.

St. Agnes had no screens over its windows, so that it was home to "flying things innumerable, with wings small and great." The hospital had "no plumbing anywhere – only earth closets." The entire facility was heated with wood, and hot water was produced on stoves in the separate wards. St. Agnes had only two small steamers for sterilization, and their "results were untrustworthy."

The hospital's laundry was done in three wash tubs and "a big iron kettle in the yard." If a need arose for ice, "a horse named Nellie with a two-wheel cart" had to carry it from downtown. "Cool water was brought in by hand from the spring to bathe the typhoid patients."

Last, St. Agnes had no electricity for years after it opened. The hospital got by with oil lamps.

From those beginnings, St. Agnes hospital persevered, although in 1940 the college still described it as "handicapped by an inadequate plant and insufficient income." It closed its doors in the early 1960s.

Raleigh

Why they vanished is unclear, but Raleigh once had cast-iron public water fountains which catered to man or beast.

At the summit of each fountain was a lion's head which dispensed water for humans. At the four-foot level were cooler-sized pans for the city's horse population. The bottom of each fountain held a smaller pan for dogs.

(There is no need to comment on the city's historic peculiarities when it came to deciding who could drink from what water fountain.)

The elegance of the cast-iron fountains, installed in 1897, may have looked out of place next to the great ornamental fountain which was placed in Moore Square. Able to shoot streams of water 20 feet in the air, the fountain was designed by a committee and looked it: its embellishments included motifs of tree trunks, ferns and squirrels. The fountain had been working for about a week when the city, acting at the request of persons best left unknown, decided to paint the plants and animals to look more lifelike.

(Now if someone would just paint camouflage on a certain monument at the Capitol, which State workers affectionately refer to as the "bowling trophy.")

Commenting in 1898 on why it had unilaterally sunk three new wells to an average depth of 130 feet, the executive committee of the Insane Asylum had this to say:

"We are not willing for our patients even to bathe in the water contaminated from hillside washings from slaughter pens and dejections from hospitals, and the water supply of Rocky Branch is getting year by year more and more contaminated and unfit."

(The executive committee's words deserve to be placed in context. In the same year, retiring Mayor W.M. Russ assured the city that "we have the best sanitary department of any city south of New York and our mortality rate now compares favorably with that of any city on earth." What if he was right?)

Raleigh opened a smallpox hospital in 1899 when the city had its last real bout with the disease, and stays in what the mayor called "this detention house" were not voluntary.

All who had been exposed to the disease were confined to the hospital for weeks, and if they contracted smallpox, city officials entered their houses, disinfected them, and burned the entire contents except for the furniture.

By the time the epidemic ended, some 80 percent of the capital's popu-

Raleigh

lation was vaccinated; unlike its neighbors, Raleigh suffered no deaths in the epidemic.

The epidemic had one side benefit in addition to updating the city's wardrobes in the closets which were torched: in the course of the vaccination program, officials were able to identify many cases of malaria in the city's poorer neighborhoods.

The first item brought before the city board in 1900 was that of impure drinking water.

"Charges had been brought to the board," a report read, "that the water was muddy and that tadpoles and other matter were coming through the faucets.

"After 20 years of investigations, discussion and action," the report went on, "the board was still debating the definition of 'pure drinking water.'" (Raleigh, of course, has progressed far beyond that point.)

The *Raleigh Times* offered this benediction on the old city Market House in 1909:

"Filthy old market house," it wrote. "A building 50 years behind its times, unsanitary, unfit for market purposes, home to countless millions of flies and billions of germs.

"Chicken coops, odorous and roughly built, are lined up on the sidewalk. Rotting fish make it a place of torture to one accustomed to decent surroundings. There are no arrangements for flushing the place... Any water turned loose on the floor must be swept out with a broom... Not even screen doors."

The *Times* continued – and this was not an editorial, but a news story – that "hordes of flies feast contentedly on the steak that is later to go to the people." The newspaper referred to "aprons boasting of long immunity from the effects of soap and water."

Then the *Times* took off its gloves and said what it really thought: "It is filth, filth, FILTH!"

(Imagine what the policemen and prisoners had experienced in the market's basement all of those years.)

Too late for Velma Barfield.... A public health report early in this century contained the following statement:

"I also note that at Oakwood Cemetery, interments are occasionally made without certificates (of the cause of death). This has occurred only in the cases of the deaths of members of the most respectable families, concerning whose decease no question could be raised."

In his *Health Survey of Raleigh* for 1918, Dr. C.E. Terry found (how to put this...?) the city still had ample opportunity for improvement.

Speaking of Raleigh's high death rates, which were 23.0 per 1,000 population among whites and 36.2 among blacks, Dr. Terry noted that "the excessive figure among Negroes is a familiar phenomenon, and reflects the conditions under which they live."

About the city's rates of infant mortality (89.3 per 1,000 whites and 225.7 among blacks), he blamed local midwives "who do not know the meaning of the phrase 'surgical cleanliness.'" Dr. Terry said that of the 80 infants who had died the year before, "half could have been saved by well-established health department activities."

(To bring the infant mortality rate into context, in 1989 the nation of Burkina Faso – generally regarded as the world's bleakest in every category – had an infant mortality rate of 138 per 1,000 live births.)

Addressing Raleigh's tuberculosis rate (189.6 cases per 100,000 whites, 374.2 among blacks), Dr. Terry observed that "the Negro rate is huge."

As Dr. Terry inspected Raleigh, he found that "the wells of the city are generally polluted"; that "there is no supply of pasteurized or certified milk in the city" (USDA certification began only in 1917); that the city's "dipped milk is dangerous"; that most food stores had unsanitary conditions; that the city's privies were neither fly-proof nor rat-proof; that "the quarter of the city occupied by the Negroes is without sewerage, for the reason that they object to the expense of installing the lines"; that too many animals were harbored in town; and that malaria mosquitoes bred not only where they were expected – along Walnut Creek – but also in the lakes at Pullen Park.

What those in authority seem to desire," wrote the *Raleigh Times* in 1918, "is that every survey begin with: 'We report the City and Commissioners to be wide-awake, alert, onto their jobs and tireless in their efforts to serve and please the public.

"'Their subordinates are trustworthy, at all times doing the best they know. How a germ of any kind ever gets by them, we don't know.'"

But rather than being "tireless" in promoting public health, the *Times* remarked, "we would have said that their tires were merely deflated."

Raleigh

What bothered the *Times* was that "so far as known, (Raleigh's) death rate continues to be twice that of the average death rate of the United States – influenza not counted."

Noting that the city spent only 50 cents per capita on public health, the newspaper observed that there was no mosquito control, the water supply was "in imminent danger of pollution by privies," and that there was "a history of typhoid on the watershed." The *Times* advocated raising health expenditures all the way up to a dollar a year per inhabitant.

"Only Two Deaths from Influenza Reported Monday."
To grasp the destruction of the flu epidemic on Raleigh in 1918, it is necessary to read only that single headline from the *Raleigh Times*.

(Not the ones describing the two or three or five or even twelve deaths in a single day; not even the report that Raleigh led the State in that October with 102 deaths, "excluding the State College and Camp Polk," which lost another twenty. "Only two" was *news.*)

The city shut down for six weeks. Schools, theaters, meeting halls and churches alike – all were closed by order of the city commission.

"There will be no sound of church bells," the *Times* reported, "to arouse the city from its Sunday morning nap; no guilty conscience to keep one from pulling down the shades to cut off the disturbing light, thumping up the pillow and turning over for another forty minutes or so... For the first time in the history of the City of RALEIGH an epidemic has closed the church doors."

Raleigh's colleges either sent their students home or quarantined them. The *Times* offered advice on how to stay healthy:

"Salute, but do not shake hands," was one precaution.

In the absence of church, Raleigh policemen doffed their hats for two minutes each evening and led prayers on the sidewalks.

Since the high school was unoccupied, the city converted its auditorium and classrooms into a quarantine hospital, and as the epidemic increased, they sent patients to it whether they wanted to go or not.

City hall, as expected, tried to vacillate. "With as much respect as it is possible for us to entertain for the opinion of the City Commission," the *Times* scolded, "all of us realize that it is not qualified to decide or solve a problem such as now confronts it... there should be none of the delay which so often characterizes Raleigh's government."

As the epidemic appeared to end, the commissioners lifted their ban on mass gatherings. With that, the number of flu cases surpassed earlier levels.

As December, 1918 ended, citizens were reporting in at city hall for something called "flu vaccine shots." An estimated 238 citizens had died, not counting students, soldiers and inmates.

Most of us prefer our drinking water straight."
That observation by the *N&O* in 1927 related to the color, odor and taste of Raleigh's tap water that summer.

After putting aside rumors that a dead body had been found in the city's reservoir, officials blamed the water's foul condition on decaying weeds at the bottom of Lake Raleigh. They said the water was safe.

"Better to mow than to drink," the *N&O* retorted.

The newspaper said that "there are many with means who pay good money to drink water from magic springs which tastes altogether as bad."

When the city engaged in one of its periodic assaults on rodents in 1935, that year's "War on Rats" began not in one of the public squares, but in West Raleigh.

Residents were advised to place Red Squill Rat Bait in comestibles left outside their homes.

"The bait causes sickness in dogs, cats, human beings and poultry," the city cautioned, "but is not fatal." (Tell that to the dogs; the city cancelled the campaign after local veterinarians had seen enough.)

The distinguished juror has found the waters of the Neuse River not guilty."

With that *bon mot*, the State Supreme Court in 1935 rebuffed the strongest challenge to that time of Raleigh's practice of dumping raw sewage into Crabtree and Walnut creeks.

"The judge subjected the question to 'trial by water,'" the Court held, "because the record discloses that His Honor had drunk of the water, bathed in it, and suffered no ill effects."

The Court added that the Town of Smithfield, which brought the lawsuit, had shown no menace from the water and that besides, the City of Raleigh lacked the money to build a treatment plant. It took 20 more years for Smithfield to prevail.

Bring me your tired, ailing, diseased, anti-New Deal free enterprisers.... Rex Hospital never achieved a modern state of conditions until 1936, when it obtained a 30-year subsidized loan from the Federal Public Works Administration of President Roosevelt.

In 1953, the Chamber of Commerce almost offhandedly reported that Raleigh still "does not own and operate a sewage disposal plant."

The Chamber noted that "raw sewage and industrial wastes from the City of Raleigh are dumped into the Neuse River. This violates the health laws of North Carolina."

What was remarkable was that the city – sued over the issue of sewage since the 1880s – had been under a court order since 1948 to build and operate an effective treatment plant by 1955.

Even with that grace period, construction had not begun when the Chamber issued its report in December, 1953.

All Pistols, Cards And Likker Must Be OK'd By The Teacher

Although the State of North Carolina promised to support public education in the Halifax Constitution of 1776, it meant to aid teachers only to "enable them to instruct at low prices."

What would be called free public education was suggested and quickly squashed in the 1800 Legislature. Raleigh's delegation voted against it.

About three-fifths of Raleigh's original inhabitants must have been illiterate.

The situation was exacerbated by laws forbidding the teaching of slaves to read and write. Yet as late as 1850, one out of seven white adults in Wake County was what today might be called "print-challenged."

One historian mourned that "the humiliating fact is... that in point of education, our State is behind all in the Union." From reading court documents, deeds, and receipt books from early Raleigh, someone from another culture might think "Mr. X. Hismark" was the leading citizen in town.

(Someone from another culture might also wonder why voters in early Raleigh were not required to pass any literacy test.)

Schoolchildren and the random outlanders who have trouble spelling "Raleigh" have reason to cheer up.

According to Nina Covington in the *North Carolina Booklet* in 1926, "... in (Sir Walter) Raleigh's time, there were about fifteen or twenty ways of spelling the name."

She revealed that in 1578, Raleigh himself signed a deed as "Rawleyghe" and also spelled his name as Rawley or Raleghe or Rawleigh. But according to Ms. Covington, "he never in a single instance spelled the name Raleigh as we spell it today."

The State Capital had no schools until 1800, when tavernkeeper Peter Casso (né Pierre Caseaux) advertised that he would broker classes for "Young Gentlemen and Young Ladies" out of his hotel.

Prior to his effort, a few Raleigh children were either taught at home or sent to private academies in nearby towns such as Louisburg or Fayetteville.

Casso imported a Mr. Guthrie from the Pittsborough Academy to teach the boys and hired a Mrs. Langley, who had tutored in the city for a few years, to instruct the girls.

Instruction was basic. Girls' courses were confined to English, geography and needle-point, but in return for this limited curriculum they received a discount: $9 per annum instead of the $13 charged to the boys, who learned sciences and read classics such as *Gil Blas*.

When the inhabitants of Raleigh decided that their children would fare better with a formal academy, they characteristically formed a committee to examine it for every potential drawback. Unable to muster a quorum for most meetings ("Members will please attend," one notice read, "for something definitely is to be done."), the committee languished.

On the other hand, Raleigh's children in 1800 may have been blissfully ignorant.

Teachers in 1800 could literally kill their scholars while "correcting" them and in most cases walk free. The State drew the line at teachers who crushed pupils' heads with iron bars, as well as those who might grab a student, "kick him to the ground, and then stomp on his belly and kill him." These latter disciplinarians could be charged with a variant of homicide.

By 1811, the Female Department at the Raleigh Academy had enough of a curriculum to spread across six grades.

The Academy's female instructor taught her charges "piano forte, painting, drawing, tambouring, embroidery and all the various branches of plain and ornamental Needle-Work," as well as new courses such as *Whelpley's Historical Compendium* and *Dilworth's Arithmetic, Including the Rule of Three*.

As for courses in literature, they were taught only by male instructors and consisted of sessions on the New Testament, *Paradise Lost* and *Young's*

Night Thoughts. The literary works in the Female Department's Library – kept segregated from the Male library – were nine volumes ranging from the picaresque to the romantic.

John Chavis founded a school in Raleigh in 1808 with an interesting mixture of pupils.

Chavis taught white children by day and black children by night, with occasional overlaps. (In other words, the school at times was *de facto* desegregated. Authorities had not yet gotten serious about keeping blacks illiterate.) All of the students cheerfully ate together. They received what was described as a "rigorous education."

Among Chavis' graduates were Governor Charles Manly, U.S. Senator Willie P. Mangum, and the sons of Chief Justice Henderson.

Present-day students in the Raleigh schools who may believe that they are oppressed need to consider the *Laws of the Raleigh Academy,* published in 1811.

Many of the regulations exist in the schools today, if in different form. "No student shall keep or use pistols," for example; or the rules which made the students responsible for the costs of vandalism; or those that prohibited gambling on the premises, or promised expulsion in the case of a duel.

Other rules, however, might seem a fraction too strict.

Male students at the Academy were not to approach female students "on any pretext whatsoever," except when they all attended the compulsory prayer sessions and church services 13 times each week. The suspicious faculty also commanded that "the Male students shall hold no correspondence with, nor gallant the Young Ladies" of the Female Department.

Students were forbidden to attend dances, or even dancing classes, "except on the 4th of July and anniversary of Washington's birthday."

Nor could they "be present at any horse race or any other scene of dissipation" or "associate with any publicly bad or disorderly company." (In effect, they could not venture out into downtown Raleigh.)

At the religious services, the students had to "behave with becoming decency and solemnity."

The Academy's principal had the absolute right of prior censorship of all student papers and orations.

Last, the students were all subject to "correction," although at the Academy, beatings were "to be considered as the last resort."

(By 1830, the Academy rules had relaxed, but in an ominous manner.

Raleigh

Students were advised that no one could "bring with him dogs, guns, dirks or any offensive weapons, unless occasions render it necessary for his safety." They also were allowed to have liquor with faculty permission.

(Yet the 1830 version was a melange. Students were guilty until proved innocent in cases of fighting. Students were expelled for profanity and blasphemy or other incendiary talk. And the prohibition against attending horse races had been extended to include "card tables, chicken pecks... or any club or combination of demoralizing character whatsoever.")

Besides the Raleigh Academy and schools of Pierre Casso and John Chavis, the early capital tried numerous experiments in its efforts to educate its residents. Some of the more noteworthy follow:

* Archibald Wills' Cheap English School. Established in 1802, it was just that: three months' schooling cost 20 shillings.

By 1809, the school had raised its tuition to $10 per year, but Mr. Wills accepted "corn, bacon, brandy or anything else that I may want" at market value, delivered to his house, as an offset against his fees.

* John Henry Gault's School. Opened in 1807, it was a place "where good Boys will be treated with kindness and levity, but the incorrigible will experience the indelible stigma of expulsion."

* The Lancastrian schools. Opened in 1814 and 1815 after English models, these schools boasted that they needed only one faculty member for every 1,000 pupils and therefore could instruct masses of students for low tuition. Raleigh did not have enough students to put their advertising to the test, but the schools' tactic was to use the older students to teach the younger. The schools were free to needy children.

The more things change... William Peace, chairman of the Raleigh Library, advertised in 1838 that "several hundred library books" were overdue and announced that the library board needed "to call them in" at the citizens' "earliest convenience."

The library soon instituted a schedule of fines.

After a visit in 1844 to see his daughter at St. Mary's School, legislator Robert Paine wrote home that the students were under control.

"I found that the girls are kept under very great restraint," he said, "and what is admirable, not one of them seem to know it."

The Rev. Aldert Smedes, who ran the school, had a knack for enforcing discipline by such methods as banning jewelry and requiring the students to wear uniforms of a single color.

When the conversation got too loud at dinner," Paine reported, Smedes would "give a rap on the table and say, 'You ladies, some of you are interrupting the conversation of your neighbors.' The conversation would then be lowered to a proper tone."

But, Paine said, the dialogue would be "deprived of none of its cheerfulness."

The status of female education in early Raleigh was addressed squarely by Susan Nye Hutchison, who taught at the Raleigh Academy's Female Department in 1815, moved to Georgia, and returned to the Academy in 1935.

In *Mrs. Hutchison's View of Female Education,* printed as part of an Academy prospectus, she found that Raleigh in 1835 still harbored the "unfortunate impression that the female mind is incapable of laborious study." Mrs. Hutchison laid the blame on parents and on the men who set curriculums in the academies.

"In the higher seminaries," Mrs. Hutchison wrote, "the startling truth bursts upon the disappointed parents that the sister's mind has neither the strength nor discipline of her brother's. Her letters are inferior to his... and her conversation, though sometimes surpassing his in vivacity, is nevertheless deficient in solidity and intelligence."

Parents then generally took a daughter out of school, to the student's "bitter mortification... just as she has begun to appreciate the value of an education."

Mrs. Hutchison said the decision on when to terminate a girl's schooling "has seemed to be whether the pupil had attained the stature and fair proportions of womanhood" – in other words, is mature enough to be marriage material – "rather than whether her mind had acquired such improvement and refinement as would fit her to adorn the circle in which she was destined to move."

Mrs. Hutchison said that female students also had trouble because they were expected to complete the same course of study as boys in about half the years. As a result, she said, girls were inundated with too much information, "all is confused and chaotic," and their minds "resemble a garden too thickly planted."

Noting that girls were required to learn such sciences as were taught in Raleigh by the time they were 14 to 16 years old, but that boys were allowed until they were 18 to 20 to gain command of the same material, Mrs.

Hutchison made a sly comment: "One is almost tempted to conclude that the expectation of anything like equal attainments under (conditions) so entirely inferior, was something like an acknowledgement of superior talents" in the girls.

She lobbied for girls to be permitted to continue their studies, arguing that "no exterior polish, however brilliant, can make amends for their deficiency."

(Mrs. Hutchison was not exactly an advocate of exterior polish in women. In her Raleigh diaries of 1815, she had been appalled at women's dress at dances in the capital. And in the Academy prospectus of 1835, she defended her policy of students' dresses having "great plainness and neatness" by observing that "it rarely happens that fondness for expensive dress is found combined with study, or slatternliness associated with the Christian virtues.")

This may not need to get around, but.... Raleigh was the home of North Carolina's first law school, founded by Chief Justice John Louis Taylor in the early 1800s.

As recently as 1911, in fact, the city had three schools of law: the Estey Law School at Shaw University, the Judge George P. Pell Law School, and the Wilbur H. Royster School of Law.

In 1911, the city had 70 licensed lawyers; by 1936, the number had risen to 195; today the total is about 1,750. Yet Raleigh is one of the few state capitals without a school of law.

Raleigh did not get its first public schools until 1841, but when they at last appeared, they did so in a bunch.

In that year, a school opened on Moore Square, another on Nash Square, a third on property owned by the Boylan family, and a fourth – the Gum Spring School – at the corner of Cabarrus and McDowell streets.

Raleigh's original public school for black students, the Garfield School, was described in 1879 as "a leaky hull of a house, and was in such a dilapidated condition that, in wet and inclement weather, it was almost impossible to stay in."

As St. Mary's students prepared for their examinations in 1883, this account appeared in the *St. Mary's Muse:*

"January 22d. Exams draw near. The numerous wills, made and duly signed, and a dejected effigy, swinging from a tree, betray the general state of mind."

Hugh Morson "himself did not teach history.... His passionate devotion to truth prevented it."

When former State Treasurer Charles Johnson recalled Principal Morson and the Raleigh Male Academy, he did so with a smile.

When Johnson attended, the academy was a three-room frame house on Bloodworth Street. It had outdoor plumbing and no lights. (Johnson remembered that boys acted up more in the winter, in part because darkness limited the hours in which they could be detained after school.)

The curriculum may not have been influenced by any Basic Education Program, but Johnson saw merits in it anyway.

"There was nothing resembling a laboratory," he told the Sandwich Club in 1953, "and because none of the teachers ever seemed to have any grasp of science, I suppose it was a good thing that science was never taught."

As for Morson, the principal's ideas about keeping order in the classroom could have been debated in the General Assembly in 1991.

"Mr. Morson's technique," Johnson reported, "was out of this world.... He would advance upon a culprit with an ominous gleam in his eye, and seize the luckless fellow by the lapel of his coat. The violent shaking that followed almost invariably expelled any thought of resistance. Then would come the application of the hickory immediately to hand. To call these bludgeons switches would be a gross understatement."

Latin: The very word seems to strike terror into the soul."

So wrote Edward P. Moses, Raleigh's original public school superintendent. His mission of acclimating the city to graded schools was not easy, but if any pupil learned to read and comprehend Moses' annual reports to the Mayor, he or she was college material.

Moses did not initially get his Latin classes, because his more important task was "to convince Raleigh's parents that public education was not a form of charity and to dispel fears of rampant immorality in the schools."

Further, Moses had to refute the argument, being propagated by some Chamber of Commerce types, that education was "an upper-class luxury that, if extended to all children, would rob the city of future laborers."

From a review of his reports, Moses had a tough go of it. Although Raleigh's schools were filled, it was because the city had too few classroom seats and "many children are seeking in vain for admission." Yet he reported that truancy was still high; no laws then existed for compulsory attendance. All Moses could do was to advocate schooling through the age of 15 years.

But when he had his hands on the schoolchildren, Moses had definite ideas about their proper instruction. The Superintendent wanted what he called "Prussian Discipline" in the Raleigh schools.

"Let men and women who suffer their daughters' minds to be filled with false views of life present in the sickly, trashy novelette of the day, and allow their sons to keep constant company, in their intellectual life, with cow-boys, thieves and cut-throats beware," he wrote. (Moses had at least mastered Prussian syntax; city department heads just don't hand in reports like his anymore.)

"There is no reason," he continued, "why a child should ever read a bad book or a silly book." (Or, a thousand eighth graders might contend, a book written in Latin.)

Moses asked the aldermen for additional appropriations to buy readers. The motion failed for lack of a sponsor.

"Boy, I wish I had a million dollars," Mr. Buck Boylan told the young Charles Johnson. "I'd spend it all for pizen and pizen Yankees with it. I'd put it in their bread."

Well, if Old Man Buck had not completely forgotten the Civil War, Charlie Johnson remained befuddled by it. Speaking of his childhood textbooks in Raleigh, Johnson observed at the Sandwich Club that "I remember I had difficulty in reconciling the fact that the South won all the battles and lost the war."

A reader of the *State Chronicle* in 1890 groused about the Baptist Female Seminary, which is now Meredith College.

"It would be the only female college in North Carolina not surrounded by large grounds," he wrote about the original location near the Capitol.

"When a man sends his daughter to school he does not want her cooped up like a chicken in a crate."

Raleigh

With a little more hardened dealmaking, Raleigh would be the site of another university.

Trinity College, now known as Duke University, decided in 1888 to move from Randolph County to a location with a more urban atmosphere. In an action which precipitated a bidding war, Trinity's trustees announced that they expected to get paid for their relocation, and that they would consider no offer of less than $20,000 from any city which wanted to be the college's new home.

Raleigh citizens quickly raised $15,000 towards the sum through private pledges. (A thousand points of sputtering arc lights?) The Chamber of Commerce then turned to the city aldermen for the remainder.

Under the city charter in effect at the time, the aldermen were at the procedural mercy of their own finance committee. The committee refused the request for funds because its members had recently made a pledge of "no new taxes."

So the creative aldermen decided to fill out the offer with 487 shares of common stock in the Raleigh and Augusta Airline Railroad Company. Coincidentally, the shares had little or no market value. Trinity College accepted the bid and signed a contract to move to Raleigh.

Enter the Duke family on behalf of the City of Durham.

Washington Duke was still steaming over the fact that Raleigh had won the Baptist Female Seminary even though Durham had offered more money. So although the City of Raleigh had a contract in hand, Duke offered Trinity College $85,000 in subscriptions and personally underwrote another $15,000 of baksheesh, making the proposal five times what Raleigh's aldermen had tendered to the Methodists. Duke also offered some advice on the trading value of the railroad stock.

Sensing that their deal was unravelling, the city aldermen raised Raleigh's offer to $35,000. Not only was that amount still well short of Duke's, but it was a signal that the city was willing to change the agreement.

The Methodists who controlled Trinity College debated for weeks before they broke the news to Raleigh. Trinity's trustees visited the aldermen with the story that their college had to be located further west in order to ease a geographical schism in the denomination. They produced letters to that effect, all written since the date of Trinity's contract with the city.

It was not the money, the trustees said, it was the need to have a unified church which could better further God's work. The aldermen released the college from its commitment.

(Note: Raleigh, at the time, already had plenty of colleges; and decades later, even Randolph County was compensated for its loss of what became Duke University. It became the home of the North Carolina Zoo.)

Raleigh

City aldermen announced in 1892 that "more than 85 percent of public school books are written by Southern authors" and claimed that the texts "did justice" to North Carolina.

In another parochial policy, Raleigh's school committee strove to hire only teachers who had graduated from colleges in North Carolina and had attended secondary schools in Wake County.

The fact that similar rules would have all but eliminated early education in Raleigh, or that reaching out for diverse perspectives might have its own benefits, seemed to be of no concern.

A minute of silent contemplation for... Raleigh School Superintendent E.P. Moses, who in 1898 assailed teachers for "neglecting the use of the Bible in classrooms" and said that he expected the faculty in the city schools to "carry the banner of Christ."

Moses' remarks, at a convention, had been preceded by a more worldly message from State Superintendent Charles H. Mebane, who advised the city that one way to upgrade its teachers was to eliminate the strong preference given to faculty who were natives of Wake County.

Raleigh's Centennial Graded School was completed in 1887 on the grounds of today's Memorial Auditorium.

The school cost $27,129.67, which was paid from the net proceeds of a $25,000 bond issue and from the city's general fund. Tuition for children was 55 cents per month.

The building, which accommodated 800 pupils – some of them in double sessions – had a pressed brick front, brownstone and a slate roof. Faced with a pupil-teacher ratio of 60 to 1, the Centennial School employed a new class of staff member: the teaching assistant.

Superintendent Moses called for a charter amendment in 1899 which would require the city's children to attend public schools for 100 days each year until they reached the age of thirteen.

"Under present law," Moses said, "we have no power over the attendance of any child except to say that if he will not attend regularly, he shall not attend at all."

As a result, nearly 60 percent of the city's white pupils attended school fewer than 60 days per year. The attendance percentage was somewhat higher among black students.

Moses called for four new small schools to be dispersed around the city "for small children who live at too great a distance from the main school to attend regularly in bad weather."

On February 7, 1889, a date which probably lived in infamy for a month or so, the Raleigh Board of Aldermen voted to eliminate eighth-grade education in the city.

The anti-tax aldermen explained that it was "the sense of this Board to disapprove of higher education in the graded schools at public expense."

Part of Superintendent Moses' difficulties were described in the 1904 report of the Associated Charities, a predecessor of United Way.

"Among the white people little value is put on education," the Board wrote. "School attendance is neglected on the smallest pretense, even when the children are small, and they are put to work in the factories at the earliest possible moment." (At Raleigh's Pilot Mills, children might earn 90 cents a day.)

The Board said that "among the colored people the school is highly valued and real sacrifices are made to keep up the regular attendance of the children." But one explanation for this pattern, warned the Board, was that "the factories are closed to the negroes," eliminating most venues for child labor.

After the agitation for the formation of a North Carolina College of Agriculture and Mechanic Arts, the City of Raleigh put together the winning bid for what is now N.C. State University.

In 1886, the city assembled $8,000 from its treasury, 20 acres of land – including donations from the Pullens and Stronachs – and a deed to the exposition building at the State Fair. The General Assembly accepted the proposal, but it was not until 1887 that agricultural science became a certified part of the curriculum.

(Several Raleigh newspapers questioned whether the State needed what they referred to as "book farming.")

Every farm has to start somewhere, and the N.C. State University School of Agriculture did so with the purchase, at $25 per oinking trio, of Poland China, Berkshire and Jersey Red hogs.

Dean B. Irby said in 1892 that a thoroughly equipped farm was needed "to let the students learn, as a first lesson, that labor is honorable.

"It is not the work that dishonors the man," Irby observed, "but the man that does dishonor to his work." (Like Shaw and St. Augustine's, the early classes at N.C. State required manual labor.)

Dean Irby would marvel at the University's livestock pool today, reputed to be the largest of any university in the nation. Counting only the animals at the Agriculture school – letting the Veterinary school and Agriculture Commissioner Jim Graham keep their own – the university has an average of 3,000 cattle, swine, sheep, goats and horses.

From its beginning of nine pigs, the university now estimates that about 7,000 swine are born each year. Nearly all are eaten.

Early in this century, the Chamber of Commerce made a case for locating what it called "The University Medical School of North Carolina" in the capital rather than in Chapel Hill.

According to the Chamber, Raleigh had two unsurpassed assets for the school: "the presence here of State-Office buildings and grounds that can be easily and inexpensively converted" into a medical school; and an assortment of inhabitants to act as subjects for medical study.

The Chamber described the latter as "clinical material." Under this heading it grouped the populations of the State Hospital for the Insane, the School for the Blind, the Colored School for the Blind, Deaf and Dumb, and Central Prison.

"The Old Soldiers' Home also offers splendid opportunities for the study of the diseases of old age," the Chamber suggested.

Had the Medical School been situated in Raleigh, the Chamber planned on using seven buildings which were then on Caswell Square, together with the beds of the Rex, Mary Elizabeth and St. Agnes hospitals. It estimated that the school could be up and running for $100,000.

In all of modern life there is no riddle harder to read than this – How shall we so help as to eliminate dependent poverty?"

That quotation is not from Ronald Reagan, although he would be the first to crack that he remembers it, but from the *Report of the Associated Charities of Raleigh* in 1905.

Part of the Associated Charities' program was to provide food, coal and firewood, medical attention, shelter and even temporary cash support to whose who were down and out in the City of Oaks.

R.S. Stephenson, the charities' superintendent, was candid about the problems which Raleigh faced 87 years ago.

His first mission, he wrote, had been to eliminate what he referred to as "many cases of fraud." Stephenson said that able-bodied "beggars have been told that they must work or suffer the consequences. The result has been that they have either found work or gone to other towns to continue their lives of deception."

Stephenson said that he had achieved "the almost total elimination of day-to-day begging which had... grown to distressing proportions."

Having satisfied those who visualized people who received assistance but had fancy buggies in their driveways, Stephenson turned to what he called the "disease of real poverty" in the city.

Poverty, he said, was what caused the "symptoms of shiftlessness, hopelessness, mismanagement, ill-health, vice, crime, ingratitude, deception, low standards and ignorance."

He wrote that even the "tenderhearted" in Raleigh had been pursuing a policy of "feed and forget" with regard to the unfortunate.

The superintendent then answered his opening hypothetical question by calling for vocational training and education for those who moved into Raleigh from rural areas.

"Street work, wood chopping and carting is about the sum of the knowledge they have brought from the farm to the town," Stephenson wrote. He predicted that unless the city did more for education, Raleigh would have a class of impoverished people for decades to come.

By 1907, students between the ages of nine and twelve were required to attend classes eight months each year until they had completed a total of 27 months' education in Raleigh's graded schools.

Teachers, who were ordered to "rule as would a kind and judicious parent," were told to use corporal punishment "only should persuasive measures fail." Principals were required to spend 3.5 hours each day in actual classroom teaching.

The city's pupils were supposed to be taught the virtues of "truth; self-control; temperance; frugality; industry; obedience to authority; reverence for the aged; forbearance to all; kindness to animals; desire for knowledge; and obedience to the laws of God." However, the school system's rules prohibited the teaching of "any partisan or sectarian views."

This one goes out for all the students at St. Mary's, Peace and Meredith who ever felt like they were imprisoned.

From the Raleigh ordinance book of 1908:

"No person, under the pretense of exercising his right to be on the streets, shall loiter near the premises of the female seminaries or schools for the purpose of... holding surreptitious conversations with the inmates thereof."

Superintendent Moses' concerns about Raleigh children spending their days in factories would have still preyed on him in 1918.

That year, a labor specialist found two sisters, ages 12 and 13, working at a downtown store wrapping merchandise for five cents an hour. They worked 12 hours each weekday and 14 hours on Saturdays. It was not their summer vacation. "Both sisters were frail," the report said, "undersized and undernourished, and had not attended school for almost six months."

Their parents were both ill and the girls worked to provide food for the home.

Fred A. Olds and his Kiddy Cotton Pickers.... No, it was not an act which played at Memorial Auditorium.

Toward the end of World War I, Olds assembled more than 200 volunteer schoolchildren to pick scrap cotton which otherwise would have been wasted in local fields after harvest. In 1918, the children collected 66.6 tons. At a penny a pound, they turned over $666 to the war effort.

Shaw University not only had a school of law, but in addition to its divinity school it also had a school of medicine and a school of pharmacy. All of the professional schools except divinity closed in 1918.

In an action which was endorsed by the Woman's Club and unified Kiwanis, the Raleigh Township School Committee adopted these teacher pay standards for 1920:

Class A: Applied to graduates of grade-A colleges who also had two years' teaching experience. (And, in a classic grandfather clause, it covered any teacher who had ten years' classroom experience, college diploma or not.) The pay was $1,200 per year for white teachers and $750 per year for black teachers.

Class B: Required three years of college; $1,100 for whites, $700 for blacks.
Class C: Two years of college; $1,000 for whites, $650 for blacks.
Class D: One year of college; $900 for whites, $600 for blacks.
Class E: Included teachers with high school diplomas who were not grandfathered into Class A: $800 for whites, $550 for blacks.

"Is the teacher worth a living wage?" The question was posed in a survey of the financial condition of Raleigh's teachers during the hard year of 1934. Although it was not answered directly, no one who read the responses of 124 instructors could reach the conclusion that they were overpaid.

A teacher's average annual salary was $674.44, spread out over eight months. (During the Depression, teacher salaries were cut across the State in an effort to avoid outright reductions in staff.) Only a few received the city maximum of $720 per year. Teachers reported that it was not enough.

Nearly 80 teachers disclosed that "they had neglected medical attention" during the preceding year; three-fourths had closed their savings accounts, with almost all the money being used to meet living expenses; one-fifth had dropped their insurance and another fifth had borrowed against it; and 80 percent of the teachers were unable to find any supplementary work during the summer.

By the time Raleigh's teachers subtracted their taxes and necessary living expenses, they had an average of $25.65 apiece to stretch over the year.

A psychologist studied children at the Murphey School in 1943 to learn whether the events of World War II were affecting them. (Remember, the events in this book are real.)

Not surprisingly – because at the time, children were put through blackout and air raid drills – the students appeared edgy when planes flew low or when they heard sharp, sudden noises which sounded like gunfire.

But the psychologist – who painstakingly collected data which she described as "a conglomerate and apparently unrelated mass of facts" – reached a conclusion of a less obvious nature.

Reading data which indicated that "hatred of the enemy was growing in the children's minds" and that some children gave vent to the "expression of horrible and blood thirsty desires toward the enemy," she concluded this:

"Often," she wrote about the children's terminator fantasies, "it may be disguised talk of hostility toward family members, probably caused by countless frustrations and deprivations which adults make children endure by bringing them up 'properly.'"

The study was approved and the psychologist awarded a Ph.D.

During what ordinarily would have been the waning days of segregated schools in Raleigh, the Chamber of Commerce issued a report in 1953 which estimated growth in school attendance, by race, through the year 1971.

The Chamber predicted that white school attendance would increase from 6,268 to 15,125 – about 140 percent – over the 18 years. It then forecast that the black pupil enrollment would increase by only 9 percent over the same period. The Chamber estimated that the number of black children in elementary schools in Raleigh would actually decrease.

How did the Chamber explain these disparities in its report, which would have been used to allocate funds for planned school construction and in locating new school buildings?

Its one comment was that the estimates "have been thoughtfully forecast."

Back in the halcyon days of 1964, before there was any wide focus on comparative school performance, the State Department of Public Instruction asked high school principals a question: What are the No. 1 and No. 2 reasons why graduates of your school fail to go on to college?

H.E. Brown, principal of the still-segregated Ligon High School, reported to the department that the greatest problem was a "lack of motivation from the home environment" and that the second problem boiled down to the "financial condition of the parents."

At the time, 45 percent of Ligon graduates went on to higher education, as compared to 58 percent of Broughton High School graduates, whose principal did not answer the question.

It may not be a flagship school, but.... In 1978, when the city sought unsuccessfully to win the N.C. School of Science and Mathematics, Broughton High School was one of the main selling points.

Broughton's "SAT scores far exceed the state averages," the city's proposal said, and it promised an exchange of students and teachers between Broughton and the new school, which it proposed to house in what were then the nearby buildings of Rex Hospital.

No Balm In Gilead

Raleigh had no church building until about 1808, when the Rev. William Glendenning opened the "Bethel" Tabernacle on Blount Street south of Morgan.

(A log meeting house further north was burned down in 1792 to make room for an estate.)

Glendenning was an expatriate Virginian who headed south either because of a schism in the Methodist Episcopal Church or because he needed a change of scenery after he got out of detention for mental disturbances.

He built Bethel in large part with his own hands, using boards and nails purchased from the Peace brothers. He attracted a regular congregation. Then he lapsed.

The Rev. Glendenning began to engage in what he believed were personal wrestling bouts with the Devil. Satan took the form of whatever citizen of Raleigh happened to be nearest at the time an attack hit. Most of the people Glendenning assaulted refused to press charges. But Bishop Francis Asbury, passing through town, wrote that if Glendenning persisted in tackling people, few would welcome him into their homes or attend his services.

The Rev. Glendenning, however, could not compromise his personal vision of Hell in Raleigh. He was brought before a body named the Wake County Jury of Inquisition, a special panel appointed to determine which citizens were lunatics. The Inquisition decided on the first ballot that the Rev. Glendenning fit the specifications.

Adjudged to be legally insane, Raleigh's first permanent minister was turned over to editor William Boylan as his guardian rather than be sent to the Poor-House or jail.

Boylan, elated that he could take care of the unfortunate Glendenning, immediately went to visit him at his house. When he assured the Rev. Glendenning that no one was going to dictate to him every particular of what he could do, Glendenning tested the limits: he threw his brandy-drinking, seegar-smoking guardian out of the house.

Upon Glendenning's death a few years later, Raleigh's first church building went with him.

It is not difficult to imagine how Raleigh's founders would have reacted to some of today's television preachers.

"False and pretended prophesies," a law read in the early 1800s, "as they raise enthusiastic jealousies in the people and terrify them with imaginary fears, are punished...."

The first time a "prophet" warned of the impending Millenium and nothing happened, he got "a fine of 100 pounds and one year's imprisonment." In the event that the prophet ventured a second prediction, the penalty was "a forfeiture of all goods and chattels, and imprisonment during life."

(Who knows how the founders would have reacted to selling phantom time shares?)

On her first tour of duty as a teacher in Raleigh, Susan Nye in 1815 tried to reconcile daily events in the city with the commandments of her religion. She couldn't manage it.

"I saw many things to reprehend," she wrote in her diary about a party. "The vitiated style of dress, oh, surely, the ladies have forgotten that even dress was necessary, or at least that they have anything to conceal. Their backs and their bosoms were all uncovered." She called them "shameless women."

She also stopped in at a "house of well-known infamy," a "detestable brothel," to help one of the young prostitutes who was ill. She left when the stricken girl began to curse her at the suggestion that she talk to a minister.

The house where Ms. Nye roomed gave her an education on slavery.

"Awakened this a.m. by the screeching of a female slave who was fleeing from the whip of her enraged master," she wrote. "I never witnessed such a scene... her neck torn and bloody, her eye swollen."

Ms. Nye wrote that "Oh, how callous are the hearts of this people. And I live it is said with the best of the masters."

Before she left for Georgia, she described "a poor negro, who lame and old, nightly limps past our house, with a basket in one hand, a cane in the other while a bunch of sticks, gathered in the woods, weighs down his venerable gray head... his profession is Presbyterianism."

"Very strange," said Judge Thomas Ruffin in 1824, "if two clergymen could not settle a dispute without calling each other hard names in print."

Ruffin was trying to mediate an epistling match between the Right Reverend John Ravenscroft of Christ Church and the Rev. Elisha Mitchell, a professor and token Presbyterian at the University in Chapel Hill.

In what archivists describe as "unpleasant" correspondence, Ravenscroft and Mitchell began their feud over whether the University should hire another Episcopalian to fill a vacancy as professor of languages.

(For those today who find the religion, much less the denomination, of a professor to be irrelevant, at the time of the feud, UNC students were compelled to attend prayer services 13 times each week. They were graded on the intensity of their devotions. God was most definitely in the state-supported classroom, and His advocates contended over who should shape the students' minds.)

The two clergymen exchanged letters, hand-delivered by their respective slaves. Inevitably, the issues broadened:

Was Ravenscroft a religious bigot who had an Episcopal chokehold on the University? Had a University faculty member threatened to "blow up the college" if the trustees did not hire a Presbyterian? Was the free distribution of Bibles to the plain people of North Carolina desirable, or would those "fools" misinterpret the Word if they read it unaided? Which minister was going to sue the other first?

Professor Mitchell may not have held the most powerful hand, but he knew how to escalate a conflict. Using words such as "reprehensible," he began writing anonymous letters to the *Raleigh Register* which tried to take some of the starch out of Ravenscroft's collar. A letter signed "Clericus" probably was the one which put Ravenscroft over the edge: it included the term "non-Christian."

Ravenscroft began to reject all initiatives to end the controversy. He remarked that one entreaty by Mitchell "contemplates only a retreat from the question to save your feelings, without any regard for mine."

Using the old apostolic one-two, Ravenscroft said that Mitchell had attacked the entire Episcopal faith *de facto* when he questioned Ravenscroft; then the rector accused Mitchell and his denomination of being "Jesuitical" and of shaking the beliefs of students by alerting them to differing concepts of Christianity.

No slouch at vituperation, Ravenscroft wrote Mitchell that "I fear your recent (illness) must have been more severe than you intimate, as your letter... is not easily reconcilable with that clearness of mind you are known to possess." After the two began to refer to each other only in the third person, Judge Ruffin bowed out.

Eventually, the University did become catholic in its hiring of faculty. Citizens of the state did receive free Bibles and no particular clergy knocked at their doors. The principals in the feud died, but not before Dr. Mitchell predicted that someday Methodists and (gasp!) Baptists might teach at UNC.

The feud would occupy only a few pages in a survey of Southern religion except for the effect it had on the Legislature, which witnessed Ravenscroft and Mitchell and froze in its tracks. Appropriations for higher education, never healthy, all but disappeared.

In the end, Ravenscroft's exclusiveness did his denomination no good. In the short term, it harmed the education of students from his own parish.

Sunday school pupils of the young persuasion may relate to the Rules for the Government of the Raleigh Episcopal Sunday School, posted in 1828.

"Every scholar," the mandates read, "shall keep from the habits of idleness, or sabbath-breaking, swearing, indecent conversation, or any other habits contrary to the word of God and the good order and peace of society."

Students, the rules continued, "must not loiter by the door of the school room or Church." They were expected to "be kind and good natured to each other." They had to "always tell the truth."

They had to "go to and from school in an orderly and quiet manner – be guilty of no rudeness or riotous conduct in the streets or roads... particularly wicked on Sunday...."

What is interesting is not so much the melange of moral and civil prescriptions in these rules, or even the fact that the church needed to post them, but the question of how the Sunday School students reacted.

Every Sunday morning in decent weather, precisely as the homily was underway in Christ Church, a gang of fox hunters, drunk or hung over, yelling and blowing horns, would canter back into town on Edenton Street, chasing their yelping hounds. The ringleader was named Boylan.

If politics and religion should not mix, it is probably because of campaigns such as the one Burwell Temple ran in Raleigh in 1844. He opposed George Thompson for the House of Commons.

Raleigh

Brother Temple, a churchgoing man, opposed a bill in the Legislature to incorporate something called the North Carolina Baptist State Convention. "The plan," he sputtered in a circular to Raleigh voters, "if not checked will be of fatal consequence." Thompson supported the bill.

Temple compared the Baptist Convention to an inquisition. He said it would lead to "the confiscation of estates, the whippings, imprisonments, tortures by fire and gibbets, the tearing asunder of living human beings, red hot spindles run in human bodies, making fast the feet in stocks, roasting the feet by the fire by degrees, boring out the eyes with augurs, and," he summed up, "death in its most horrid forms."

"All of these," Temple wrote his would-be constituents, "followed the establishment of institutions as harmless as these now incorporated in North Carolina."

All of that rhetoric was too much for Raleigh voters, who elected Thompson and looked forward to revenues when the Convention met in town. (As for the Baptists setting up an inquisition, except for practicing a little suppression now and then at Meredith College, Brother Temple had it wrong.)

The date: November 7, 1860. The occasion: the largest church service in Raleigh's history up to that time.

Why did the members of the city's Methodist and Presbyterian congregations gather together that Sunday?

Their purpose, as *The Standard* described it, was "to humble themselves before God, and to pray that He will avert the selection of a sectional candidate to the Presidency." (In other words, Abraham Lincoln, who was not even on the ballots to be cast in Raleigh later that week.)

The same Constitutional Convention which met in 1861 to secede from the Union decided, once it got to Raleigh, to operate on the State Constitution as well.

In what appears on the surface to be a fraction ironic, the secession convention voted to end what had been a discriminatory provision in the State Constitution for more than 80 years: the prohibition against members of the Jewish faith from holding office.

Raleigh's delegation of George Badger, Kemp Battle and W.W. Holden were strict constructionists.

During the debate, they had to respond to one delegate who said that although he was "in favor of removing the restriction, so far as it applied to

Raleigh

Jews," he was "not in favor of everybody of all religions and of no religion – Turks, Pagans, Coolies – to be eligible to office in the State."

Raleigh's stalwart delegates assured the doubter that the new provision was "intended to apply only to Jews," several of whom were about to enter Jefferson Davis' cabinet.

Early in what was called the "War of Northern Aggression," the city's Baptist, Methodist, Presbyterian and Episcopal churches volunteered "to give up their bells with a view to their being cast into cannon."

In April, 1862, the Baptist Church appointed a committee of the Rev. T.E. Skinner, Jr., P.F. Pescud and W.J. Palmer to haul down the bell – estimated to weigh 1,300 pounds – and send it to Fayetteville, where it was to be melted down and transfigured into three six-pounders. *The Raleigh Register* and *The Standard* reported that the other churches tendered their bells a week later.

"They will be devoted to a holy and sacred work," observed the *Register*. "God will smile upon them in their new vocation of hurling death and destruction upon the infidels and vandals... as benignly as He did when their chimes summoned worshippers to his altars."

The *Register* predicted that if the South lost the war, "our church edifices will be of little use to us, as their pulpits will be occupied by puritanical, Praise-God-Bare-Bones, cropp-eared, round-head, Yankee Abolition parsons, who will preach blasphemy through their noses and compel us to pay for it."

To fight or not to fight in the Civil War may have been a question of conscience, but for two Raleigh ministers, it became a down-to-earth matter before the State Supreme Court.

The two – one who wanted to serve, but not as a draftee, and the other who wanted to continue his ministries – were caught up in the Confederacy's ever-tightening conscription laws.

Like many other Raleigh residents who were stopped at bayonet point, asked to produce their certificates of draft exemption from service, and then arrested if they were not carrying them, the Revs. Samuel Curtis and William H. Cunninggim were marched to the Confederate training center at Camp Holmes near the city.

The Rev. Curtis was a Primitive Baptist minister who had decided to hire out as a substitute in the Army of Virginia. He planned to send his soldier's pay back to his congregation. Curtis was on his way out of Raleigh to report for duty when local officers stopped him and took him to Major Peter Mallett, the commandant of the camp.

At the time, the Confederacy maintained that conscripts lacked the right even to *habeas corpus* in state courts in order to protest their imprisonment. (The State Supreme Court disagreed in a lengthy series of cases, usually with Major Mallett as a defendant.)

In Curtis's case, the Court concluded that "the duties of a soldier or officer and a minister of religion are not incompatible." It cited instances of North Carolina ministers in the Revolutionary War, "fighting or preaching as (the) occasion offered." (Gary Cooper could have played these parts.)

Once Curtis contracted out as a substitute, the Court said, he instantly waived his exemption and became fair game for Major Mallett. The minister ended up serving not for a Virginia regiment, but in North Carolina.

The case of the Rev. Cunninggim presented a different set of facts.

As an ordained and practicing minister of the Methodist Episcopal South Church, Cunninggim seemed to qualify for the exemption from combat which was given to clergymen. (That exemption was narrowed during the course of the war as all sorts of men discovered preaching as a calling.)

But in the eyes of Major Mallett, Rev. Cunninggim had a disqualification: he took no salary from either of the congregations he served, but instead lived off his earnings as the owner and manager of a Raleigh hotel. Mallett decided that he was not a bona fide minister and attempted to make his arrest stick.

Church and state may be separate in North Carolina, but they had more than a passing acquaintance when the Court took up the plea of the Rev. Cunninggim to be released from Camp Holmes.

Justice Battle started his opinion with the example of St. Paul, whom he wrote was "the greatest preacher whom the world has ever known, who worked with his own hands at his occupation as a tent-maker, so that his support might not be a burden to the churches of Corinth and Ephesus." The unanimous Court said that unpaid ministers did much good "by working for nothing of an earthly nature and supporting themselves."

The Confederate Congress, the Court explained, had exempted ministers from duty in order "to afford to all who should not be called into the field – to the men, women and children, who should remain at home – the services of all ministers of religion, of every grade in every denomination."

"Can any good reason be given," the Court asked, "why these ministrations may not be useful and productive of much good, though rendered by unpaid ministers?"

The Supreme Court concluded that "the fact that they take nothing from the coffers of their church for their support, renders (the church) more able to sustain those who are laboring in the higher grades of the ministry. They occupy an important, though it may be an humble, field of labor, and are deemed essential in... furnishing the means whereby 'the poor have the gospel preached to them.'"

Besides, the Court said, it had never heard of a regularly practicing preacher being shipped out to combat against his will. The Rev. Cunninggim remained with his two congregations in the capital.

(Losing an occasional conscript by court decision was the least of Major Mallett's worries. Lacking enough men either to guard the conscripts during training or to escort them to their units, Mallett watched as escapes from Camp Holmes became epidemic. For that and other reasons, it was impossible for Mallett to keep an accurate count of the state's conscripts.

(The escapes led to Mallett's receiving a blistering telegram from his own commander in Richmond, saying that the major's "gross errors" had made his monthly reports "utterly false and unreliable" and that Mallett's "explanation cannot be accepted."

(As Memory F. Mitchell observed about most histories of the Civil War, which depict cheerful Rebels running to volunteer for service, "little attention has been paid to those whose enthusiasm for military service was less than ardent.")

From a churchgoing legislator in 1866: "All the congregations here take up collections every sermon," he wrote about a new Raleigh custom.

He remarked in a letter to his wife that his friends in Raleigh had "gone to the Baptist Church tonight to hear a sermon on Baptism," and speculated that "all that go will be apt to come back with the same notions they started with."

The Senator fretted that "the preacher will lose his labor save the basket collections which will likely be considerable."

It happens only occasionally – a minister gets out of step with a majority of the congregation, refuses to go quietly, and a divisive meeting results in his ouster.

But when members of the Second Baptist Church of Raleigh tried to fire the Rev. Henry M. Tupper in 1872, they received a surprise:

Tupper threw *them* out and changed the locks on the church building. It took five decisions by the State Supreme Court before the dispute was resolved.

As best as can be determined from conflicting accounts and from about one foot of handwritten affidavits and pleadings, this is what happened:

Tupper, who was the founder and first president of what today is Shaw University, became pastor in the 1860s of a local Baptist church. Using his earnings as a soldier, he purchased land at the corner of Blount and Cabarrus streets. The members of the church then built a sanctuary by hand.

("I and several members worked in the woods getting the timber," church trustee Gideon Perry testified in his lawsuit to get the church back from Tupper. "I struck the first lick.")

Problems first arose when Tupper asked to lease the second story of the church for use by the new college. The members refused, and a debate began over how closely – if at all – the Second Baptist Church should be affiliated with the Shaw Institute.

Tupper provoked further controversy by trying to tell his congregation how to vote in elections.

Shortly before 82 percent of the church members voted to fire him, Tupper responded to his critics. He said that "the church was his own, and he intended to govern it as he pleased. If any of them did not want to hear him, they could leave." Tupper added that the members were "fools" if they did not vote as he directed.

With that, the congregation called a special meeting to consider resolutions against the pastor.

"Whereas our beloved Pastor Eld'r H.M. Tupper," one resolution opened, "has transcended the bounds of Christian propriety and violated openly and flagrantly the rules of our church and thereby has made himself odious to a majority of the congregation...."

Another resolution accused Tupper of "attempting to constrain the political opinion of his congregation and to force them to vote for a political candidate in accordance with his, Tupper's, political views and contrary to their own views."

Rumors also made it into print that Tupper had whipped, kicked and had sex with blacks. (Not at the same time.) A division occurred over whether the church could tolerate having any white minister. It was a memorable church meeting.

The congregation voted 54 to 13 to oust Tupper. "There was a dead silence for a while," one participant recalled in a deposition. Then the Rev. Tupper arose to speak.

Tupper pulled from his pocket a document which he said was a 999-year lease of the church building. He remarked that "he owned that church for 999 years." He added that "those that did not want him to preach might leave for there he was going to stay." He walked out of the meeting.

The next Sunday, all of the deacons of the church, all but one of its trustees, and two-thirds of the congregation attended services at Joel Evans' house. They issued a call for a new minister. But when they returned to the church they had built, Tupper had barred the doors. He said the members who had met at Evans' house had seceded from the church, and that he was therefore in charge of the only Second Baptist Church in Raleigh.

The members sought the informal advice of former Governor W.W. Holden.

"I advised them," Holden later testified, "that the right to control the whole matter was in the congregation, and not in the minister, who was only the servant of the church or congregation; that they should proceed prudently and slowly to maintain their rights, and should do this in a Christian spirit." The members retained lawyers.

By that time, the Shaw Institute was using the church building for classes on the first floor and sleeping quarters on the second. The "lease" Tupper held still contained no consideration, no seal affixed as required by law, and no official action by the church trustees to grant it.

"That there were mistakes and failures must be admitted," Henry L. Morehouse later wrote. He ascribed the controversy to the "ignorance and folly of the colored people" as well as to "hostility from very many whites" towards the Shaw Institute.

In one of its many reviews of the standoff, the State Supreme Court decided in favor of the church members.

"By the arbitrary and high-handed conduct of the defendant," the Court wrote about Tupper, the minister in effect had forced the congregation to leave. The Court described the members as "colored people... unwilling to do any act that might lead to open force on the part of the white man who had acted as their 'shepherd.'"

The controversy raged for years, and as it did, use of the church building would be withdrawn from Tupper and then reinstated. Walls were installed and removed depending on who was in control at the moment.

The Rev. Tupper did mount an aggressive defense of his position. Among other things, he alleged that the dissenting trustees were not really members of the church; that some were drunkards and others thieves and sexual transgressors; that "ignorant colored men" were being used as "tools" in a plot against him by the white First Baptist Church; that the Baptists were in collusion with Raleigh's Roman Catholic mayor; and that he was the victim of a "bitter persecution" which included even the Klan.

Tupper also insisted that those juries which decided against him had been packed by the Baptist-Catholic-Klan alliance. It was quite a ministry to want to keep.

Today, Tupper lies buried on the Shaw University campus which he developed despite his problems with religious litigation. A brick church bearing his name is on the site of the disputed Second Baptist Church. The litigating church members scattered elsewhere.

Former State Treasurer Charles Johnson once recalled a local angler who caught a string of what he termed "Baptist fish."
When Johnson pressed for the derivation of the name, the fisherman said that it was "because they spile so soon after they gets out of the water."

"Outraged" was the word used by the unanimous vestry of Christ Church to describe their reaction to an assault on their choir director in the sanctuary during Easter Week of 1878.

Major William L. Gulick had been rehearsing the choir when a renowned Raleigh matron arrived late, made no apologies, and then began criticizing the length of certain notes in a hymn.

"I then said to Mrs. ___," Gulick later swore, "that the choir was under my charge, that the music was sung according to my directions, and that I could not allow anyone to interfere with it."

Both Gulick and the lady agreed about her reply – "I did not come here to be insulted," she huffed – and witnesses recalled her threatening to send her sons after him as she stalked out the door.

Choir practice was still going *in excelsis* when the sons arrived. They came equipped with "tree limbs and cudgels." Gulick, who was "armed only with a hymnal," was beaten senseless and bleeding to the sanctuary floor. Female choir members shrieked and leapt out of the chapel windows to find help. Several members who arrived to aid Gulick were also clubbed by the brothers.

When Rector M.M. Marshall heard about the assault, he was less than amused. He wrote the woman to inform her that she was "suspended indefinitely" from communion because of her role in the affray.

What happened next is instructive in the politics of churches and wealthy congregants.

The woman's husband – as prominent a lawyer as Raleigh had in 1878 – waited a few days ("For my natural indignation... to cool," he wrote) and then came at the Rev. Marshall full force.

Leading with the proposition that the Rev. Marshall had acted as "prosecutor, judge and executioner" of the matron, her husband said that the minister had "wounded her good repute, as a Christian matron, a good citizen, a refined gentlewoman." (How this could be true, since Marshall wrote his letter in private, is an open question.)

The lawyer described his wife as "a Garibaldian of GOD" and said that he was confident of "her rank in the great army of Christ." He then threatened a slander suit and said he was taking the suspension upstairs to Bishop Thomas Atkinson in Wilmington.

At that point, fending off the local newspapers who smelled a good scandal, the Christ Church vestry adopted its resolution in support of the Rector. "Whether a lady was insulted or not," its conclusion read, "had nothing to do with the matter... there are proper times and proper places for resenting insults of whatever kind, but... the Church of God is not the place."

But although the vestry supported the Rev. Marshall – and he did remain at Christ Church for 29 more years— his longevity owed nothing to Bishop Atkinson. Fearing a lawsuit, the Bishop ordered that Marshall's edict be lifted. The Bishop quibbled that the word "indefinitely" was too harsh, and Marshall himself said he had intended the suspension to be only temporary.

"You have a tendency to impatience and intemperance," the Bishop chastised Marshall.

That tendency, Marshall wrote back, "is certainly not the least of my besetting sins." He added, however, that he expected the Bishop to back his decision and that if not, he would lose his effectiveness at Christ Church.

Atkinson implored the Rev. Marshall not to resign. "In this particular matter I would recommend you to *say* as little as possible and to *do* nothing hasty," he wrote.

The denouement was swift and private: indicted for assault and placed under $200 bond each, the sons settled their case without going to jail; and feeling no longer welcome at Christ Church, the parents and their sons ended years of attendance.

(Although Easter service hymns were listed in the Raleigh newspapers for 1878, no one reviewed the singing at Christ Church as to whether the notes were too long, too short, or just right.)

However, the definitive word on church choirs had been handed down five years earlier by the State Supreme Court, only a block from the sanctuary. The case involved a singer whose enthusiasm exceeded his talents.

"His voice is heard after all other singers have ceased," the Court found, and the quality of his tones was such that "the irreligious and frivolous enjoyed it as fun while the serious and devout were indignant." (When the voice was imitated in court, it had the effect of "convulsing alike the spectators, the bar, the jury" and the judge.)

The man was arrested and charged with disrupting a religious service. The music-loving Supreme Court reversed his conviction and referred the matter back to religious rather than judicial authorities.

A case of steeple envy arose in Raleigh when the original Edenton Street Methodist Church had the temerity to erect a spire higher than that of the white First Baptist Church.

As Robert Lawrence recollected, he was so concerned by the construction that he hurried to visit the ailing Dr. Thomas E. Skinner at the minister's home. (The young Lawrence thought that Skinner was near death until he realized that he was not wearing his customary toupee.) He learned that the issue of steeples had infiltrated even city government.

"He, too," Lawrence recalled of Dr. Skinner, "had been deeply concerned about the action of the pesky Methodists, and said that he had conferred with Mayor Dodd (who was a Baptist) to see if something could not be done to prevent it, but had been told by his Honor that the plagued Methodists had a majority on the Board of Aldermen, and so nothing could be done about it."

(Both the new church and its successor burned, proving to some that there was a higher power in Raleigh than the aldermen.)

When the Rev. Sarah A. Hughes was ordained in Raleigh in 1885, she became the first woman minister in the African Methodist Episcopal Church.

Installed by Bishop H.M. Turner, she went directly from the church to preach to "a great colored camp meeting" near the site of the present Motor Vehicles building. An estimated 6,000 heard her.

One of Raleigh's random religious debates occurred in 1895, when some churches began using individual cups for communion and a few physicians endorsed the practice as a public health measure.

Ptooey, wrote Josephus Daniels for the *N&O*. He could find no evidence that disease was spread by the use of common communion cups and regarded the change by several Baptist churches in the city as "the next innovation against the old-time customs of Christianity.

"There is just as much danger of contracting disease," Daniels wrote, "by sitting for an hour or more next to a person who has incipient germs or grip or some other disease.

"Why not divide the churches up into stalls like horse-stables in order to make sure that disease shall not be communicated by personal contact? There is just as much reason for it as for providing separate communion cups, and more scripture for it."

Noting that he had witnessed as many as 25 Baptists be immersed at one time in a common pool of water, and that several who were baptized were wearing soiled clothes under their robes, Daniels wryly suggested that the Baptists consider the consequences for public health of that ritual.

"These were immersed with microbes that may have been upon them," Daniels wrote, "and according to the ancient practice, their heads, including their mouths, nostrils, eyes and ears, were all put under the same water, occasionally accompanied by coughing and strangling."

Look away from Christ Church with its historic weathercock (by legend, the only chicken left in Raleigh when General Sherman's troops decamped). At least as interesting is a church just down Wilmington Street, even if it did not hang a Confederate flag in its sanctuary during its centennial.

The First Baptist Church – Raleigh's city directories used to append the abbreviation "col." to its name – was founded in 1812 by the Rev. Robert D. Daniel. Together with its brother, the *other* First Baptist Church across Capitol Square, it is the oldest continuous church in terms of congregations in the city.

According to accounts at the time, the Rev. Daniel had "an eloquence which arrested and held the attention of any audience." His original members, fourteen blacks and nine whites, "included no wealth but was from the working class."

(The church was integrated until it split into two congregations in 1868. In 1859, for instance, its membership consisted of 228 whites and 208 blacks. Who knows; both churches may be integrated again today.)

By 1822, the church had a small sanctuary on Moore Square, which for years afterward was called Baptist Grove. It was "a plain little house, no modern comforts, the only lights a few feeble candles." The Rev. Daniel built it for $600 in current dollars, and by the time he departed in 1826, the church had 224 members and was the largest then in the capital.

A teacher at the Raleigh Academy remembered attending services there: "The room was crowded with black and white. The candles one after another gave out." The service ended in darkness.

Daniel's replacement was Dr. Amos J. Battle. He had been a real estate entrepreneur when he rode through Georgia on the way to inspect an investment in Florida. He "stopped at a little wayside church to rest his tired horse. Services were in progress. When Amos returned to his steed he was a changed man."

Battle visited the church again on his way back north, arrived home, "quickly abandoned his business," and began to study the Gospel.

In 1839, one of the city's surviving founders, seegar chewing Willie Jones, deeded a lot to Battle so that a permanent church could be built away from Moore Square. To say that the new church was "a house of worship erected at great personal sacrifice" is all too accurate.

In 1841, the Rev. Battle was arrested for debt and booked at the Wake County jail. Although he was not imprisoned for the $1,750 at issue, the mortgage which was tendered to the Court to secure his release tells much about the First Baptist Church.

In the mortgage to satisfy Dr. Battle's creditors, "it appear(ed) not only that there was $400 due him on salary, but he had spent (personally) $3,300 building the church."

Out of one financial problem, the church encountered another only three years later when its mortgage holders foreclosed on the sanctuary over a late payment of $400. The present First Baptist Church adopted the name of the New Baptist Church and did not regain its original name until the schism after the Civil War.

Over the years, the church has had ministers such as P.W. Dowd, who was the first president of the Baptist State Convention, and the Rev. O.S. Bullock, who pioneered the use of free bus transportation to the services.

Battle was not the only minister of the First Baptist Church – either branch – to experience a spiritual transformation. In Marshall D. Haywood's address at the centennial celebration of the State Supreme Court, he related a story about a university student who stopped at the well of Col. J.T.C. Wiatt, then the Marshal of the Court.

The student picked a fight with Wiatt's bulldog and, using a whip and "accompanied by such a torrent of profanity as had never before been heard in North Carolina since the days of John Burrington," he drove the dog under Wiatt's porch.

"You have shown me," Wiatt told the young man, "that there is one man in North Carolina who can swear louder and longer than I can. The world is likely to hear from you before it gets much older."

Some years later, Wiatt was introduced to a familiar-looking man who had just been assigned to the pastorate of one of Raleigh's largest churches.

"I once had the pleasure of hearing this gentleman talk," Wiatt said to his companion, "but he was not then preaching the gospel – according to my recollection." Wiatt said that "he was confident that no man with such fluency in expressing himself could fail to be entertaining as a preacher." He planned to attend the new minister's services but died shortly before the Rev. Thomas E. Skinner was installed at the First Baptist Church.

(The successor to this vibrant history stands today at the corner of Wilmington and Morgan streets. The building seems endangered again, not by creditors or schisms, but by those who dream of high-rise offices and bigger parking decks. If only young Tom Skinner could talk.)

Back up Wilmington Street, Christ Church demonstrated that even affluent congregations can have cash flow problems.

In 1897, the church vestry took the step of formally notifying the parishioners that they had to sweeten their donations or else witness church activities sink into a pool of red ink.

The communique listed the members of the church in alphabetical order together with their respective pledges, right down to the Liberty Head quarter. The vestry cautioned that based on past experience, it could not count on receiving more than 80 percent of the donations promised by the communicants.

It must have made for spirited conversation at the church: the occupants of, say, Pew No. 11 knew what the denizens of Pew No. 112 contributed as well as how much seating space they took up in the sanctuary. (More about the church's pews in a moment.)

(As a professor of religious history phrased it, the members could now distinguish the *pillars* of the church from the *caterpillars,* who only crawled in and out.)

In the interest of preserving privacy – which is more than the vestry had – suffice it to say that the two leading benefactors of Christ Church were women: Mrs. R.S. Tucker with an annual pledge of $250 and Ms. Annie M. Parker with $100. The average for all 103 who made pledges was $17 per year, or not quite 14 cents apiece each week when the two women were factored out.

If the vestry seemed desperate, it was because Christ Church had little beyond the pledges in the way of income. Together with the $5 per week which it received in its collection plates, the pledges left the church with an anticipated deficit of $667.80.

Yet by 1897, the parishioners should have been accustomed to warnings of deficits. After 1878, when the church's income exceeded its expenses by exactly one dollar, the church had generally operated in the red.

"You are summoned to a very important meeting" of the congregation, the vestry wrote one year. In extraordinary tones, it continued that "you should make no engagements conflicting with this meeting. Should you not attend and the meeting prove a failure, regrets will not remedy the wrong done."

Christ Church became uncomfortably concerned about money. (Other churches may share the same affliction, but their transcripts are not in the Archives.) Its vestry repeatedly delayed improving the sidewalks outside the church until the City of Raleigh sent threatening notices from the police chief. The vestry argued for months with Thomas Briggs over a small bill for covering the walkway between the sanctuary and the tower. They argued with the Episcopal diocese over whether they could drop their support for certain charities. They ended up in court over claims.

When Rector M.M. Marshall fell ill, the vestry decided to cancel all services for months rather than to pay for an interim pastor. After the third stern letter from Bishop Joseph B. Cheshire, Jr., who pointed out that Christ Church should at least be open for Easter week, the vestry relented.

It was financial necessity, in fact, which led the church to adopt a "free pew" system in 1891. (Prior to that, most of the pews were owned in fee simple by members who had bought them decades before when the church raised money for its sanctuary. Pews were handed down in estates and, in a few instances, were sold on the open market.)

"Passing over the spiritual aspect of the question," the vestry told the congregation about its desire for free pews, "the Parish is in financial straits." Pew-holders were not contributing to the church and could not be forced to, but there was no room for new members who would give money.

"We have all the disadvantages of both the new and free church systems with the advantages of neither," the vestry wrote. It asked the members to sign over quitclaim deeds to return their pews to the church.

Looking at the church's financial prospects, the vestry found that "under the present system, most of the increase in membership is from within – in the growth of families, which financially amounts to little if anything more than a breaking up into smaller sums of the amounts now subscribed.

"Our only hope is, therefore, getting a larger number of moderate means. But we have no seats to offer."

With three-quarters of the pews as the target, the church began its campaign to secure the deeds. It categorized its members as "likely" to donate back the pews, "doubtful," and likely "not to donate."

Some members attached conditions to their signatures, some preferred that Christ Church rent out their pews and use the income, and some refused to return their property altogether.

But the church had enough willing members so that after about a year it achieved its goal, helped along by some highly creative arithmetic.

Based on the financial report of 1897, the adoption of free pews scarcely healed the financial condition of Christ Church. But the congregation persevered and today the church continues in style.

As the Revs. Bill Finlator and Coy Privette might attest today, politics and religion do mix in Raleigh, but the resulting brew causes some people to swear off.

Writing in 1897, former N.C. Attorney General Theodore Davidson said that he had canceled his plans to attend Christ Church one Sunday with several legislators.

"Having heard that Dr. Marshall and Mr. Ottinger were blatant 'goldbugs,' " he wrote, "I'll have nothing to do with them." (It is unlikely that the men would have declaimed on the topic of the nation's monetary policy.)

Occasionally out-of-town preachers would alight in Raleigh for extended meetings. At least one of them left a memorable record.

In 1898, the renowned Rev. Dr. Len G. Broughton of Atlanta drew some of the "largest crowds ever seen in a church" during his ten days in town. (Towards the end of his visit, the Reverend also drew some anonymous hate mail objecting to his critique of the city.)

Discussing morality in Raleigh, the Rev. Broughton said that "I must tell you that you've got the rottenest town, as far as the whiskey traffic is concerned, that I've ever seen. You've got 15,000 inhabitants and 30 barrooms." He contrasted those statistics with Atlanta's, which he said had about 100 saloons for 125,000 citizens.

"More whiskey is consumed here," Broughton continued, "by the young men than in any other town of this size that I have ever known." (His sermons were transcribed and printed daily in the *N&O*.)

"Not content with debauching the manhood of the city on week days, you allow whiskey to be sold on Sunday," he raged. "Oh yes you do. A man told me that only last Sunday, he saw a fellow coming out of a bar-room here with a bottle of whiskey."

Perhaps sensing that this evidence was circumstantial, the Rev. Broughton added "if anybody wants that man's name I can give it. I suppose he'll stand up to his statement. If he backs down he'll have me to lick."

He closed the sermon by declaring that "not only is the city rotten and reeking with whiskey, but gambling dens are openly run." He denounced the city government as "corrupt" and implored it to get rid of "screens and side doors" in taverns and to eliminate free lunch tables and gaming in saloons.

In a further attack on city hall, the Rev. Broughton said that while he did not blame the "poor souls" who abused alcohol or even sold it, he had complete contempt for those who issued licenses to "enable" its use. He suggested that "Christian men" in public positions should resign before they stooped to issue a single saloon permit.

Neither was the Rev. Broughton an adherent of cigarette smoking. The transcript of his remarks is incongruous, juxtaposed as it was against the *N&O*'s advertisements for tobacco products.

"There can be no question," Broughton told another overflow crowd, "about the pernicious effects of cigarette smoking. And nobody knows it better than the man who makes them.

"The paper in which they are wrapped is bleached with arsenic. The tobacco is soaked in alcohol and opium. The smoke is full of nicotine. Hot and poison-charged, it passes into the lungs and saturates the tissue until it causes decomposition. And consumption, deadly and rapid, sets in. It is self-murder.... There's no way around it."

(To put the Rev. Broughton's remarks in context, 1898 was the year when Methodists in North Carolina wrung their hands for days at their convention over whether to accept an endowment from a Mr. Duke in Durham. As Carrie Nation verified on her later visit to Raleigh, the Methodists took the money.)

What a friend they had in Jesse.... In 1958, city councilman Jesse Helms had some ideas about a forthcoming meeting in the Institute of Religion series at the United Church.

"You consult with our chief-of-police," Helms wrote to City Manager William Carper, "and make sure that sufficient law enforcement officers are inconspicuously available to keep order."

Helms said his demand was motivated by a desire "to protect the rights of people with whom we may be in disagreement."

(The series had run for several years without incident and included speakers such as Martin Luther King, Jr. Carper simply filed the letter.)

The first composition to be played on the new pipe organ at White Memorial Presbyterian Church in the 1960s was "Whole Lotta Shaking Going On," which was in full swing at the hands of one of the crew which installed the organ just as the church's minister walked in to inquire about their progress.

He did not recognize the piece.

Hands Off Our Weak-Brained Women

In early Raleigh, any Justice of the Peace could advertise a missing slave as an "Out-Law." If the slave did not return after publication of the notice (how could he or she read it?), any person in Raleigh could "kill and destroy such slave, by such means as he or they may think fit."

The Intendant of Police was empowered by Raleigh's charter to whip any male slave who was "guilty of rude, indecent or offensive behavior toward any white female, in any of the streets or public grounds of the city, either by night or day, so as to alarm or insult such female."

One almost has to admire, or at least notice, a newspaper which would run a column entitled, "Repository of Genius."
The publishers of the *Raleigh Register* were named Gales, not Limbaugh, but their sentiments toward women were fat-headed even on a constant fat-head basis. Consider one poem by "Simon Henpeckt."
Explaining how he could win a claim for a perpetual motion machine at the U.S. Patent Office, Mr. Henpeckt rhymed: *"I'll send them my wife, whose perpetual clatter/ Cannot help but convince of the truth of the matter."*

(Nearly all such items were done anonymously in early Raleigh. Men may have defeated the British Empire and been masters of what state law called their "castle houses," but when it came to writing to a newspaper, they were almost universally spineless.)

Raleigh

This editorial, also from the *Register* about 1800, speaks for itself:
"The Fair Sex. The charming prattle of the fair sex has certainly been specially granted them by nature as a relief to their confinement and sedentary occupations. It is unjust, therefore, to censure their propensity to chat.

"A learned and ingenious friar, once preaching to a convent...assured that our Saviour, when he arose, appeared first to a woman, (so) that the news of his resurrection might be the sooner spread about."

And the Baptist State Convention thought it took a hard line against dancing.... In early Raleigh, any free black who permitted slaves to dance on his property was fined five pounds and expelled from the city.

(Free blacks were prohibited from living in Raleigh unless they received a license from the Intendant or the city commissioners. The blacks were required to prove that they had "an honest, industrious and peaceable character." They could reside in Raleigh only "during good behaviour.")

Long before Reaganomics, the citizens of Raleigh knew that economic discrimination not only existed, but that it was institutionalized. All they had to do in 1800 was to take a look at the Legislature.

The State Senate had been conceived as a body which "should represent the wealth of the country, and ... its members be men of the most temperate habits."

But even the House of Commons was less than a hotbed of populism.

In 1800, Rep. Henry Seawell of Raleigh was described in a debate as "the Gentleman from Wake (who) seems to think that all the indulgences of the government ought to be reserved for the rich, opulent and powerful."

(All Seawell had said was that "counties ought to be represented according to their ability to pay taxes.")

Why did the laws which prohibited the teaching of slaves to read and write permit them to be instructed in arithmetic?

The slaves went to market and to make pickups at businesses for their masters. Well into the 1800s, no fewer than four kinds of currency circulated in Raleigh, including British. A slave needed to be able to convert them and make change like any international traveler.

Some early Raleigh institutions made limited stabs at expanding their clientele beyond the white male Protestant elite.

The Raleigh Peace Society, which advocated holding debates instead of wars, put on a membership drive in 1824 before it folded from what its founders called "apathy."

"In general," the Revs. Thomas Daniel and Amos Battle wrote, "members of all peace societies are found to be intelligent, moral, responsible characters." But there were too few of those in the capital.

So "if illiterate persons show a desire to give or receive benefits through our society, (we) see no reasonable objection to their membership."

In fact, Dr. Battle added, "I have deemed <u>females,</u> as well as <u>males,</u> eligible.... You may perhaps think this objectionable."

Typical of the discourse about Raleigh's women was a diatribe in *The Microcosm* in 1838, in which Ephraim Grabwell defended his right to remain a bachelor.

"When I was a young man," he wrote, "the ladies were worth looking at, and deserved attention. They showed a full front, like a seventy-four, and walked all points like a race horse; they dressed neat and tasty; their manners were simple and sincere.

"But now how is it?" he cried. "They are all tapered to a grasshopper waist; and when they move (for 'taint walking), they totter along, mincing like a Chinese. Their manners are so artificial and affected, that you can't get one word from the heart – all is frozen hypocrisy...."

Uncle Ephy may have cemented his marital status with those words, but he was taking no chances and continued.

"Now nobody knows what they are, by their fantastic mode of dress; and they just play the part in the drawing room that their mothers made them rehearse upstairs. Besides this, I've proved them; they are altogether mercenary. Look how soon they lay aside their gracious airs and sweet smiles after they get a poor wretch to say 'yes'...."

That was enough for one female reader, who urged subscribers to "never mind Ephy; Ma says, he came to her house one day and just looked into the bung hole of a right new barrel of cider, and the next day it was <u>sharp, strong vinegar.</u>"

Another woman wrote in to question why females wanted marriage at all. "Poor creature," she wrote of a friend, "she is going to be married – she says to a 'charming man' – Poh! what silly creatures girls are to get married so soon after they leave school. They no sooner get clear of the leading lines, than they quietly submit to have the halter tied around their necks."

But most of the correspondence was derogatory to Raleigh women, or at least to their dress. "The waists of our belles were literally compressed into the dimensions of a gourd handle," a correspondent wrote about one style, and others described costumes as "apish fantastics" with "feathers enough to officer a brigade."

In addition, one wrote, "the 'Grecian bend' was introduced, which deprived a large part of them of the privilege of standing erect." He feared that the capital's women would "degenerate into a race of cripples and hunchbacks."

"Just give the ladies a chance," a Raleigh advocate of equality wrote before 1850.

"Let them mix with the world, let them legislate, kill bears, or build railroads, at their own good pleasure, and we rather calculate they'll show you some brighter tricks than... boiling cabbage or making pants."

(Totally off the topic, cabbage apparently was a much more popular vegetable in the 1800s than it is in Raleigh today. One owner of the Joel Lane grounds had the disrespect to plant a cabbage patch over the grave of Raleigh's founder. He sold the produce at the city market.)

The graduating class of the Raleigh Female Seminary in 1859 got to listen to these words of wisdom from editor W.W. Holden, their commencement speaker, who later was impeached as Governor.

"The duties of women," Holden counseled them, "if not so diversified, so extended, so world-pervading as those of a man, are yet quite as important in their sphere as his. And as much of the happiness of society depends on their just performance."

Holden told the students that "man is rough, aggressive, warlike, aspiring; woman is soft, retiring, modest and loving. Man's duty is to subdue nature, to till the earth, to govern, to establish and sustain visible society; woman's task is to encourage him with her sympathy, to cheer him in his despondency, to give shape and tone to domestic government...."

(A man who made a speech like that today would never be impeached as Governor because he could not get nominated. But in fairness to Holden, other than the legendary Thornton J. Melon, who else has failed to sound like a sap when giving a commencement address?)

Raleigh

State Treasurer and Governor Jonathan Worth is remembered for many things, but his sense of timing was not always prophetic.

In January, 1865 – with the end of the Civil War less than three months away – some people in Raleigh were still buying 6 percent tax-exempt Confederate bonds, payable two years after the end of hostilities. Others, by law, were still handing over 10 percent tithes of crops and bacon to the army.

But Treasurer Worth went those people one better: he decided to go into the slave business.

On January 6, 1865, he paid Emma C. White the sum of $400 to hire one of her slaves for the remainder of the year.

Two weeks later, Worth handed over $5,000 to William N. Ledbetter for a "negro man Archer," together with another $5,000 for a pair of mules, gear and a wagon. He was all set to start a plantation.

Despite the fact that by 1865, prices in Raleigh had "gone through the roof," $10,400 was still a meaningful amount of money.

So several weeks after Appomattox, with his slaves emancipated and little need for farm equipment which had cost many times its value, Worth started to sell off portions of his lands and sharecrop others. Raleigh's short-term financial decline had begun.

How preoccupied was Raleigh with race in the years immediately after the Civil War?

In 1872, the State Senate passed a city charter amendment which would have authorized a referendum on installing three new cisterns for fire protection.

The legislation, wrote the *Daily Sentinel,* "might properly be termed a bill to take negro laborers from the farm to be fed in Raleigh."

So much of Raleigh's oldest money was built on slavery that Dr. Kemp Battle of UNC, orating in the city in 1876, had to scrounge around to name citizens who had built their holdings by other means.

Newspaper publisher William Boylan, for instance, at one point was so aggrieved about his purchase of one lethargic slave for $350 that he prepared to sue the seller. The slave then commenced to bear the first of 24 children, "fifteen of whom grew up to be valuable."

Boylan withdrew his lawsuit in 1800, watched as his valuable slave population grew, and inadvertently taught a lesson about infant mortality on a "good" plantation.

Raleigh

Racism in Raleigh scarcely commenced when Josephus Daniels arrived in town.

The *Sentinel,* in questioning some voting tactics in 1868 among the new freedmen, printed a ditty which read in part:

"Whar's de tickets? Fetch 'em straight!
I vote early— I vote late—
I vote often— I vote right—
I' se no ignoramus white."

Reconstruction was an era when the city fathers held unauthorized elections, believing that the General Assembly would later validate their results. (It did not.)

It was an era when Raleigh had a city board which barricaded itself in the mayor's office one day and took possession of all city documents. (The board believed, and the *Sentinel* agreed, that they had been thrown out of office by "an unconstitutional act of the bogus legislature." They stayed ousted.)

"Elections," one historian wrote about Raleigh during Reconstruction, "were so largely concerned with Negroes, and carpetbaggers, that at times they resolved themselves into orgies of drinking and brawling. Freedmen crowded to the polls deliberately making themselves offensive to whites."

To the horror of the city's white citizens, the new city board which was recognized by Governor Holden included two Negroes, and the board proceeded to hire a Negro as assistant constable and placed three Negroes on night patrol of the police department. After that action, Holden could not count on even his hometown in the approaching impeachment struggle.

In an anecdote which had something to offend most every sensitive reader, the *Observer* related this in 1877:

"At the Wilmington Street entrance to the city market there is an old 'coon' vending out a patent cement. We can especially recommend it as an invaluable article to married men. He sold a bottle to a married man four days ago, his wife injudiciously got some of it on her lips, and she has not opened her mouth since."

Before a child could be enrolled at the Institution for the Deaf, Dumb and Blind in 1881, school officials had to be satisfied with 28 answers on an admissions questionnaire.

Raleigh

Question No. 1 asked the child's name. Question No. 2 asked the child's race. Not until Question No. 18 did the State ask whether the child had typhoid, scarlet fever, or other contagious diseases.

The *Chronicle* in 1884 decided that one raconteur's remarks about women deserved to be printed on Page One.

"Money can't always buy a woman," the man advised, "at least they vary in price.

"We read in the Scriptures how Rebecca's sweetheart gave her bracelets worth a shekel or two shekels. That was just sixty-two and a half cents. You catch any fellow getting a modern Rebecca with that kind of jewelry."

The *N&O* reported in 1885 that "even the women folk could take a pot shot at being intellectual with the aid of the Female Classical Institute on Hillsborough Street."

When Raleigh staged the Northern Settlers' Convention in 1886 (the city fathers openly desired to attract more Yankee residents who had money), it paid the transportation costs of travel writers from across the Eastern seaboard.

Naturally, no Northern writer could travel into the South without touching on race relations in his dispatches. A sampling about Raleigh from the nation's newspapers in 1886:

• One writer deplored the state's convict lease system and its prison population which at the time was 80 percent black. The writer expressed shock at "convicts in regular convicts' garb" who were working on the new Wake County courthouse project under the eyes of "state guards patrolling with rifles." Yet he found it remarkable that when he interviewed the black and white masons who were laying stone blocks between the streetcar rails, all worked side by side for the same $2 per day.

• Another reporter from Maryland pointed out that when Shaw University was founded, the presence of the black college ended all construction of homes for whites on the south side of Raleigh. He reported that Shaw's presence also depressed the values of existing white-owned homes.

"There is now no sale, except at great sacrifice, for what was 15 years ago fine property," he wrote. "All the new and handsome buildings are now going up on the other side of the city."

• One of the more bizarre reports was by a reporter from the *Boston Evening Transcript* who took pains to describe himself as a black Republican. He had this to say about the capital:

"The negroes seem to go everywhere the whites do – into the same cars, into the same buildings, at the same counters for lunch. The whites do not appear to notice their presence, though they have to put up with some acts of social equality which we at the North would not stand."

Referring to "two plantation darkies, smoking dirty cigars" who were in the same train car as several white women, the reporter commented that "I doubt if we at the North would put up with this, even on cattle-show week."

Reporting on a speech by Booker T. Washington in Raleigh in 1893, Josephus Daniels commented that Washington's "father was a white man and he shows in his face, in his speech, and in his executive ability, his white blood."

If one negro can control six white men, then the six white men deserve no sympathy nor any place on any board."

How 'bout dem racists? And that was not the *N&O*, which probably would have used a word other than "negro," but *The Progressive Farmer*. The issue was the presence of James H. Young, a black politician, on the board of directors of the N.C. Institution for the Deaf, Dumb and Blind.

The Progressive Farmer was incensed at the *N&O*'s campaign to force Young off of the board.

The *N&O*'s cartoons, "with their vulgar suggestions and the premeditated, deliberate, willful and malicious and slanderous lies which accompany them," the *Farmer* said, "should forfeit the respect of honest people for the perpetuators and drive their filthy sheet from the homes of decent, self-respecting people."

(And all the "News and Distorter," as editor Clarence Poe called it, had done was to print cartoons of Young alone in the school's dormitory rooms with unsighted white girls.)

"Oh no," the *Farmer* said, "the ladies of the State are too intelligent to be fooled by the cry of 'nigger'." (Perhaps so, but since women were not yet allowed to vote, the relationship of that remark to the gubernatorial campaign of 1900 – when Young was an issue – is obscure.)

"Certainly, they howl nigger," Poe continued. "It's to keep the people from reasoning. It's to draw attention from their disgraceful management of

Raleigh

State affairs. It's done in order that they may slip in and disfranchise the poor and the unlettered."

Poe had a point. At the time, the *N&O* was promoting a literacy test amendment to the State Constitution. "Shall the negro cease to be a political power to do evil?" the *N&O* asked.

"Those who would have the negro eliminated will vote for the amendment."

The *N&O* also explained the proposed amendment to its readers – in 1900, there were no women voters to form a League – by stating that "It Allows All White Men Who Register Under It before 1908 to Vote For All Time, Whether They Can Read And Write or Not."

Assorted Raleigh headlines from the 1898 campaign, which was kinder and gentler only than a media lynching:

"The Wake County mongrel ticket appealed yesterday...."

"Is There a Negro on the Fusion Magistrate Ticket in Raleigh Township – Rumor Says There Is – Some Suspicious Circumstances."

"Shall the White Man or the Black Man Rule in North Carolina?"

"W.W._____, white of skin and black of heart, got his head punched."

Well, so much for the headlines on the news stories. Some of the news items themselves add to the flavor:

"All business was suspended and the pavements were thronged with a pipe-smoking, bet-making crowd."

"When you said, 'Down with the dust, boys,' they had little money but a good excuse."

"The white men were on one side, and the negroes and a measley little gang of office-seekers and their heelers were on the other side."

Maybe Josephus Daniels was correct in one of his autobiographies. Maybe he did go a little too far in the election campaign of 1898. (His activities also appear in the sections on communications and on entertainment.)

"NOT ONE TWENTIETH of the Horrors of Negro Domination Has Been Printed in the Papers," Daniels wrote.

"The Almighty has made the Anglo-Saxon race his hope in the world's evangelization. That is a truth that all the world now accepts," Daniels wrote.

"Populists are expected to walk down the central aisle to the tune 'All Coons Look Alike to Me,'" Daniels wrote.

"They are vastly superior to their brothers in the African swamps," Daniels wrote, "but we do agree... they are unfit to govern."

Daniels wrote that "under negro committee men (he did not want a single black to serve on a single local board of education) the standard of the public schools would be lowered, the attendance would fall off, and the interest of the people in the public schools would give place to a feeling of revulsion and neglect."

Daniels edified his readers one morning with the news that "so long as the management of the schools is entrusted to a gentry advanced in civilization only a few paces beyond the breech-clout stage, no self-respecting white man is going to vote one cent more tax upon himself to support them."

(How would the man have felt about having a desegregated middle school named in his honor?)

Josephus Daniels was not content merely to win the 1898 White Supremacy Election. He meant what he wrote, and he wanted to follow through and permanently end black political influence in the state.

Thus, about a month later, readers picked up their Sunday *N&O*s to find the front page dominated by a scheme to prevent blacks from holding public office.

The idea, which Daniels hammered on as the Legislative session neared, was simple: although the 13th, 14th and 15th amendments to the U.S. Constitution guaranteed many things, holding public office was not among them. (It really is unfortunate that Daniels did not live long enough to meet House Speaker Dan Blue of Raleigh.)

The *N&O* also printed a poem authored by the "Yellow Kid" in praise of the White Supremacy rally in November. Among its verses, all written in dialect, were these:

> *"Dere wan't a single nigger*
> *Fer us ter guy er fight*
> *We took it out in tootin'*
> *And yelled wid all our might.*
>
> *Josephus Daniels run it*
> *So course 'twas de best stuff*
> *De Radicals wuz roasted*
> *Jess zackly brown enuff."*

Raleigh

(Critic's note: The above poem may belie the theory that white Southerners, while willing to go to extreme in mocking the dialect of any minority group, never listened to how they spoke themselves. On the other hand, the Yellow Kid may simply have forgotten his poetic voice.)

Daniels had other admirers, including the correspondent who wrote that the White Supremacy rally in Raleigh had been more fun "than throwing baseball at the 'nigger head' at the Fair" – an attraction which bothered Daniels less than the Fair's gambling booths and girlie shows.

Old Josephus was one of 'em. He later claimed in his many autobiographies that racism was only a political expedient of the 1898 campaign, but the man was preoccupied with race years later.

"Drapped the Wrong Nigger," was a headline in the *N&O* in 1907 about a fatal shooting at a picnic.

"His face was so smooty and greasy that he could hardly be recognized as a white man," was a line gratuitously inserted into a news story about firefighters. (And people wonder why the *Carolinian* newspaper has survived in the city's black community.)

Then there was the *N&O* headline, "Cost Him $28.15," which described the "Case in which a Negro Pays a Good Fine for Getting Knocked Down." The report tells as much about race relations in Raleigh in the early 1900s as it does about Daniels.

It seems that a white man on Wilmington Street "brushed against a Negro, who stopped and said, 'You better run over me, you big fat rascal.' Wherefor _____ knocked him down with his fist."

Both men were taken into court for engaging in an affray. Charges against the batterer were dismissed; the black man may have felt lucky to avoid the city chain gang. And Daniels had his headline.

Raleigh could have a splendid bicentennial debate over who holds the title of the all-time media bigot.

No one should get the impression that the *N&O* was Raleigh's only newspaper which flunked Community Relations 101.

The *Caucasian* was a political fusion newspaper which opposed the *N&O* in its White Supremacy campaign, but it was hard to distinguish one from the other by their rhetoric.

When Daniels hired the city's first political cartoonist, the *Caucasian* reciprocated with a cartoon of its own captioned "Democratic Niggers." (Most of these cartoons ran on the newspapers' respective front pages.)

In an era when photographs were unfamiliar in Raleigh's newspapers, the *Caucasian* printed one under the headline, "More Nigger Outrages." The photo was of a capias which deputized a black officer to arrest a white woman. The deputy was described by the newspaper as "A Big Burly Black Nigger." The *Caucasian*'s stated intent was to show that Democrats as well as Fusionists were complicit in placing blacks in positions above their proper status.

The *Caucasian* directed its hate at more than blacks. In the process of disagreeing with an editor in Rocky Mount, the newspaper attacked him for being "a small mouthpiece of the money-changers Christ drove from the Temple."

Yet as lowlife as the *N&O* and *Caucasian* appear today, Raleigh need not despair. Their commentary was meek at the turn of the century when compared to the *Wilmington Messenger* or the *Oxford Public Ledger*.

The *Messenger*, which wrote that a white mob which killed 11 blacks provided "a splendid example of forbearance and moderation," and which mused over lynching as one means of silencing a black editor, finally concluded that "it is true it would be best if the negro were eliminated completely." It was not talking about politics.

And a few miles up the road from Raleigh, the *Public Ledger* redesigned its masthead. On the left side was a depiction of a white man with one arm raised, aiming to the right, where a black man lay spread-eagle as a corpse.

The nearest that Raleigh seems to have come to a race riot was not following the assassination of Dr. Martin Luther King, Jr., but – when else? – toward the end of the White Supremacy campaign of 1898.

Raleigh at the time was home to the Second Infantry Company, which was stationed near today's Little Theater while it waited to be released from duty after the Spanish-American War.

With little to do but prepare for inspections, and with the citizens of Raleigh regarding them with increasing distaste, the soldiers did not get along with a spectrum of people. (The city's police dockets were replete with warrants for vandalism, for troops who got "tanked up on Wilmington Street bug juice," for knifings and for terrorizing neighborhoods.)

But in particular, the soldiers did not get along with the black community in what was then called East Raleigh.

(East Raleigh was described by a correspondent of the *Charlotte Observer* as "the tough suburb... it is known by the county authorities that whiskey is sold there by 'blind tigers.' The mayor is powerless there. Some very bad negroes live in that quarter and some extremely low white men frequent it, especially on Sundays.")

Raleigh

Several evenings before they left town, three enlisted men struck up a conversation with some blacks on East Street; the discussion concerned prostitutes. The soldiers ended up being pelted with stones and a brick, and beaten with sticks.

The next afternoon, several hundred soldiers and a similar number of blacks lined up on East Martin Street for the showdown.

This time they carried guns.

According to the *N&O*, the two sides "fired enough rounds to kill scores of men." Fortunately, however, neither the members of the United States Army nor the residents of East Raleigh were good shots. No one was killed, and most of the wounds were superficial.

(In fact, most of the wounds came from the back. The *Observer*, reporting on the fusillade, said with a straight face that "two negroes are reported to be wounded, but as the negro, like the Indian, carries off and hides his dead and wounded, the (injuries are) rather hard to verify.")

With Raleigh's streets smelling of cordite, the Governor and the mayor called out the militia to preserve order. Raleigh citizens began to buy up every firearm which was for sale in the city. One hardware clerk downtown sold 50 boxes of Winchester ammunition in one day. (It was all that he had in stock.) The blacks stayed in East Raleigh and prepared for their defense.

With the militia standing guard, rumors began to circulate that there would be another confrontation and that this time, the soldiers planned to burn every house on East Martin Street. The day before it was to happen, the Army decided to release the Second Regiment from duty.

The incident was just the kind of prelude which the White Supremacists had needed in their campaign.

Speaking on Emancipation Day in 1900, Dr. C.N. Hunter addressed himself to the proposals which would soon disenfranchise most black voters for decades.

As for the injustice of requiring blacks to pass literacy tests when only two generations before it had been unlawful to teach them to read and write, Hunter asked the crowd, "What would Jesus do?"

"Would He taunt them of their ignorance which was forced upon them by the laws of the State?"

Hunter then pursued a more immediate argument for whites: their pocketbooks and paranoia.

If the disenfranchisement measure passed, Hunter said, "your lands will be depopulated of the best and cheapest labor that will ever be available to you. The great industrial progress of your cities will be checked. The situation will invite from the over-crowded cities of the North a class of laborers who will bring to you every conceivable element of lawlessness."

The amendment passed in Raleigh by a huge majority.

The reading room is free to all white persons of good character" over the age of twelve – those were among the rules of the Olivia Raney library in 1901.

Once the eligible patrons got inside the place, however, they found a designated Smoking Room, which depending on one's attitude was either a further discrimination or a blessing which is missing today.

The realities of "separate but equal" education cannot be made more clear than in Dr. Richard H. Lewis' report early in this century about the grade school then on Oberlin Road.

(The Oberlin community, steadily nibbled away at by development in recent decades, has been a residential area for Raleigh's blacks since after the Civil War. At one point, there was a master plan for a new black city of San Domingo, to be located off Wade Avenue, but the scheme failed.)

Lewis' committee found that the Oberlin school's roof leaked because its shingles were "in a state of crumbling decay"; the chimneys were "falling away from the building"; the floor showed "unsteadiness" and contained numerous holes; the stoves were "broken or inadequate as well as improperly located"; the privies were "in a most dilapidated condition and must soon fall down" (nor were they sanitary); and coal ashes were taking over the playground behind the building.

The Oberlin school also had non-complying handmade desks and used them well into the 20th century after the city's other schools had patent models.

Dr. Lewis said that in addition to correcting the school's defects, the School Board needed to finance an auditorium not only for the students, but for the Oberlin community.

Other than the foregoing, Dr. Lewis commended the educational climate at the school.

One problem inherent in writing about Raleigh is illustrated by the case of the preeminent local attorney, long deceased, who had the habit of writing racist letters to national figures. His letters ended up in the State Archives.

Is the lawyer and former judge to be remembered exclusively for writing to the president of the NAACP and suggesting that the Federal government set aside a reservation for blacks? Or for writing to Chief Justice William Howard Taft and saying that the South would be much happier if certain inscriptions were chiseled off the Lincoln Memorial?

(Taft thought little of the idea, replying that it "would awaken great discussion and do great harm.")

How can the lawyer's periodic outbursts be balanced short of giving a chronicle of his other activities? The answer is to omit his name, leaving him as an anonymous example of the kooks who lurk among us.

No matter how far-flung, almost any political issue in old Raleigh could be tinged by racism.

Consider the upright, morally-correct crusade in 1920 in favor of granting women the right to vote. These are some of the arguments which were made by the *proponents:*

"Woman Suffrage Raises No Race Issue... Color cannot be dragged in by the utmost strain of construction... The qualifications that now apply to negro men will apply to negro women (That is, they would be effectively disenfranchised.)...."

And, "If white domination is threatened in the South, it is... DOUBLY EXPEDIENT TO ENFRANCHISE THE WHITE WOMEN QUICKLY IN ORDER THAT IT BE PRESERVED."

If the "Suffs" in 1920 were reduced to making such arguments in seeking the vote, what were Raleigh's more conservative "antis" saying?

Raleigh was home to the *State's Defense* newsletter, a broadside which was exactly that. "We plead in the name of Virginia Dare, that North Carolina Remain White," it importuned.

Then there was the catechism written by the antis and entitled "The Feminist and Our Bible." Full of citations to prove that women were created to be subservient, its saving grace was the Raleigh author's disclaimer that she was not qualified to interpret the Scripture.

Not content with invoking God and Virginia Dare, the Raleigh antis also likened the proponents to the recently vanquished Kaiser of Germany:

"The Suffs say it's bound to come," they wrote, "but don't be misled by that propaganda. The Huns said they would be in Paris by Christmas."

Under fire from such uplifting arguments as those, made by the Society for the Rejection of the Susan B. Anthony Amendment, the Suffs went back to the basics.

"Just as the East allows the West to regulate the Jap problem," they advised, "so the North has accustomed itself to hands off in the negro question."

They added that in case the Yankees tried something sneaky, "250,000 North Carolina White Women Are Prepared to Vote for White Supremacy."

Either despite or because of these frothings by both sides – and these were Raleigh's "society women" – the General Assembly did give all deliberate consideration in 1920 to adopting the Nineteenth Amendment. And it did so in 1971.

Although Raleigh's entire delegation to the General Assembly voted against woman suffrage in 1920, the city was somewhat more progressive than those four troglodytes might indicate.

Months before the amendment was killed in the Legislature, Raleigh sent five women to the State Democratic Convention. (In reality, the city's Democrats had little choice. In a tactic which anticipated what McCarthy and McGovern supporters tried in the Presidential contests in 1968 and 1972, dozens of women, unannounced, had "invaded the late March precinct meetings" and secured representation.)

As for the four legislators, all had been lame ducks when they voted against suffrage in 1920. None of them ever chose to face the voters again.

Some women in Raleigh had begun to question their confinement to the home and exclusion from politics before North Carolina began to seriously consider the suffrage issue.

The home was no haven from political matters, wrote Martha Haywood in 1916. "Politics governs alike the purity of the milk supply and the efficiency of the city medical department," she argued. "Politics comes into the home and gets inside of the baby whenever the milkman with a 'pull' and a dirty farm leaves a bottle of milk at the front door."

Haywood's remarks, in *Everywoman's Magazine* which was founded in Raleigh, were so direct that the magazine disassociated itself from her views two issues later, swearing that it was not "a suffrage publication" and that opinions from all sides were welcome.

But Haywood, president of the Suffrage League of Raleigh, persisted. To rebut the argument that new women voters might be manipulated by the Republicans, Haywood promised that "260,000 North Carolina white women" would "stand against any measure, any man or woman, who proposes to question Anglo-Saxon supremacy."

Raleigh

"We should take steps to keep them out – and don't make much difference what kind."

Those charming words, which were followed by a public appeal to the Ku Klux Klan, were uttered at an Indignation Meeting held in 1927 at the Hayes Barton Baptist Church.

At issue was whether a Raleigh family should be permitted to build a home in the 1600 block of Glenwood Avenue so that its children could attend the grade school across the street.

Nominally, the head of the household fit the pattern of many well-to-do residents of Hayes Barton. He was a successful self-made businessman. He was patriotic. He had never run afoul of the law. He supported the Chamber of Commerce. He made large and regular contributions to such local institutions as Rex and St. Agnes hospitals, Peace and Meredith colleges, and the Community Chest. He planned to build a large, dignified brick house which would be the equal of any going up in the neighborhood.

The only problem was the man's name: call him Mr. R.

"Greeks should live with Greeks and Americans with Americans," read one of the anonymous letters which Mr. R. received after he acquired an option on the Glenwood Avenue lot. (He had lived in the United States for more than 20 years and been a citizen for nine; no one had questioned his heritage while he donated for the war effort.)

"We do not think that you or anyone else would want to build and live where the neighbors do not want you," read a second letter, this one signed by housewives named Lundy, Mangum and Beddingfield.

"We expect to appeal to the Ku Klux Klan for protection... if you keep up this disturbance," read another letter signed by "the neighbors" which U.S. postal authorities thought was written on the same stationery and typed using the same typewriter as the epistle from the three women.

More than 60 residents of Hayes Barton turned out for the church meeting, which was later described as "anything but Christian."

They determined to appeal to the City Commission to deny Mr. R. a building permit so that he would have to sue in order to begin work. They told the commissioners that if Mr. R. moved in, property values would plummet and the city would lose tax revenues.

The persecutors called for a boycott of Mr. R.'s businesses if he did not desist. They decided to form a neighborhood syndicate to see whether they could buy him out. They enlisted real estate agents to promote parcels of land elsewhere in Raleigh where Mr. R. might be induced to build. They talked about getting a restraining order. They talked some more about the Klan.

(In general, they reacted in exactly the way black people in Raleigh have come to recognize, only more out in the open. The reason they did not try red-lining was that Mr. R. planned to build his home with cash.)

The persecutors were not your run-of-the-mill rednecks; they had surnames such as Howison, Briggs, Williamson, Smith, Danielson and Parker.

As for obtaining the restraining order, the *N&O* did not think that the Hayes Barton residents had a chance, because it said that the only restrictive covenants in Hayes Barton deeds concerned "house footage and persons of African descent."

The *N&O* came to Mr. R.'s defense, remarking that if the principle of the residents were carried to its logical extreme, "all the brunettes may be summarily chased out because the gentlemen in Hayes-Barton prefer blondes."

When it was suggested that an injunction be sought against Mr. R. for being an "undesirable person," someone pointed out that to seek one was risky because based on the tone of the Indignation Meeting, "there might already be some undesirable citizens in Hayes-Barton."

The would-be seller of the lot commented that "just why it is more ethical or patriotic to offer to sell a Greek a lot near the Thompson School rather than the Hayes-Barton School does not appear on the surface."

The controversy stewed for weeks as the residents of Hayes Barton failed to put their money where their prejudices were. Newspapers around the State picked up the story and began to print accounts which made the neighborhood an unqualified laughingstock.

"It would seem," wrote the *Goldsboro News*, "to the ordinary human not endowed with royal prerogatives, that the good citizens of Hayes-Barton are making a pitiable spectacle of themselves."

The *Asheville Citizen* stepped in. "Judging from their present attitude," the newspaper observed, "if Jesus the Carpenter, or Peter the fisherman, or Paul the tent-maker were to undertake to locate in Hayes-Barton, the residents would object." (Mr. R owned two shoe and hat businesses.)

By the time that the Rev. S.J. Betts expressed surprise that the Hayes Barton Baptist Church – a part of his own denomination – "had not publicly announced their disapproval and apologies for the unfortunate matter" of having the Indignation Meeting in the church, the congregation was becoming unraveled. There was talk of seeking to expel church members at the next congregational meeting.

Mr. R. remained cool despite his frustration. "I don't particularly care about living in Hayes-Barton," he told the *N&O*. "There are other good places in that section convenient to the school, and with just as good people."

Amen. Particularly after some of the Hayes Barton homeowners, reeling under the publicity caused by their own actions, tried to make out Mr. R. to be a bigot himself. At one of the persecution meetings, a resident alleged that Mr. R. had proclaimed, "American come to Greece, put him with the best people. Greek come to America, try to put him with the niggers." The attempted diversion failed.

Toward the end, Josephus Daniels pointed out in essence that at the time Mr. R.'s ancestors were completing the Parthenon, the ancestors of Hayes Barton residents were still wearing skins and clubbing their lunch to death.

Mr. R. made four visits to the city's building permit bureau before anyone would see him. He was informed that he would be issued a permit as soon as he submitted formal architectural plans for the house. He had delayed on commissioning the drafting because of threatened litigation by the neighbors.

But by the time the plans were drawn, Mr. R. had decided to forego what newspapers were calling the "high fliers" of Hayes Barton. (Perhaps he had found – as is said of Trump Tower in New York – that if you can afford to live there, you can live somewhere better, or at least more hospitable.)

In the 1930s, the Raleigh city directory listed all black-owned restaurants as "Eating Houses" and the corresponding white establishments as "Restaurants."

Who invited *him* to speak?... The scene was the dignified chamber of the North Carolina Supreme Court. The occasion was the presentation in 1933 of an oil portrait of the late Justice Alphonzo Calhoun Avery. The speaker was the *N&O*'s Josephus Daniels, chosen to extol his mentor's life and career.

Daniels revealed to the gathering that Judge Avery had been a founder of the Ku Klux Klan in North Carolina. Then he warmed to the subject.

"The true story... of the Ku Klux Klan, in days when terror stalked abroad, is yet to be fully told," Daniels said. "When it is written, the courage of brave men in stress will constitute a new chapter of devotion."

Daniels said that "the spirit of men who rode by night and put their lives in jeopardy in that distressful period bound them together with hooks of steel." He related a political incident when he had questioned Avery about his support of a candidate for statewide office whose views did not conform to his on an important issue. "He took me off to one side," Daniels remembers, and whispered that the candidate had also been a night-rider.

Daniels did contrast the Klan of the 1870s to the renewed version of 1933, which he called "spurious" and "pseudo." He explained that the original KKK operated "for the protection of womanhood" and out of a lack of respect for State government following the reconstruction years. "Real chivalry," he said of the Klan's mission.

The publisher never wrote the true story of the KKK. After his speech, to the accompaniment of the American Legion drum and bugle corps, Daniels boarded the train in Raleigh on his way south as the new U.S. Ambassador to Mexico.

The official book of Raleigh's sesquicentennial in 1942 dedicated eight and one-half pages to white churches in the city and four paragraphs to those attended by blacks. At the time, their percentages of the city's congregants were estimated to be about equal.

When the Spaulding family of Durham bought the Montague Building at the corner of Moore Square, one of its tenants operated a soda shop.

One afternoon, a Spaulding brother stopped at the shop, ordered a soda, and began to drink it while standing at the fountain. His lessee kicked him out into the street, telling him that blacks were not allowed to consume beverages on the premises.

When the lease expired, the Spauldings found a different tenant.

In Raleigh, the accentuation was on the "deliberate" rather than on the "speed" as the city grappled with desegregation of the public schools after the *Brown* decisions.

The city government knew, assuming that it read its own reports, that although education in Raleigh had been racially separate, it had been nowhere close to equal.

At Ligon High School in 1954-55, per-pupil expenditures for the library were $1, as compared to $2.16 at Broughton High School. At Ligon, teachers had average classes of 22.48 students, as compared to 16.6 students in an average class at Broughton. (Incidentally, high school teachers in Raleigh today have higher average class sizes than Ligon did in 1954. But class sizes increase when fewer students drop out of school.)

When the *Brown* decisions were reported, the city responded by forming a Council on Preparation for Integration. It met and issued reports.

Raleigh

Time and again, the School Board voted to deny school transfers to black students, among them current City Councilman Ralph Campbell, Jr. The Board was willing to spend thousands of dollars to bus black seventh-graders across town from Oberlin Road rather than permit them to walk down the street to what is now the Daniels Middle School.

Raleigh's leading State Senator said he had canvassed his black friends and had been assured that they believed integrated schools were "unnatural."

It took seven years after *Brown* for the first three black students to enter Broughton High School. (One pupil had enrolled at the Murphey Elementary School in 1960.) One arrived as part of a settlement of a desegregation lawsuit, and another was thrust into the role because the denial of this particular student would have embarrassed Raleigh's gentry on a daily basis. All three were females.

Although the foot-draggers won, there had been other voices in Raleigh.

Cy King, concerned about Governor Luther Hodges' pronouncement that white schools could close rather than integrate, wrote Hodges in 1955:

"I have never tried to judge Southern politicians on their utterances on race, for it is obvious that any politician in the South who advocates integration of the races is dead politically."

However, King added, "I had hoped that you would be spared the necessity of sounding like a Southern politician on this issue."

Hodges replied in essence that he did not place much stock in his own remarks and was using the Pearsall Plan, which embodied them, as an escape valve for public tension.

By 1965, more than a decade after *Brown*, the school system was desegregated to the satisfaction of the city fathers. And they expressed pleasure at their accomplishments. Out of 20,941 students in the system that year, the complexion was this: "negroes at white schools, 70; whites at negro schools, 0."

All but unnoticed was the fact that the city's parochial schools had integrated back in 1955, with racially-mixed classrooms two blocks from the Confederate Memorial.

Nothing Is Too Much Of A Humbug

Early celebrations of the Fourth of July were special for residents of Raleigh, since the Revolution was near enough to mean something tangible.

In 1800, Raleigh celebrated with a parade up what was then called Fayetteville Road to the State-House, complete with state and federal officials and guns and cannons firing.

After a ceremony at the State-House, Raleigh's founding fathers repaired to a stag luncheon at a spring, catered by innkeeper Peter Casso. They drank "sixteen official toasts and several excellent volunteer" ones, with a cannon volley after each drink.

Darkness halted the old sports, who then returned to the State-House where Raleigh's women awaited for a dance and more drinking. (Who knows what frame of mind the women were in when the men wobbled through the State-House doors. It appears, at least, that the toasts on most official occasions were drunk with scuppernong wine and not whiskey.)

The *Minerva* was grateful that the Fourth passed with only four serious injuries from the festivities. It suggested that in 1801, amateurs be kept from firing off the cannons and shooting muskets.

At Casso's tavern, cockfighting was part of the regular entertainment, but not all the action was confined to the pit.

After several incidents, the nearby General Assembly passed an act to prohibit "the reprehensible practice of cock-throwing" – that is, flinging a spurred rooster into the face of a human adversary.

Raleigh

Although the City of Durham occasionally gets bent out of shape by the *N&O*'s reporting of crime there, the *Durham Herald* has rarely hesitated to pounce on the state capital's less desirable features.

In the 1940s and 1950s, the *Herald* dredged up a series of stories about public executions which happened in Raleigh more than a century earlier.

Describing a hanging in 1830, the *Herald* wrote that "the day before a hanging, most husbands made sure that they had plenty of whiskey on hand to carry on the trip. (Evidently the burghers of Durham would ride over to Raleigh to witness executions.)

"The women baked a cake or two and packed a large basket of lunch," the *Herald* continued. "The children were well scrubbed and their best clothes laid out for the big event."

(Well, those people were from Durham. And if Durham's early newspapers could be found, there should be similar accounts about its own hangings.) Nonetheless, the *Herald* did capture the mood in Raleigh when it discussed more than 3,000 spectators on Fayetteville Street.

"During the morning," it reported, "every avenue leading to town was literally blocked with human beings of both sexes, and of all colors, and ages.

"As the hour of noon approached the crowd became stationed near the jail. We feel it our duty to state the humiliating fact that a large proportion of the crowd... were females."

The *Herald* – drawing on Raleigh newspaper accounts – said that the crowd waited for "two hours in the mid-day sun" before the hanging and amused itself with the "drinking, fighting and gambling (which) were common at all executions."

One of the better descriptions of a cockfight is contained in a letter by a Raleigh woman in 1833.

"We had a barbecue and a chicken peck... on Easter," she wrote in her own spelling.

"The first fight we had they let our chicken get out of the ringe and in catching him he ran in some timber and in getting him out they cilled him so we lost the fight the next fight we heald our chicken droped him in the pit when he only maid a few jerks both (gaves?) out of the leathers we then picked up our cock and gived up the fight we had two other fights and wone both fast two and wone two and came off two dollars and a half winners after all of our bad misfortune we would have wone the other two fights with all ease if it had not been for what I have jest toled you of...."

(Not even William Faulkner could argue with that sentence structure.)

Raleigh

Two sentences later she took time to mention another Easter Sunday pastime in Raleigh:

"It appears," she wrote, "as if religion is in rather a declined state in this neighborhood at this time. I thought wonce the religious party would rule this nation of people like all other countrys...."

Even political campaigns can amount to entertainment – they can even be pleasant, the innovations of recent decades notwithstanding – and the Presidential contest of 1840 was one of the most colorful in the city's history.

The intellectual level of the campaign can be summarized as this: when he was attacked for being a cider-drinking, cabin-dwelling rube, Whig challenger William Harrison turned the criticism around; he depicted President Martin Van Buren as an effete snob who had lost touch with ordinary Americans. In what many regard as the least logical campaign in U.S. history, Harrison was elected.

At the height of the campaign, pro-Harrison delegations literally rolled into the state capital. Each county group traveled with a log cabin built on wheels, with "stick and dirt chimneys on which was stretched a coonskin." The wagons paraded from the Governor's Palace to the State House.

A highlight of the parade occurred when a promotional wagon for the *Raleigh Register* overturned. "A wheel ran off and down came Stephen, press, types and all in a heap," a competitor reported. Democrats cheered the incident as an anti-Whig omen.

(It is interesting that the production facilities of Raleigh's chief newspaper were small enough to fit into a wagon.)

The Harrison wagons stayed in the city for weeks. Some of them began to sport red petticoats which were intended to be a slur on the war record of the Democrats. Fistfights occurred on a daily basis. Open cider barrels awaited all potential voters.

Not content with their cabin village, the Whigs built a wigwam in the mud on Fayetteville Street, and "in the center... suspended from the joists was what the Whigs claimed to be a Democratic scalp." (Historian R.H. Whitaker later identified the object as "a handful of hair which Mr. William G. Hill pulled from the head of a Democratic candidate for the Legislature, in a little affair.")

The wigwam, manned day and night and kept stocked with cider of its own, served as Harrison's headquarters.

Decades later, the Rev. Whitaker recalled, businesses in Raleigh still displayed a coonskin or petticoat from the campaign, along with the "scalp."

Raleigh

(The city has collected some interesting trophies in addition to stolen art. W.W. Holden's newspaper office, for instance, prized a cutting from the rope which was used to hang John Brown. Who knows what treasures might be donated to a downtown museum?)

For every retired CP&L vice president who had an opinion at his lunch club, Raleigh had another person with different ideas.

Back in 1841, the Raleigh Mechanics' Association celebrated the Fourth of July with an unusual toast:

"Repentance and Reformation," the toast began, "to those profligate scamps and pumpkin-headed fops, who affect to despise mechanics because they are such."

(That toast could have been written by the ancestor of the person who brought us the "nattering nabobs of negativism.") Next to it, *The Rasp* carried a plain news item:

"Wonder who attended the Chicken Peck the present week? There were lots of $5 bets."

When Henry Clay came to Raleigh in 1844, he did more than review the city's militia.

"Clear the Way for Harry Clay," was the message on a banner which the *Raleigh Register* said the "Ladies of Raleigh" made and suspended across Fayetteville Street for Clay's appearance. They clearly had excelled in banner-making.

"On the right of the picture," the newspaper reported, "a female figure, robed in the National Flag, is endeavoring, altho' weak and exhausted, to raise herself from the ground...." She was surrounded by menacing clouds which were labeled "envy" and "discord" and the like. In the center of the banner stood Clay, helping the woman up with one arm while pointing with the other to a beautiful, sunlit land toward the left end of the drapery.

But as fine as that banner must have been to orate under, it was the barbecue fundraiser the night before Clay's speech which should get the attention of present-day politicians.

According to the *Register,* more than 8,000 persons attended the pig-picking on Capitol Square – a crowd enough to excite most candidates 150 years later. The campaign took in today's equivalent of $80 per plate.

In 1853, the *Southern Advertiser* reported on the first annual fair of the State Agricultural Society.

Admission was twenty-five cents per person, fifty cents for buggies, and one dollar for carriages. The Fair offered a music band each day.

Primarily an agricultural and homemaking exposition, the Fair paid premiums for the same kinds of products as today. The Society was also interested in any soil experiments which could improve the State's farming; one involved the output of privies.

But several decades later, the *Progressive Farmer* concluded that although the privy experiment had been discontinued, excrement still existed at the Fair's new midway.

"Nothing is too much of a humbug," the paper groaned about the entertainments, "and nothing too vulgar or indecent to obtain admission, provided it pays a percentage of its worse-than-blood money into the hands of the (Fair) managers."

The journal said that the midway had "the usual array of fakirs, gamblers and immoral shows" which had the aims of "robbing the people and corrupting public morals." It recommended that the State should deny financial aid to future Fairs until its managers at least admitted that vice was an annual occurrence.

No one should conclude that the early State fairs were dull, despite the fact that "midways had not then introduced the fakirs, the thimble riggers, the 'Orientals,' and the 'hoochee coochees,'" and "nobody was alarmed about pickpockets."

Raleigh in the 1850s was graced by the "Don Quixote Invincibles," a group of men known informally as the DQIs, who appeared one October.

"They were all dressed as knights," recalled one participant, "wearing masks, helmets and shields, and carrying spears, and were mounted on the poorest horses, mules and no-horned oxen that could be found."

More than 100 of the DQIs, "who beggared description," paraded up Fayetteville Street, and at their epicenter was "a wagon drawn by a mule and a steer, in which sat Colonel Buck Tucker, who, dressed as a woman, with a bonnet on his head big enough for a buggy top," portrayed the fair Dulcinea.

Once they reached the Fair Grounds, the DQIs held jousts to see who would win from "Dulcinea" an ultimate trophy: "The victor's wreath, made of collard and mullen leaves." Yes, the participant mused, "we had good times at the fairs of long ago."

Raleigh

Forget, hell.... In 1866, a legislator wrote home from Raleigh that "our little dancing girls have mortified some of their friends by insulting a Federal Major and his Lady at Mr. Yarborough's house by refusing their hands in a dance and otherwise insulting them."

Emotional recovery from the Civil War appears to have taken time in Raleigh – some in fact never got over it – if a report in the *Daily News* in 1872 is any measure.

Describing the city's activities on the Fourth of July that year, the newspaper wrote that "the ringing of the bell over the Market House at 4 o'clock, A.M., the firing of about $100 worth of fire crackers, a desultory artillery firing at Camp Russell, and a street full of lounging negroes was the only spirit of '76 to be seen in the Metropolitan city of North Carolina....

"The glory of this great national day has serenely departed, and we say – let her slide."

The joys of restaurant management....
In 1872, the Raleigh newspaper *We Know* criticized the practice of "bar-room tenders who step in, at stated times, to indulge their appetites."

(The newspaper particularly resented the fact that their free food and drink was added to the costs of paying customers.)

We Know called for "some means by which these pests may be kept in the background, or dispensed with entirely. Gentlemen who go to a restaurant for oysters and wine at eleven prefer privacy, and the control of their own purse strings."

The tribal rite of "hanging out" began to disturb Raleigh merchants and pedestrians long before someone discovered that playing booming Barry Manilow music would cause loiterers to disperse.

The *Daily News* in 1872 described a scene of utter congestion at the city Market House.

"At all times, nights especially, the entire pavement is occupied and blocked by loungers and loafers," the newspaper reported.

"In order to pass, it becomes necessary to pull and press your way through... at night it is almost impossible for a gentleman and lady to pass."

The newspaper asked the Board of Aldermen and police to remove the crowds – which were of all ages, sexes and races – from the Market as a public nuisance.

Raleigh

Between the State Fair, Robinson's circus and exploding newspaper buildings, October 1872 in Raleigh had enough entertainment for anybody.

The *Daily News,* which admitted that "we derive our information from madame rumor," ballyhooed the festivities by describing everything from a 99-foot snake to a man who promised to throw a 40-pound cannonball over the State Capitol.

Two events which actually happened both involved animals.

"Bryan with his bears arrived today," the newspaper announced, "and has already matched one to fight Smith's dog for one thousand dollars." Tickets were on sale at downtown hotels. As for the outcome, the SPCA would not like it.

About the same day, "a game cock man" from Chatham County arrived in the city with his roosters, and he "put them on the Yarboro House baggage wagon without marks or instructions.

"They duly arrived" at the hotel, the *News* went on, "and went the way of all flesh. By the time Mr. S. made his appearance they were all killed and half picked."

The newspaper said that Mr. S., armed with a stick and a brick bat, advanced on the employees of the hotel's kitchen and that the resulting cursing and melee "disrupted the usual genteel calm" of the establishment.

(There was no report on what Mr. S. ate for supper.)

The newspaper *We Know* lamented the new fashion of wigs on Raleigh women in 1872.

It called for a return to the days of "natural hair, and a universal letting alone of flax imitations, and the exhumed ringlets of some poor wretch whose bones are bleaching beneath the sod."

The Don Quixote Invincibles, with their Knight of the Jolly Nose and Knight of the Rusty Nail, were not the only impromptu legions who paraded through Raleigh in the 1800s during State Fair week.

In 1858, the Royal Raleigh Ringtail Rousers, described as "a crowd of grotesque beings... unworthy of mention," shimmied up Fayetteville Street "dressed in rags with pumpkin heads."

In 1875 – in a satire of Civil War remembrance which hit so close to home that they never made another appearance in the city – came the "Mulligan Guards and the Grand Panjandrums of the Noble Order of Flapdoodles."

Raleigh

Led by the Oak City Band, the local troupe poked fun at every form of warfare until the procession was halted by a fistfight.

"The serenading mania has this season developed into alarming proportions," the *Observer* reported in 1879.

"The most discordant sounds seem to be thought melodious by sentimental vocalists. Many complaints are made by people all over town."

June serenaders had to watch their step as they navigated from the city's grog shops into its streets. For the *Observer* also noted that "the cow mania is in no wise abated, and these animals still have the freedom of the city." The newspaper said that the cows' "depredations are very trying to the part of people who own front yards."

The more things change.... After an exposition at the State Fairgrounds in 1880, Raleigh's *Journal of Industry* felt compelled to print this notice:

"The managers of the *Journal* desire to say that they were in no way, shape nor form, responsible for the games on the Fair Ground by which many people were swindled out of their money."

The *Journal* was a short-lived publication allied with the Chamber of Commerce. It began in 1879 with the motto, "God Will Help Those Who Help Themselves." Then, after consulting with some of Raleigh's clergy, the newspaper amended its banner in 1880 to read, "God Will Help Those Who Try to Help Themselves." (The *Journal* failed for lack of help from a more secular source: its advertisers.)

"The latest sport," the *Observer* reported about downtown in 1879, "is rat-catching, the rats then being turned loose for the edification of dogs and bystanders."

When a wooden house on the northwest corner of Capitol Square burned in 1880, newspapers reported that "the capitol bell was melted in its belfry. Many persons carried off pieces of it as souvenirs."

Tell me some more about that initiation... Raleigh in 1880 was home of a club named the Eunuch Lodge No. 38.

Raleigh

"As a club, we occupy a rather unusual and trying position – a large club in a small town in which everyone's affairs are everybody else's business."

With those words, Dr. Richard Lewis began a debate over whether the Capital Club should clean up its activities on the eve of local Prohibition in 1886.

Lewis noted in his president's report that drinking and high-stakes card games went on nonstop in the club. He put much of the blame on Raleigh's "floating population out of all proportion to its size." He urged the club to restrict the number of legislative lobbyists who operated there each week.

"We could not stand a flood-tide of public opinion against us," Lewis concluded. The members agreed and at least temporarily, the card games and lobbyists moved to another location.

How is that again?... The charter for the YMCA in Raleigh, granted by the General Assembly in 1887, declared that the organization's purposes were to improve "the spiritual, mental, social and physical (sic) condition of young men... provided, that the same not be repugnant to the Constitution and laws of this State or of the United States."

One fine spring day in 1887, the merchants of Wilmington Street challenged their counterparts on Fayetteville Street to a game of "base-ball."

"There were some astonishing results," the *N&O* reported, "among which was that nobody got killed and the umpire got home in good condition."

After listening to the gamesmanship which preceded the charity contest, the *N&O* had entertained doubts.

One of the players "was asked if he could catch a foul on the fly," the *N&O* offered. "He said it depended on how old the chicken was and how far it could fly. Another was asked if he knew how to hold a bat. He said, 'No, I don't, and I don't want to know. The last time I got hold of one the blamed thing made its teeth meet in the end of my forefinger.'

"Such as these are the well-posted champions who will play the game," the *N&O* said. "There is fun ahead and plenty of it."

Fayetteville Street was ahead by 26 to 10 when the game was called after six innings. Sportsmanship had been paramount.

One of the players, "Jonathan Cross, discovered a black eye 4" in diameter... and offered to wipe up the earth with the man that made it with his right hand tied behind him," the newspaper recounted. Others could have gone directly to St. John's hospital, which received $23.15 from the gate.

Pullen Park may have been criticized in the first city plan, but much more needs to be said about its history. Some random facts:
• R. Stanhope Pullen, when he donated the property next to what is now N.C. State University, provided that a section of the park be deeded over to any cotton factory worth more than $50,000 which would locate there within five years. None appeared.
• The reason the park has a lake and pool, at least in their present locations, is because the Catholic orphanage donated 13 acres so that the park could run along Rocky Branch creek.
• The first swimming pool, built in 1890, was wooden and was filled with water taken directly from Rocky Branch. Until the city fathers set aside a special day each week for women, the pool was open to men only. They swam nude.
• Starting with two raccoons which the superintendent bought from a farmer at the city market, Pullen Park developed a semblance of a zoo. A circus presented the park with a pair of grizzled lions, the Town of Dunn made a gift of a bison, and the park acquired the entire contents of a bankrupt zoo near Norfolk.

In its heyday, the Pullen Park zoo contained an alligator pond (Raleigh's suburban alligator of 1991 had its antecedents), bears, coyotes, foxes, golden eagles, waterfowl, monkeys and groundhogs.

N.C. State students used to kidnap the bears and put them in the school's chapel on Saturday nights so that services the next morning would be canceled.
• When the merry-go-round was purchased from Bloomsbury Park near Lassiter's Mill, John Bray was the commissioner of public works and "was roundly cussed for thus spending the city's money."

But, an observer wrote a few years later, "no one would dare remove it now." (Eventually, as the park fell into disrepair, the carousel was shut down for several years. It has been restored.)
• The park in the early 20th century had a dance hall and was the scene of musicales, magic shows and outdoor entertainments. Pullen Park was one of the mandatory stops on the national vaudeville circuit.
• Superintendent Wiley A. Howell, who managed the park and pool for 47 years, took it as his mission to limit the obvious romantic potential of the landscape. He failed and was fondly remembered. ("Mr. Howell, give me a towel," adults would call to him on downtown streets.)

- Those crafty N.C. State students surveyed the grade of the railroad tracks running through the park and determined that if they greased them, a train slowly climbing out of downtown Raleigh could not get enough traction to make it through the campus.
- For years, Pullen Park was the site of celebrations on the Fourth of July, including mock Revolutionary War battles. The practice ended when "a sham battle was fought and somehow in the fight a loaded cartridge was fired and a soldier was killed."
- At one stage, the city planted the park with 12 acres of oats, two acres of clover, and an acre of rice along the creek. (William Boylan's slaves had pioneered rice cultivation along Rocky Branch.)
- Had it not been for reversion clauses in Pullen's will, the city would have cut thoroughfares across the park in two directions decades ago.

It took the *Charlotte Observer*, of all newspapers, to provide the clearest account of one of Raleigh's public executions in the 1890s.

"Many people waited patiently in front of the jail for hours," the correspondent wrote, "merely to see (the condemned man) take a few steps in the open between the jail door and the gate of the gallows enclosure. Such is human curiosity in its most morbid phase."

(The correspondent took no exception to the half-price beers which were offered on the day of the execution. The throngs on Fayetteville Street should have been happy that this particular hanging was closed to all who didn't have a ticket; the noose on the prisoner slipped and instead of having his neck snapped, he strangled for 13 minutes before being pronounced dead.)

On August 5, 1892, the singing dog "Dan" of the Yarborough House hotel was struck and killed by a streetcar.

The dog had been to Raleigh what ducks are to the Peabody hotels, only Dan had not been franchised.

"He was a musical prodigy and was the only singing dog ever known," Dan's obituary read. (If he was the only one, how could the newspaper tell that he was a prodigy? It can be concluded that given the noise and speed of Raleigh's streetcars, the dog must have been more than tone deaf.)

Raleigh recovered sufficiently from the Civil War to celebrate the Fourth of July in 1892 despite a downpour.

Among the entertainments which an estimated 3,000 citizens enjoyed were a "greasy-pole contest" in front of the Post Office – the prize at the top was a solid silver watch – and a barbecue at Brookside Park "to which all orderly white people are invited."

Conflict between the bicycle and other vehicles hardly originated with Raleigh's increasing traffic congestion.

In 1895, the *N&O* reported that "many complaints have arisen among the bicyclists of this city." The riders had discovered that "the drivers of vehicles are not disposed to recognize the rights of wheelmen."

Indeed, other than three streets downtown, no traffic rights-of-way existed in the city. Buggy drivers had little inclination to yield to faster-moving bicycles, which they regarded as nuisances that alarmed their animals and tailgated in packs.

One of the original purposes of the Capital City Cycle Club, formed in 1894, had been to champion street improvements. Club members would pick out a scenic route, set off through the ruts or the mud, and later regale non-riders about how enjoyable the trip would have been for all citizens if only the city would pave more streets.

Given road conditions and the frail materials used in early bicycles, it is little wonder that club members never seemed to complete a run together.

A member had to be 18 years old to qualify as a "wheelman," had to stay in line behind the club's captain or else be fined 50 cents for passing, and was subject to expulsion for "any improper or obnoxious conduct."

After one Raleigh man was hanged in 1903, frustrated citizens who had been unable to secure a ticket to the execution set up a chant on Fayetteville Street. In a few minutes, "the remains were placed in the coffin and brought out for those who were outside to see."

He don't look like a daredevil because he's short and fat, but he acts like one, and no mistake."

The *N&O* was describing one James J. Grant, who leapt off a 91-foot ladder into a tub of water during the great street carnival of 1903. From the descriptions, turning Raleigh's streets into a circus for six days pleased both merchants and thousands of spectators alike.

As for the daredevil, "he finally completed his change of costume in a little tent nearby and came prancing out as nimbly as his 200 plus of

Raleigh

avoirdupois would permit. Then he ran up the tall ladder, yes, ran, and stood at the little platform at the top blowing and puffing just like any other fat man who has run upstairs."

Grant then steeled himself for the jump from behind the Post Office. As the *N&O* reported it, "'Look, he's saying his prayers,' said a little girl. Maybe he was. Some people would in his position." The daredevil landed without incident in five feet of water.

The carnival also featured a high-wire artist who traversed Fayetteville Street (part of his act was to carry out a mattress, pillow and blanket onto the wire and profess to sleep the night in mid-air), an assortment of midway attractions ("If you are not on the lookout you will be called on to pay a dollar to have a fake fortune told by some fakerette. Find out what it costs before you get in too deep."), and exotic animals ("The big snake got his trimonthly meal. He was served yesterday with a number of live chickens, which be proceeded to squeeze into a pulp and draw into his internals.").

Other than the matter of an escaped mountain lion, only the Oriental Show – a hootchy-kootchy tent in the middle of Fayetteville street – ruffled the town fathers. "It ought to have been closed up two days before it opened," fumed one. The *N&O*, the Mayor and the Chief of Police formed an ad hoc decency squad and tamed the offending performers.

The mountain lion – a cub, actually, but not according to the rumors which fanned through the city – was also tamed once it was captured.

Raleigh in 1904 had what is believed to have been the nation's first organized Squirrel Feeders Club.

According to Billy Arthur, members of the club had "to report for duty on benches facing Fayetteville Street at 10 a.m., always have some of their fathers' money... and raise their hats to every lady that passes."

The curious in 1903 could, for the low-low price of ten cents, peer through tubes in the dirt and see a man buried alive on Fayetteville Street.

Staged as a fundraiser for the city's firefighters, the burial was accomplished after one Professor Corby hypnotized the adolescent R.W. Williams of Wilson and planted him in a vat of dirt at the express office. The lad's feet and face were visible through pay-for-view eyepieces.

After three days, Professor Corby carted Williams to the Academy of Music, where he summoned him from his trance. Admission for that was twenty-five cents.

Raleigh

As the end approached for Metropolitan Hall, its critics found their voices and remembered the building in less than sentimental terms.

"Barn-like," wrote the *N&O*, which opposed a suggestion in 1907 by the Board of Aldermen that the old hall be expanded by adding two overhanging stories onto it. (One-third of the audience would have had to use ladders to reach their seats.)

"Metropolitan Hall is wholly unsuited for speaking," the *N&O* said, "because it is so situated that no speaker can he heard for the noises and rumbling that is incident to the location." (This is not exactly the description of downtown which the Chamber of Commerce had in print at the time.)

Opponents of the aldermen argued that the heightened building, at 56 by 204 feet, would be no improvement over the old hall, which was 16 feet narrower. "The noisiest place in town," complained one. "Too narrow," another commented. They prevailed, and for once, the case for better design won.

Championship Wrestling, which oozed onto Raleigh television screens courtesy of that arbiter of taste, WRAL-TV, had nothing on the Great Aviation Meet held here in 1910.

(Not to suggest that WRAL created wrestling; Raleigh residents could watch 641-pound wrestlers grope with each other at Memorial Auditorium long before television, or even see Jack Dempsey fight an exhibition.)

The lure of the Great Aviation Meet was the question of whether a motorcar could outrun a Curtiss biplane, then the state-of-the-art barnstorming aircraft. The course was one which Ralph Nader would have loved: the half-mile racetrack at the State Fairgrounds which now encircles the Raleigh Little Theater. In theory, the roadster would hug the track for ten laps while the biplane, 100 feet up, would veer wide at the turns to avoid what can only be described as barrage balloons.

When the Great Race began, it pitted the 70-mph biplane against a 20-horsepower Hudson convertible. Thousands paid admission (50 cents for adults; children under ten admitted free) to stand unprotected and wait for crashing metal to come from the oval or the sky.

(In the spirit of fairness in media, the meet was sponsored by another arbiter of taste, the *N&O*, which flogged it for days on half of its front page.)

Unfortunately, the Curtiss had trouble getting into the air. On its first sally, one of its bicycle wheels fell off. On the next try, the plane's engine failed, and if the race had been to see who could drive into a culvert, the biplane would have triumphed.

The biplane was airborne on its third try when its engine quit again and it glided serenely into one of N.C. State's demonstration cotton fields. Mercifully for everyone but the spectators, officials decided that it was too late for another attempt. (The spectators received "wind checks," but one had to persevere and read the fine print inside the *N&O* to learn that there was no race the next day.)

At a minimum, citizens did get to see the biplanes in their practice sessions, soaring to an estimated 1,000 feet above Raleigh before landing. Their pilots dutifully pronounced that "it was cold up there." And hundreds paid to watch the roadsters qualify.

Two days after sponsoring the meet, the *N&O* – without a trace of irony – printed an editorial which condemned the "speed lust" of local drivers and demanded that they be put in prison.

The *N&O* could have been more chary about whether the Great Aviation Meet would be consummated.

In 1888, the drawing card at the State Fair had been a giant hot-air balloon. Piloted by "Professor Myers, Miss Carlotta and Leon Dare," the balloon was scheduled to ascend to 1,000 feet, whereupon brave Leon would parachute to the ground. Thousands of onlookers, many of whom paid for special train excursions, came to Raleigh to witness the feat.

On Day One, Professor Myers told the Fair manager that he could not attempt an ascension because of high winds. The manager, eyeing the crowds which were becoming impatient, pushed the professor to try. He did and the balloon rolled over, struck the ground, and sustained a five-foot tear.

The professor vowed to try again and many spectators arranged overnight accommodations in the capital.

Although the weather forecast was poor (the 1888 equivalent of a meteorologist simply figured out which way the wind was blowing, in this case telegraphed Atlanta, and learned what was happening there), the Fair manager believed that he had leverage. The Fair had included a provision in the professor's contract stating that the parachute leap had to be completed "before he received his compensation."

But the weather on Day Two did not matter. Professor Myers, Miss Carlotta, Leon Dare and their torn balloon had caught the midnight train out of Raleigh. They did not return. (Nor were they seen again, unlike the "wild man of the Brazils," who was spotted as a waiter in a Baltimore restaurant.)

The next year, with another balloon company, the parachute jump succeeded. Balloons became a fixture at the Fair until they were preempted by the Wright Brothers.

"There were no pickings," a report about a local train wreck read in 1907, but "the wreck as a spectacle was worth the trip."

Gaping at train wrecks was a Raleigh pastime along with executions. And although the city's scavenger corps carried little away from the 1907 freight car derailment (lugging coal and wood up a 30-foot embankment and a mile back into town was not an inviting prospect on a summer afternoon), they had fared better in 1903, when a passenger train went off the same Walnut Creek bridge.

"In an almost incredibly short time," the N&O reported back then, "and by all ways and in every sort of vehicle or on foot, the people poured in great streams to the wreck."

Even as rescuers were bandaging the injured, other citizens were rifling through scattered luggage and personal effects.

Today's entertainment police could take a lesson from Raleigh Mayor J.S. Wynne, who in 1910 decided to stop the play, "The Girl from Rectors," from being performed at the Raleigh Academy of Music.

Wynne thought that the traveling performance was indecent and said that it had been banned in Grand Rapids, Michigan. The day before the show, he threatened to arrest the Academy's manager, J.S. Upchurch, who also happened to be a city alderman.

Upchurch's public response – "There are not enough police in Raleigh to arrest me in my own theater" – was, as he recalled it, the "finest publicity imaginable" and "sold out the house." More than veteran theater-goers decided to visit the Academy on opening night to see what would happen.

"The night of the show," Upchurch related, "the Mayor took the entire police force of the city and lined them up in front of the academy." (In 1910, that would have been thirteen officers.) More than 2,000 people jammed the streets, cheering Upchurch, jeering the police, and setting off false fire alarms to add to the confusion. The Academy doors remained locked.

In the ensuing chaos, the police thought twice about arresting Alderman Upchurch, but they did carry off the Academy's stage manager, electrician and janitor in the city patrol wagon. With that, Upchurch said, "the acting company got scared and refused to perform."

"Indecent Show Shut Out By the Mayor of Raleigh," trumpeted a banner headline in the N&O the next morning. "The bold stand of Mayor Wynne," the newspaper wrote, "will find ample commendation with the best thinking people of Raleigh, the state and the entire country."

(Not *all* of the best thinking people; the State Supreme Court upheld $25,000 in damages against the city for false arrest and loss of profits.)

And what indecency did Mayor Wynne protect the playgoers from seeing? "The Girl from Rectors" contained this exchange, from a male customer in a cabaret to a female coming onstage: "Where be your room?" he asked. "Down the aisle to the altar," she replied.

That had been enough for the mayor, who periodically deputized censorship committees to view rehearsals of plays such as Hammerstein's "Kissing Time" and decide whether they were suitable for Raleigh audiences.

Well, times do change. "Now when a musical comes through," Upchurch observed several decades later, "they want to find out what the show is carrying, and it is usually three carloads of scenery and about fifteen cents worth of lingerie."

Every reader knows the caliber of artists who play at the Friends of the College series or who thunder from the loudspeakers at the new Walnut Creek amphitheater.

Many can recall when Elvis Presley, Hank Williams, James Brown or Otis Redding used to get things moving at Memorial Auditorium and the Cow Palace. A few may even recall when Bette Midler played at the Frog and Nightgown.

But putting musicians aside, who else played in Raleigh in the old days? Try John and Ethel Barrymore. Will Rogers. W.C. Fields. John Drew. Al Fields. Irene Castle. Charlie Chaplin. And the inimitable Sally Rand. (If only Mayor Wynne had been here to see her.)

A great sports trivia question: What are the most points ever scored in one game against an N.C. State athletic team?

(The apparent answer might seem to be 124, scored against the Wolfpack basketball team by Maryland in 1979. But that would be wrong.)

The answer is 128 points, scored against the State *football* team by Georgia Tech in 1918.

That year, the State football team was hampered both by the influenza epidemic and by inductions into the armed services. A further complication was the Georgia Tech coach, who was named John Heisman, as in the Trophy.

Heisman wanted to run up a score that would impress the East Coast sports writers. But ever the gentleman, he agreed to halt the game after three quarters in Atlanta with his team leading by 128 to 0.

Euphoria at defeating the Kaiser reached such a level in 1919 that even the old Market House was paid a compliment – albeit a backhanded one.

"For once," the *N&O* reported, "the shabby old structure was not an eyesore." The newspaper then explained that the building was almost entirely obscured by a temporary reviewing stand, bunting and banners for a parade to welcome the troops back from World War I.

In a celebration not unlike the one held in 1991 for troops returning from Operation Desert Storm, Raleigh's doughboys were treated to bands, speeches, photo opportunities, honors, a barbecue, fireworks at the Fairgrounds, and – here the parallel stops – a baseball doubleheader.

Raleigh's Red Cross made use of the occasion to announce its final war drive, this time for clothing to send to the liberated nations in Europe.

Observers said it was the largest crowd at a celebration since 20,000 had come for the unveiling of the Confederate monument on Capitol Square.

Courtroom drama in Raleigh passed for high theater on Spectator's Day, when the courthouse would be clogged whenever something interesting appeared on the docket.

Even so lowly a matter as an eviction could command a crowd's attention, as witnessed by a case in 1920 which resulted from C.M. Jones' efforts to eject Hannie Thomas from her apartment.

As reported in the *N&O*, "this action on the part of Jones seemed scandalous to Hannie, and she proceeded to play the role of Carrie Nation with right good will.

"She availed herself of an axe, and tore a hole anywhere from one to two feet high in the weatherboarding of the store occupied by Mr. Jones, and thereby destroyed much of his merchandise."

While the courtroom went into hysterics, "Mr. Jones declared that she cursed him as much as she could in English and he couldn't tell just how much in Syrian, but he had his inferences from her manner of delivery," the *N&O* added.

The damages cost Ms. Thomas $15 and she had to seek a new place to live. As for the courtroom audience, it sat waiting for the next case.

For reasons that were unclear even at the time, Raleigh staged a Mardi Gras celebration in 1922, not in connection with Lent, but on a Wednesday and Thursday in November.

("We didn't have the nerve to ask," commented the *N&O*.)

Raleigh

An estimated 20,000 people crowded Fayetteville Street, milling and dancing in costume between bands, floats and fireworks. The festivities included motorcycle races and an attempt at a radio concert. ("Unfortunately," wrote the *N&O,* "the chief soprano of the evening was Miss Static.")

Raleigh observed its time-honored tradition of cross-dressing at public functions. "Some well-shaven young gentlemen," reported the newspaper, "masqueraded as ladies and vamped old gentlemen with whiskers."

Although legislators had banned wire-balancing and rope-dancing apparatus from the State-House in 1811, the Mardi Gras spilled onto Capitol Square, where a man named Raymond Craig was straight-jacketed, hoisted up "to a dizzy height tied by his feet," and left to extricate himself before he blacked out and plunged to the steps. Craig succeeded, of course, and "unfurled a pocket edition of the Stars and Stripes to the autumn breeze."

The *N&O* reported that souvenir sales were brisk. "Every small kid that had a dime to spend sported a mustache and 'looked like papa,'" it said, and added that a few adolescents got into some beer and "bug juice" and "smelled like papa."

Writing about black-owned businesses in Raleigh around 1930, Frank Hicks discussed the social role of the city's barbershops.

"One outstanding feature of the barbershop is the checker board," he wrote. "Not a single shop in the city was found without such an outfit. Many an hour of labor is lost in playing the game, which runs without a break from morning until night."

On the last day of his tenure as Wake County chairman of the Republican Party, D.P. Franks wrote to Willis Briggs that "I will be in to get the cigar soon that you lost to me on Landon. Please have a 25-cent one on hand."

(Franks hoped that his resignation would be "one of the first steps in the disbandment of the Republican Party" after the 1936 elections. He wanted a new American Party whose mascot would be an eagle, not an elephant.)

Occasionally, a football fan proves to be more single-minded than all others, and without even wearing a loony hat to the game.

On December 20, 1941, Governor J. Melville Broughton of Raleigh commented on the abrupt decision to relocate the Rose Bowl game from California to Durham.

Raleigh

"It is indeed a stroke of good fortune," the Governor wrote, "that this game is coming to our state."

Maybe the sense of values of New York boys is all screwed up, I don't know."

When he made that diagnosis, Coach Everett Case had just seen several of his basketball players indicted for point-shaving. It was the beginning of proceedings which limited N.C. State's scholarships, eliminated summer basketball, and closed down the Dixie Classic basketball tournament, at the time the most economically important entertainment in Raleigh other than the State Fair.

Case himself had called in the State Bureau of Investigation.

"When I saw the finish of our game with Georgia Tech, I was suspicious," he said. The coach had also lectured his players repeatedly about the need to disassociate themselves from gamblers.

Three of the players failed to heed the warnings.

About one of them, who was charged with taking $1,250 for influencing the outcome of a game with Duke University, a teammate said that "he'd gamble on anything. You throw a feather in the air and he'd bet on whether it would hit the floor or not."

What kind of book about the City of Raleigh can omit sports? After all, more people have been known to plop down in Carter-Finley Stadium for an N.C. State football game than *lived* in the city when F.D.R. was President. Season tickets have been a greater issue than child custody in divorce settlements. If one counts the fans who are glued to their television sets and radios – and sometimes both at once – it becomes clear that sports in Raleigh is more popular than, well, Mayor Upchurch.

So for the benefit of the city's sports fans, in addition to the descriptions of cockfights, here is an account of the Greatest Golf Hole ever played in the area.

(Note: Raleigh somehow got along without golf courses until early in this century. This means that the early residents who dressed like golfers were in all likelihood homosexuals.)

The Greatest Hole was born out of boredom one afternoon in the 1960s at the Raleigh Golf Association. A few inveterate players had grown tired of teeing off on the same holes every day – that was as tedious as holding down a full-time job – and they also had lost their enthusiasm for several creative alternatives: playing eighteen holes backwards; 700-yard crossover;

Raleigh

rounds using Superballs instead of Titleists; and even the challenge of first-one-in-the-hole-who-caroms-the-ball-off-the-clubhouse.

And ever since a sportsman had lost the title to his car in the twilight while betting that he could two-putt every hole on the practice green, that game had no takers. Nor would anyone at R.G.A. gamble again on how many ounces of sleet could accumulate on a golfer's woolly hat on the back nine in February. (A hustler had tried it before, using a Stewart Sandwich oven to melt down the evidence.)

The R.G.A. players took their golf seriously. One morning, for instance, one of their number turned up dead – shot by an estranged husband who proved that a .38 Special is faster than a four-iron. When word of the shooting reached the R.G.A. clubhouse, a low handicapper immediately asked, "What club did he use?" and then shook his head and remarked that the deceased had never mastered his long game.

The survivors decided that they needed a new hole, but nothing within the confines of the golf course. They agreed to meet before daybreak and to play from the first tee at R.G.A. to the sixth green at the Par Golf pitch-and-putt course, which was then on U.S. 401 next to the Montlawn cemetery. In a straight line on a city map, the hole would play about 2,150 yards.

The rules were practical for a hole which no one had ever played. There was no par; a lost ball cost only one penalty stroke from the place where it disappeared; there were no penalties for balls which rolled into storm drains; a player was entitled to a free drop from any lie where, if he played his shot, he might get arrested; and it was every man for himself in choosing the route to Par Golf.

The stakes were considerably less than a car; they were more on the order of bail money.

Shortly before 5 a.m., four players and four spotters convened in the R.G.A. parking lot. After a final discussion of the rules, they concluded that they could not trust one another to keep honest scores. By a coin toss, they agreed to play by an identical route.

The Greatest Hole in the history of Raleigh began with a drive that had to clear hedges, parking lots and Tryon Road before it landed somewhere down the 13th fairway. It was one of the least perilous shots of the day.

Some players hit their second shots down thirteen with irons, others with woods. But except for one (who had skulled his tee shot into another player's car in the parking lot), they played their third shots due east, across the Southern Railway gulch and into the scrub pines, weeds and wine bottles which lay in the direction of the old Raleigh Municipal Airport.

Hacking and cursing, putting down one old ball after another, and startling rabbits, the players forged through the undergrowth.

("Once you have played through a forest – I mean *through* it – you'll never see a bad lie again," one of the golfers remarked recently.) Somewhere in the woods the four spotters deserted their jobs, grabbed clubs, and started their own match. After a while they glimpsed a clearing.

None of the players knows what the man in the airport control tower *thought* when he saw the eightsome emerge from the trees and begin to launch three-woods up the runway. But what he *said*, over the loudspeaker, is remembered as "Clear the runway. What the... Whoever the hell you people are, clear the runway. Get out!"

The runway offered huge rolls if a golf ball landed on its surface. (It is a vicious lie that the runway was softer than the fairways of R.G.A., which are acceptable today but were unwatered in the 1960s. One player did comment that in spots there was not much difference.)

It must have required discipline for a player to keep his eye on the ball while simultaneously looking for incoming aircraft or police. But the players persevered. Up the runway, they were confronted with two avenues of attack in getting to U.S. 401: through the airport parking lot, with its hostile loudspeaker, or across the roof of King's Department Store.

If a solid shot hit in the direction of King's got lucky, it could carry onto the roof, miss the ventilation units, and bound clear across the store's parking lot onto the shoulder of 401. If a ball wriggled back into one of the drains in the oft-flooded lot, that meant a free drop and a club-gouging swing from the asphalt.

In the worst scenario, even if a ball stayed up on the roof, the department store had a ladder behind it. One player reasoned that the roof amounted to a dandy elevated tee for his first shot up the highway. (That kind of resourcefulness later helped him win two city golf championships.)

Another quandary faced the players once they reached 401. Because they had spent so much time slashing through the woods, commuter traffic was starting to roll into downtown Raleigh.

Was it the responsible thing to do, under the circumstances, to play it safe up the shoulder of the highway? To steadily pitch shots up the median? Or did the nature of the competition require that the players go for distance by playing on the road itself? It was no time for debate.

"The quicker I get off this bleeping road the better," was one player's analysis as he smoked a driver up the northbound lanes. He figured that even if he struck a car, the damage would be minimal because the cars were traveling in the same direction as his shot. The trick was to avoid a duck-hook into the windshield of some soul who was motoring south. A power fade was the correct shot, and with no posing after each swing; a player had to be prepared to run for cover *before* an errant ball landed on something.

Up the highway, the players made their last decision: whether to play around or through Montlawn Memorial Park.

Playing in a cemetery had been a crime in Raleigh since 1819, but Montlawn was the shortest route to Number Six at Par Golf. (Of course, playing up U.S. 401 was probably also a crime, not to mention the airport, but the golfers were ready with the story that they were volunteers out collecting litter.)

None of Montlawn's staff was in sight. From a distance, the turf in the cemetery appeared to be lush, if a little unmowed. There also was the question of whether, if the golfers skirted the cemetery and played through Par Golf, they could identify their balls among the hundreds scattered on the driving range.

On the other hand, those monuments in the cemetery could interfere with a backswing. A penalty shot for an unplayable lie would have been crucial at that moment, because the match was close. There was also the question of respect for the dead.

Two players finally lined up their putts in the summer dew on Number Six, missed them, and tied at 74 strokes for the expedition.

Some of their shots had covered 400 yards and others – struck with equal ferocity – no more than four feet. But there was neither broken glass nor blood nor handcuffs.

(Hindsight says the golfers probably took the wrong route to Par Golf. Had they played due north up the Southern railroad tracks, and then generally followed Carolina Pines Avenue to the east, they could have cleared U.S. 401 with one shot. However, the Carolina Pines neighborhood had some spirited dogs at the time.)

Raleigh's luncheon clubs may be sedate institutions, but occasionally one gets a speaker such as the Five Points Coffee Club had in February, 1968.

The club's sessions had previously been taken up by discourses on wills, trusts and stock options when a retired vice-president of the Carolina Power & Light Company got his turn at the dais:

"Has the paternalistic Federal government," he began as the members ate their apple pie, "spawned an indolent, unshaven, unwashed, long haired generation which disdains everything that you and I hold dear?" He continued to question everything from rock music to speed limits.

(Who knows what he would have added if he had spoken after the riots at the Chicago Democratic convention? The club quietly changed its guidelines for luncheon topics.)

Fetch My Squirrel-gun, Ma! They're A'pavin' Our Poppy Patch!

Today's dissension over the Boylan Heights cut-through is no more acid than a road dispute in 1800.

When Seth Jones petitioned the county court for a new thoroughfare to the south, Willie Jones and other planters struck back with a petition of their own.

They alleged that "there are scarcely enough hands to keep (existing roads) in tolerable repair." They asserted that roads within four miles of each other were already too close.

Willie also charged that some of Seth's petitioners had been gulled into signing through "misrepresentation." (Both petitions contained numerous marks made by illiterates; Seth retorted that Willie was not above duping a few people himself.) Willie asked the court to reject Seth's proposal as "entirely unnecessary except for the private convenience of Seth Jones and a few others."

This early debate about Raleigh's infrastructure is haunting.

Seth, in a primitive vehicular traffic study, argued that his road would reduce the need to cross over the Neuse ("Nuse") River. He reported that the Neuse's bridges "are very often down and out of repair." Willie answered that maintaining the bridges was Seth's responsibility and that in any event, it was time to hold down public spending.

(The winner of the dispute is not known. But based on today's road maps, Willie Jones' vision of four-mile separations went the way of Neuse River navigation schemes. At least in 1800 no one demanded noise baffles.)

"We will not say that overgrown trade leads to personal misery," a Raleigh newspaper said in 1800, "or national corruption.

"But we will say, that the best support of individual felicity and national prosperity, is a responsible body of men, who derive their subsistence from the earth, and depend upon the manly labors of the plough for their independence of mind and health of the body."

(Two of the crops Raleigh's independent-minded founders engaged in ploughing were hemp and opium poppies.)

In early Raleigh, a person didn't need a lawyer so much as a naturalist when he executed a deed for property.

Metes and bounds were marked not only by stakes and roads, but by rocks, streams and trees. An early deed for 586 acres which today are in the corporate limits twisted and turned around the following species: small gum, plum, water oak, pine, white oak, spanish oak and red oak.

The survey ended by going "down a branch to a slow pond."

Any contemporary homebuilder can identify with Treasurer John Haywood's experience in building his house on New Bern Avenue.

"Not a room is yet finished," he wrote his wife Betsey in 1799, reporting that wet and cold weather had stymied his plasterers and painters.

"I have several carpenters employed," he wrote again, "and they are hurried by me without ceasing, yet the repairs appear to go on slowly." His correspondence concerning the house went on for months, while he lived in an apartment in the State-House, heated with its own fireplace.

"Our garden is ploughed up for the first time," he advised Betsey, "but is neither laid off nor freed from rubbish. Having no Gardener, I am under the necessity of attending to the laying off of the walks."

But as the house appeared to be nearing completion, Haywood's letters took on a more optimistic tone.

"Our hall is sufficiently large to dance in," he wrote after the staircase was finished, and he promised to hire Betsey a male dance instructor "to teach you as many new Dances in the course of the Summer as you please."

Haywood told his wife that he had added a window into the garden salon downstairs so that Betsey could gaze into the garden while she played her piano. (In defense of the carpenters, some of Haywood's decisions appear much like change orders.) He predicted that the house "will look I think pretty smart" when wallpaper arrived from Petersburg, Va.

Raleigh

Unfortunately, though, Haywood was far from through with his house when he imagined Betsey playing the piano.

Not until October, 1801 was he able to buy 90 window panes and ten pounds of putty from the Peace brothers' store and seal out the approaching winter. (The eight-by-ten panes, most of them still in the house, cost Haywood the present-day equivalent of $2.20 apiece.)

In November, Haywood returned to the store and bought provisions for the house, including flatware, plates, glasses and condiments. What Raleigh knows as Haywood Hall was occupied, two years after groundbreaking.

As for Haywood Hall's supposed New England influence, some of the Treasurer's considerations were simply practical.

He wrote Betsey that "the outside of the House is to be white, as being the most cool-colour," and the inside was designed to accommodate the political crowds which she said exhausted her.

In 1802, two lots facing Moore Square sold for "$100 and a breakfast table."

Kemp Battle, orating in 1876, said that the purchasers of Raleigh's original lots – men with names such as Ashe, Bloodworth, Davie, Hawkins, Dawson and Lane – were "politicians who bought on speculation and lost money on the resale."

Battle reported that by 1876, the descendants of Thomas Bennehan of Orange County were the only remaining family to own original lots continuously in the city. (They are still there in the Marshall D. Haywood House on East Edenton Street.)

The more things change... Junk mail became such a problem for John Haywood in 1803 that he paid for an advertisement in the *Register* announcing that he would no longer pick up letters which lacked prepaid postage.

If Raleigh gets a new museum of local history downtown, it ought not to suffer the fate of the city's first such enterprise.

Raleigh opened a history museum in 1818, which also functioned as a reading room and the place where parishioners of Christ Church worshiped before they built their first frame sanctuary across from the State-House.

(The reading room admitted strangers for no charge but cost Raleigh residents $4 per year or fifty cents each month.)

One of the motivations for building Christ Church was an advertisement which appeared one morning, offering for sale the Museum and all of its historic contents. Less than four years after it appeared, Raleigh's first museum was gone.

(Done correctly, a contemporary Raleigh museum need not fear of having its memorabilia sold. Imagine, for instance, a display case containing a photograph of the antebellum Heartt House side-by-side with a chunk of cracked asphalt from the parking lot which replaced it. Who would want to buy something like that?)

The naysayers who have hesitated for years to support rail transit for Raleigh and the Triangle might be interested in the experience of the investors in the Raleigh and Quarry Experimental Rail-Road.

Created in 1833 after the State-House burned, the corporation completed a rail line in less than a year from the city's eastern quarry to Union Square. But the project went forward "not without encountering many difficulties, occasioned by want of confidence in some as to the political utility of the Road."

(Among other fears, citizens had a "distrust of the intention of the Legislature," which was still considering moving the capital to Fayetteville.)

The legend in Raleigh – that "one horse pulled the Capitol a mile" – is apocryphal. According to the railroad's board of directors, the company used three horses which hauled stone from the quarry to the square. The animals and two train cars were "procured from the North."

Initial fares for the citizens who wanted to ride on the cars were 25 cents for all persons over the age of twelve and 12.5 cents for children. So many people wanted to ride on the train that the company was soon able to cancel its leases and buy its own stock.

"The managers were compelled to *hire* them before," the board reported, "sometimes at exorbitant prices."

By 1834, the board of directors had so much cash that it raised its quarterly dividend from 10 percent to 25 percent, a smart return for a single line which had cost less than $1,800 to build. (The costs included cut wood, iron rails, rock, slave labor, overseers and temporary housing for workers.)

More important than the monetary return for its investors, the railroad proved that Raleigh had civic initiative in its efforts to rebuild the Capitol and keep it in the city.

(There were certain parallels to today. When the idea of a railroad was first floated in 1832, one prominent citizen argued that "further information ought to be obtained on the subject before the company was organized." The matter was referred to a committee which took action only after it was frightened by the Legislature. More than 150 years ago, the city usually acted in response to crises.)

A sense of the smallness of Raleigh, even 40 years after its founding, is conveyed by a promotion for the Raleigh Academy in 1835.

Students should enroll, the prospectus said, because of the "beautiful retired situation of the Institution..." which offered "the agreeable quietness of the country."

Considering that the Academy sat where the Governor's Mansion is today, the rural tranquility seems remarkable. (Although as Raleigh continued to have fires – burning down the State-House and entire blocks – the business center was actually getting farther away from the school.)

As for activities in town – the Academy's circular called them "the refinements of the city" – the school had a raft of regulations to prohibit the students from enjoying them.

Benjamin F. Seaborn may have burned up the first forty years' worth of deeds in Raleigh, but there are surviving indications of what the city's founders paid for property. They paid too much.

The *Star* was mortified in 1831 when it was suggested that the smoldering State-House be rebuilt in Fayetteville.

"The Legislature," the *Star* wrote, "have at various times sold the remainder of their lands (in Raleigh) at enormous prices.

"The *citizens of Raleigh* purchased this property, and paid the earnings of a laborious life into the coffers of the public, while they knew (and any one with half sense knows), that this property would never have brought one hundredth part of the prices given for it, had not the faith of the People of North Carolina been pledged to preserve its value, by maintaining the seat of government at Raleigh."

The *Star*, after noting that the citizens of Raleigh had also made costly improvements to the property they had bought "at extravagant prices," said that moving the capital would "bring ruin upon a very large proportion of the population."

According to contemporary reports, it took up to 20 hours to take the early trains from Raleigh to Gaston.

On one occasion, a Raleigh clerk missed the train which was to carry him and his family on a vacation, hired a carriage, and beat the locomotive to Wake Forest.

The principal problem with the early railroad was the rails themselves: they were made of wood with iron strips running along the top. Even if the wood did not splinter or rot, the iron strips would come loose and puncture floors of passenger cars. These wayward rails, called "snakes" by the engineers, might split a car up the middle in addition to causing a derailment.

Besides the fact that eastern Raleigh was "flatter, dustier, and more swampy" and received the effluvium of the city's untreated wastewater, why did the capital grow to the north and west?

Professor Adam Clarke Davis of N.C. State University pointed out that "when textile mills were being built in Raleigh... the smoke from their operations drifted eastward on the prevailing winds." Those with means, and who were not excluded by the city's racial covenants, built upwind.

Didn't anything right ever happen here...?" *Gleason's Pictoral Drawing-Room Companion,* printed in Boston in 1852, said that "Raleigh is laid out with great regularity and is altogether one of the prettiest cities in the Union, and it is enjoying a flourishing trade."

Frederick Law Olmsted, who later designed New York City's Central Park on his way to becoming one of the nation's premier landscape architects, passed through Raleigh in the early 1850s.

Christ Church in particular struck him. "A church, near the Capitol, not yet completed, is very beautiful," he wrote. "Cruciform in plan, the walls of stone, and the interior woodwork of oiled native pine, and with, thus far, none of the irreligious falsities in stucco and paint that so generally disenchant all experiences of worship in our city meeting-houses," he added.

Olmsted admired the stands of evergreens which grew near the Capitol and suggested that they would make better ornamental trees than the oaks which the city kept planting. (Some of the few firs which remain are in the yard of Christ Church.)

But the architect was not entirely complimentary. He noted in his journal that "North Carolina has a proven reputation for the ignorance and torpidity of her people" and remarked that more than 25 percent of white adults were found to be illiterate in the 1850 census.

Olmsted also wrote that "the country, for miles around Raleigh, is nearly all pine forest, unfertile, and so little cultivated, that it is a mystery how a town of 2500 inhabitants can obtain sufficient supplies for it to exist."

Some 30 years later, Olmsted would take part in the design of western North Carolina's premier showplace, the Biltmore House. But what was he doing in Raleigh, at this early date? He stopped to "repair damages to my clothing and baggage on the Weldon stage."

Oh! That awful Reconstruction!... Historian Fred Olds recalled that "money was spent in every conceivable way in the years from 1865 to 1870" in Raleigh.

He said that Reconstruction years were "undoubtedly the flush times of Raleigh" which resulted in a "golden harvest" of new stores and dwellings. Despite losses from the Civil War, the city's population nearly doubled from that of 1860.

Come forward, mystery solvers.... In 1878, citizens of Raleigh obtained an injunction to prevent the State of North Carolina from selling off Moore Square. (The State, in default and all but bankrupt, was in struggles with its creditors and looking for every dollar it could find.)

By the time local residents gummed up the proceedings, the State had surveyed the square into lots and advertised them for auction. Yet despite references in newspapers that the controversy was pending before the State Supreme Court, no opinion seems to have been handed down.

The outcome is apparent – Moore Square sits today without so much as a townhome or swimming pool on it – but how did the citizens win?

Herbert H. Brimley, who became the director of the State Museum, arrived in town in 1880.

"Raleigh gives the impression of being completely raw," wrote a man given to accuracy, "the cows and hogs roaming the streets giving it something of a rural atmosphere. The city had only occasional board sidewalks.

"However," he ended, "there was a restless, pushing air about the place and its people."

Raleigh

Not only cows, but geese commingled with Raleigh residents in 1880.

"A liberal reward will be paid," an advertisement read in the Daily Dispatch, "for the goose that swallowed the gold watch key of Mr. Pritchard... we should term that a *golden goose*."

In the same year, the *N&O* noted that "complaints are daily made about the geese on the streets, not the sort that talk, but the sort that cackle."

As Raleigh approached its centennial without any surfaced streets, T.D. Hogg thought he had diagnosed a part of the problem: the city's streets were simply too wide to make for affordable paving.

"Fayetteville Street," he wrote in a campaign leaflet in 1881, "is wider than Broadway, with its 1,500,000 people at noon, and the Strand in London, with 4,000,000 people, is narrower than Broadway."

Hogg suggested that in the case of Raleigh's four principal streets radiating from the Capitol, medians be created with grass, shrubbery and trees in order to reduce their 99-foot breadth.

As for the 66-foot streets, he proposed to narrow their traffic area by planting the sides of their rights-of-way with trees. If traffic grew to the point that the remaining roadways were inadequate, Hogg said that the trees could be cut down and used for firewood for the needy.

With those actions, Hogg thought the area which needed paving would drop to a manageable amount. He had no takers. (At least not in his lifetime; recently, Halifax and Fayetteville streets were wiped out altogether.)

Of the 1,155 acres in Raleigh in 1881, about 180 acres were devoted to streets. Given his focus, Hogg would have been interested to see that ratio skyrocket after the introduction of the automobile, when the city also discovered the allure of parking lots.

Raleigh's image as a bustling city in search of new industry was not helped by reports from the nation's travel writers who attended the Northern Settlers' Convention in the 1880s.

After "inspection of the post office and of the commodious residence of the Governor now in process of erection and a visit to the cotton market... we have seen almost everything of interest in the place," one reporter advised at least 20 newspapers across the United States.

Nor was the Maryland writer overwhelmed by the city's cotton factory.

After he described the press, which could squeeze a bale of cotton

Raleigh

"into the dimensions of a Saratoga trunk," the writer had this to say about the production of 500 gallons per day of cotton seed oil:

"When it leaves Raleigh it is plain, unvarnished cotton seed oil, but when it gets into the hands of the manipulator, it soon changes into olive oil, and into other oils equally delusive."

One of his colleagues from Pennsylvania reported that the oil was sold in New York in containers with Italian or Spanish labels. Worse, he discovered that the kitchen at the Yarborough Hotel, only blocks from the cotton seed press, used the "imported" stuff.

The (cough, hack) slog of progress.... J.C.S. Lumsden in 1884 donated to each Wake County farmer who wanted it enough free seed to cultivate one acre of tobacco. Left to their own devices, most local farmers had been planting other crops.

The annals of boosterism.... In 1884, Josephus Daniels wrote in the *Chronicle* that "the drift of recent development shows that this city is destined to be one of the most important manufacturing centres in the South."

Charlie Johnson once recalled the Raleigh of 1890, when 12,500 people fit into the boundaries of Boylan, Johnson, Swain and South Boundary streets.

"There was ample place to grow vegetables, graze cows, and stable horses," he said. "So there were plenty of flies.

"My grandmother had a mechanical fly-fan in the middle of the table which I was allowed to wind up before our three-o-clock dinner."

Johnson and his compatriots used to play "cord ball" in the city's streets using sticks and twine wrapped around a rock.

Just dial 1-800-NUCLEAR... Raleigh's first electric utility was such a mom-and-pop operation that it is near to unfathomable that within 90 years, its successor was moving dirt for the Shearon Harris plant, which cost more money than the utility had managed to raise since its storefront beginning.

The city's first electric company used to wait until it received a request for a new residential connection before buying a mail-order meter from New

York. Its largest order in the first two years was for three meters at $12 apiece.

The utility bought items in small and odd lots from Briggs Hardware (nails, pliers and the like); from pharmacies (acid, for acid tests); and from Barkley's Restaurant (oyster shells for paving around its power plant).

The utility bought 4,000 shingles for $12. (Unfortunately, they were made of wood, and when the power plant caught fire a few years later, those shingles demonstrated what accelerated depreciation is all about.)

It bought coal from Egypt Depot, N.C. and water from the Raleigh Water Company for $12.93 for 64,628 gallons. (It seems like one could run a power company then for average expenditures of $12, much like one can repair anything on a house today for $950.)

The company bought an Otto gas engine. It paid stable bills for its horses. And even in the 1880s, the utility went through adversity as the new monopoly on the block: for every ton of Tennessee coal which it bought for an average of $1.30 per ton, the freight charges to Raleigh were $3.

(Generations later, CP&L Chairman Sherwood Smith may have gotten the last laugh. Confronted with rail cars full of frozen coal during a power emergency one winter, CP&L freed the coal the old-fashioned way: with dynamite. It should have bought the explosives from Briggs Hardware.)

Raleigh's first electric lights in the 1880s "burned great sticks of carbon which sizzled and hummed continuously and attracted great swarms of insects of all kinds." (Well, not really continuously; the city sued the electric company repeatedly for poor service.)

When the first incandescent lights were introduced, the "feeble yellow light" which was emitted from their fragile filaments would last only a few hours until the wires burned through. If anyone in Raleigh appreciated them, it was "Jack the Grabber," a pervert who lurked in the dark on Edenton Street and was never apprehended for his lunges at women.

Led by "a dissipated 'Colonel' from Texas, with a white beard that was habitually discolored and a diction that was a harmonica of profanity," a parade crept up Fayetteville Street on Christmas Day, 1886.

No matter that the parade leader, after his horse slipped and they both rolled over through the mud, abandoned his post and went off in search of another drink. No matter that the steeds in the parade looked suspiciously like mules. Raleigh at last had a streetcar.

A little girl rang the bell on the first car, hundreds of citizens took free rides, and Raleigh's first public transportation system was declared a success.

Three years after its soggy beginning, the enterprise had five miles of tracks, eight cars, 25 horses and 15 surviving mules. When it advanced further and began to use electricity for its traction power, the Raleigh Electric Company became a precursor of the Carolina Power & Light Company.

Traction power for the streetcars was the company's primary business, and initially, electric power sales were simply a way to use surplus capacity from the utility's engines when the streetcars were not in full operation.

The streetcar system almost defined a seasonal industry.

"With respect to traction operations," one observer wrote, "the Raleigh Electric Company was in the odd position of having to operate fifty-two weeks of the year with net profits largely determined by the business of one week... State Fair Week."

Indeed, weather and the corresponding attendance at the Fair was critical "in determining the financial profit or loss for the company" in each early year.

Those years were difficult. In 1894, the company had to sell out to local investors for $4,000, although the value of its assets had been estimated at $50,000 shortly before. The company lost money on a cash basis in four of its first ten years and was in a deficit position for nine of its first eleven.

Yet the streetcar carried what seems like a horde of passengers, particularly since Raleigh fared poorly when compared to streetcar ridership in other cities. (The most common explanation was that Raleigh lacked the steep terrain to encourage people to ride rather than walk.)

From a total of 527,935 passengers and transfers in 1889, the ridership rose to 1,531,981 passengers in 1908 and to 3.3 million in 1924. By comparison, in 1990 about three million passengers rode the city bus system, even though Raleigh's population, miles of routes, and number of transit vehicles all have multiplied.

(In 1930, more than 40 percent of Raleigh's citizens used the streetcar; today, perhaps two percent take the bus.)

CP&L closed down the streetcar in the 1930s. Bloomsbury Park's carousel, which had been installed to encourage riders to take the Glenwood Avenue line, was moved to Pullen Park. All that remains is a berm, next to the Carolina Country Club, where the streetcar left the median on Glenwood Avenue.

Raleigh

In view of its financial gaspings in early years, it perhaps was fortunate that the Raleigh Electric Company associated itself with the General Electric Company of New York.

But that association carried with it several adjustments in the price of electricity in the capital.

Initially, the new consortium worked well. For example, when the entire power plant burned in 1896, it was estimated that Raleigh would be without electricity for three months. But by using its industrial connections, G.E. managed to restore full service in 20 days. (If that seems long, it is because there were no interconnections in the area until well after 1896.)

G.E. was reputed "to know the location of practically every piece of idle equipment in the eastern division," bought much of it, and saved the city a bundle by quickly rebuilding the power station.

On the other hand, G.E. in 1906 created an entity called the Electric Bond and Share Company of New York. If today's electric supplier in Raleigh once bore a resemblance to a homegrown enterprise, that resemblance vanished in 1906.

Under later antitrust laws, the Bond and Share outfit was named a "holding company." It proceeded to buy up all of the stock in Raleigh Electric. And in 1908, another push of the corporate paper on Wall Street resulted in a merger and the name of the "Carolina Power & Light Company." Bond and Share held controlling interests in three of the utilities involved in the consolidation.

In the next move in that era of lax regulation, CP&L signed a contract with its parent, Bond and Share. More money began to change hands.

Bond and Share agreed to manage CP&L – right down to preparing its filings for rate increases – and all it took was $25,000 per year and 1.5 percent of CP&L's gross operating income. The potential for what the Federal government later termed "excessive fees" was clear.

In 1926, CP&L grabbed for the brass ring. It reorganized again into the present-day utility.

In a maneuver which drew more attention from the Federal Trade Commission than it ever did from CP&L's corporate biographers, CP&L and its subsidiaries decided that they could reverse the rules of depreciation. On the eve of their reorganization, the utilities took a write-up of the values of their respective assets. The write-up, done without any regulatory oversight, jacked up CP&L's rate base and its charges for electricity.

The effect was a huge rate increase for Raleigh. After many complaints were heard, the FTC and the U.S. Senate in hearings found "no competent evidence" that the write-ups were supported by sound accounting principles. Other bodies charged that CP&L had "violated its monopoly privileges" by "claiming and receiving returns on fraudulent and inflated values."

CP&L viewed the issue differently. In a study sponsored by the company, an economist wrote that "CP&L feels that it was perfectly justified, in that its properties had appreciated in value by the amount of the write-up and, therefore, it was permissible to make such an increase in its asset accounts."

The utility did not offer the first word about the depreciation it had been taking for years on these same properties – charges which were a part of its rates – nor did it offer an explanation of how it decided the amount of the write-ups.

Finally, one of CP&L's own witnesses said that the company wore no clothes; under oath, he described CP&L's position as "circular reasoning."

After more than 10,000 pages of transcript and what CP&L official Jack Riley described as threats of criminal action against the utility's officers, CP&L settled its case with the Federal Trade Commission. The company's refund of $18.6 million to consumers – a startling amount of money given the cost of early power plants – would today be the lion's share of a billion dollars.

What has development cost the city? Consider a story about one vanished house.

According to Perrin Busbee in the *North Carolina University Magazine* of 1893, when Judge William Gaston died one winter at his home on Hargett Street, he was laid out for a week in the parlor with the windows open.

In the greenhouse in back (now a parking lot), the "furnace was kept at a red heat during the whole of the cold snap" which Raleigh suffered during the mourning period. Then, after the funeral party left, attendants opened the two glass doors separating the greenhouse from the parlor.

"The cold arctic air of the parlor, rushing in on the moist tropical atmosphere of the greenhouse, produced a perfect but artificial snowstorm," Busbee related. He said that the snowstorm, complete with "large flakes," lasted for three minutes.

Apocryphal story or not, the house of the author of "The Old North State" was later demolished.

In an effort to secure a tobacco factory, a committee set out in 1888 to sell Raleigh citizens 1,000 shares of stock at $25 a pop.

The sales pitch suggests better than any statute why Secretary of State

Raleigh

Rufus Edmisten needs an active staff to watch over the securities business.

"Citizens; young and old," the promotion went, "When the committee approaches you, don't say 'I don't want any stock.'

"You *do* want it... Will you? Are you a whole-souled Raleighite? Do you want your city on a big boom?... It's time for business now!"

The solicitation, which was devoid of financial statements, was directed specifically at residents who might be able to afford only one share of tobacco stock. It promised that in lieu of any prospectus, the committee members would drop by to answer questions.

Although the promotion failed and citizens lined up to try to retrieve their money, Raleigh did ultimately get its tobacco factories. They manufactured cigars – well insulated from the competitive forces of the cigarette makers in Durham.

Even when Raleigh did attract a new industry – say, the Pioneer Tobacco Warehouse in 1884, at the time predicted to be the start of Raleigh's ascension to become the mightiest tobacco center in the South – the city's lack of civic initiative emerged.

(Not to say that the rhetoric was pallid: "Raleigh yesterday turned over a new leaf," wrote *The News and Observer*. "It was a tobacco leaf and upon it were inscribed the words, 'Progress and Prosperity.'") The newspaper predicted that "in time Raleigh will become a famous tobacco market," and indeed for a few years, the city made headway in catching up with Durham.

At the warehouse's opening, however, Governor Thomas J. Jarvis had to observe that "in Raleigh, individual enterprise (has) done much... yet as great as individual enterprise has been, there has not been the combining of energy which has marked some other towns in North Carolina."

Keep raking up the yard, Junior, we can go into business....
In 1884, citizens from Raleigh offered for sale at an exposition wigs which they had fashioned from long-leaf pine needles.

Most of what could be obtained on Fayetteville Street in 1880 is available there today; what has been lost is about 95 percent of the street's charm, and except for a random construction site, all of its dust and mud.

Consider a few of the enterprises which operated *legally* on the street in 1880:

Raleigh

Seven newspaper offices; two cigar manufacturers; an oyster company; a billiard saloon; two bookbinders; a bakery; an auction house; two candy manufacturers; two drama theaters; a butcher shop which specialized in wild game; three boarding houses; and the city market.

But not to be too nostalgic: Fayetteville Street in 1880 did have its deficiencies. There were only 16 lawyers on the street, most of them quartered in the Courthouse building. And the street offered only one real estate agent.

Tell it to IBM: Under the headline, "Do We Want Immigration," the *State Chronicle* in 1886 noted that "Raleighites, used to a comfortable homogeneity of people and ideas, want the newcomers to be copies of themselves."

Not all who passed through Raleigh shared the Main Street view: Walter Hines Page, who edited the *Chronicle* for several years, wrote that "in the year 1883, the thing that most impressed observers in Raleigh was its inertia."

Warming up, Page said that "if you were to go there now you would soon lose your reckonings. The sense of responsibility would slip from you. The days would come and go, every one like every other one. You would hear the same remarks made at the same time-of-the-day that were made there at that time-of-the-day in the years of your grandfather."

Page described life in Raleigh as "an intangible continuity of a vacuous monotony."

He concluded his analysis by remarking that "while he lives, a man there may study himself dead – touch his own corpse and commune with his own suspended intellect.... It's the clearest case of arrested development to be found in human annals." And Page moved North to edit *The Atlantic* magazine.

The more things change.... "It has been nearly a year now since the railroad companies decided to build," the *N&O* fussed in 1890, "and not a brick has been laid yet. This breaks the record for delay."

Like the First Citizens and the RJR Nabiscos of today, the railroads left the city with an unplanned open space, causing "the doubting Thomases to begin their carping again." The city was particularly vexed because it had already spent money to grade the unpaved streets to the site.

Raleigh

The owners of the new Hygienic Ice Factory in 1892 complained about Raleigh's lack of interest in their product.

Built after an old plant burned down, the business had two machines which could produce 6,000 pounds of ice every eight days.

"There is scarcely business enough for one machine," the proprietors said.

Give me your tired, your poor, your huddled masses.... The Chamber of Commerce and Industry, in a promotional book about the capital published in 1894, assured potential residents that Raleigh had none of the "scum" populations of Northern cities and would make every effort to keep things homogeneous.

Historian R.H. Whitaker was less than enthralled by the rise of what he called the "time merchants" in Raleigh – those who would sell fertilizer for $18 cash or $30 credit against next year's crop – and their role in driving agriculture out of town.

He described an early crop lien from a Raleigh finance wizard to a local farmer. The Rev. Whitaker said that the local pronunciation sounded like "crap" lien. He wrote:

"At the winding up of the year the crop lien began to draw and it kept on drawing. It drew all the cotton and corn, the wheat and oats, the shucks, the hay and the fodder... the biscuits and molasses from the kitchen table..."

"And when it had gotten everything else," he wrote, "it reached for the dish rag and wiped up the whole concern, not leaving even a grease spot."

RALEIGH, NORTH CAROLINA within 15 hours of NEW YORK CITY. The ideal winter home for Semi-Invalids and Pleasure Seekers from New England."

Well, who's not to be attracted by an advertisement like that, courtesy of the Chamber of Commerce in 1897?

Among the enticements listed were "a Home for Old Ladies and Incurables, etc." and optimism that "within a few years good roads will be the rule and... bad roads will be the exception."

The Chamber added that "a hop culture is now being tested" which it expected could be gathered, cured and sold before the New England hops even ripened each season. It also promised that "special inducements are being offered for a pants factory."

The auction in 1898 of the Pullen estate was said to be "the largest public sale of real estate ever known in Raleigh." (The Resolution Trust Corporation was not around in those days.)

That October, 31 properties were sold at an average pace of four minutes each. They brought in a total of $52,000, which was estimated by the *N&O* to represent about 75 percent of their value if they had been trickled into the market over time. The highest prices paid at the auction were by Pullen heirs.

What was available in Raleigh in 1898? Nine and one-quarter acres off Hillsborough Street went for $343. A store and land on Hargett Street between Fayetteville and Salisbury commanded $950.

For $1,650, a buyer got an eight-room house and lot on the corner of Oakwood and Polk streets. Another buyer spent $1,700 for a similar house with 50 percent more land on Elm Street; it was the highest price in the sale.

Every citizen should... talk for Raleigh. Commend her merits, for she has many, and keep silent concerning her weaknesses, if any there should be." – Alderman John C. Drewry, 1899.

The more things change.... In 1907, the Raleigh Merchants' Association underwrote the publication of a new book for businesses. It contained the "credit ratings of every resident in the city."

Although the book was supposed to be distributed only to Association members, questions immediately arose about the confidentiality of the data and the difficulty of correcting errors.

As late as 1907, a letter could be mailed from across the nation addressed only to "Mr. X. at the Yarborough House" and it would be delivered in Raleigh. The hotel burned in 1928.

Some of the promotional material for Raleigh's new suburbs at the turn of the century is at least quaint today.

To try to encourage buyers to settle in Cameron Park, the Parker-Hunter Realty Company hailed the advantages of agreements it had worked out for sidewalks and for the free delivery of groceries and medicine.

"One who has never lived in a suburban section can hardly realize what the advantages mean," the company wrote. "To be alone in a detached house with serious illness in the family...." (All the brochure lacked was an endorsement from Mrs. Fletcher, the fallen woman in those emergency-service commercials.)

"There are no poor sections," the realtors promised. "There are no bad approaches."

In another section, they pointed out that there would be "no negroes or persons of negro blood." (In common with most subdivisions in Raleigh, the deeds contained restrictive covenants. Servants were excepted.)

The company proclaimed that all "barns, stables and outhouses" in Cameron Park would be limited to those built for the residents.

On a somewhat higher plane.... When the General Assembly killed the first effort to annex Cameron Park in 1919, members ridiculed what they called the "Let George Do It" spirit of the neighborhood.

"Those people out there," one politician noted, "are living off Raleigh and they ought to come in and bear a portion of the burden." The annexation bill failed when its own sponsor turned against it.

Anyone can mourn over the buildings in Raleigh which were demolished in the name of profit. Raleigh has never treated its historic properties well or coherently.

(It is revealing that the bones of Joel Lane are thought to repose under an asphalt parking lot, but researchers are not quite certain.)

Of the 60 "landmarks" listed in the city's sesquicentennial history – a short list even in 1942, and it was padded with some suspect entries – nearly a third are gone today. If celebrants of the bicentennial want to see a baseball game, for instance, they will have to drive to Durham or Zebulon. But if they want to see garbage trucks at rest, they can go to what once was Devereux Meadow.

If Raleigh's lack of respect for its traditions has a pattern, it is typified by the fate of a general store on Hargett Street owned by "Snuff Bill" Upchurch. He retired in 1896 after doing business in the same wooden building since 1835.

"It is one of the landmarks of Raleigh," the *N&O* rhapsodized, "filled with a storehouse of historical relics that a true antiquary might revel in for months and not exhaust." The newspaper described the "bladders of snuff," still in use, "just like they were when our grandmothers sent to town." The building was then flattened without so much as a champagne breakfast to celebrate the demolition.

But of equal interest to the demolitions are a few projects which, despite heated prodding by the business community, the city failed to obtain. They would have transformed the capital.

The Chamber of Commerce, and its predecessor, the Chamber of Commerce and Industry, had big aspirations for Raleigh toward the end of the 19th century.

For example, the Chamber complained that Raleigh had insufficient heavy industry and also needed a few chemical production plants. The Chamber's members said a "safety first approach" to development was to blame, and that in terms of industry, Raleigh needed to be more "daring."

So it may not come as a surprise that the business community, once it lost the battle against the building of Central Prison, decided that Raleigh would be the perfect site for what later became the Federal penitentiary in Atlanta. (After all, by 1886, Central Prison held a few dozen Federal inmates as well as those imprisoned for State offenses, and the Federal inmates seemed to make fewer escapes.)

To understand what Raleigh would be like today if the Chamber had succeeded, take 350 acres – the size of the Atlanta penitentiary campus – and append it to the southern and western sides of the Central Prison grounds.

That amount of land, almost identical to the original grid of streets laid out in 1792, would contain 37 walled acres (about eight times that of Capitol Square), 1,400 prisoners, and 521 employees. Another 500 inmates would be held on a Federal prison farm near to the city, probably about where the Art Museum is situated.

Add in a stream of visitors to some of the nation's meaner felons and the image comes into focus. Raleigh lost the bid, it was announced, because Atlanta had better railroad connections. (Not only that, but the railroads and the city donated the land.)

The Federal prison would have been picayune, on the other hand, compared to the Chamber's next project.

The Chamber – whose members could remember armies in town throughout the 1860s – nonetheless decided that Raleigh needed a permanent U.S. military base.

Not some podunk tank camp, either: this time the Chamber and the city pledged to buy $200,000 worth of property contiguous with the city limits and to donate it to the United States government if it would give Raleigh a full-fledged base.

Once again, it helps to visualize what our local Babbitts would have created.

In 1896, the sum of $200,000 would have bought enough land to accommodate a six-square-mile base. That amount of land, nearly 4,000 acres, would have represented a third of the city until annexations exploded starting in the 1950s. And the military base would undoubtedly have expanded.

(The Chamber was altogether earnest in seeking the camp. It formed committees, issued press releases, and went to Washington to testify in support of authorizing legislation. The *N&O* thought the base was a "fine prospect.")

But the Chamber was not through. In 1918, it tried to make permanent the tank camp at the old Fairgrounds.

A Federal prison; military bases; heavy industries; chemical plants. These are only some of the stuff of Chamber dreams found in the public records.

As Robert Fomon remarked while he was chairman of E.F. Hutton, "sometimes the best deals are the ones you don't make."

Those who remember the demolition of the historic Woman's Club Building on Hillsborough Street to make room for the round Holiday Inn will find incongruous what the club did for Raleigh in 1912.

Concerned that the city was developing with no apparent plan – when it was moving forward at all – the club raised funds to import a landscape architect to study the city and develop a plan for its esthetic improvement.

To review Charles Robinson's plan, published by the Woman's Club in 1913, is to get the sinking feeling that some urban problems refuse to go away. Remember that it was written nearly 80 years ago.

For downtown, Robinson recommended putting utility poles underground. He said the poles were a "disfigurement," caused a "serious menace in case of fires," and resulted in the "beheading and mutilation of trees." Speaking of the city ordinance which required all poles to be neatly painted, Robinson wrote that "one would never suspect the existence of such a statute from looking at the city streets."

Next, Robinson focused on the handling of trash. He proposed nighttime collection downtown so that merchants would stop leaving trash bins standing all day on the city's sidewalks. He also urged citizens to recycle and make use of their household refuse, specifically glass, paper and metal cans. Calling the landfill a "municipally-made nuisance," he speculated about the dangers to well water from continuing to bury garbage. Robinson proposed a city "crematory," or incinerator, for trash which could not be sold for recycling. (He did not, however, recommend where to build it.)

Next Robinson proposed a sign ordinance. He believed that protruding signs on stores were "dangerous to human life" (they fell on pedestrians and hindered firemen) and were unsightly.

Even the electric signs, valued because they augmented Raleigh's feeble street lights, were to be banished because other than a few hours, they were "nothing but an unsightly advertisement sticking out over the public sidewalk."

And if Robinson had been emperor, there would be no discussion today about the Side Street Cafe's painted wall advertising Coca Cola, because painted advertisements would also have been prohibited. (What especially irked Robinson was signs which marred the landscape and did not even plug products made in Raleigh.) Of course, if the emperor today were someone who enforced historic accuracy, Raleigh would have many more painted signs on walls, not fewer.

Robinson assayed Fayetteville Street and found on it "alone a tendency to descend to the ordinary level of a very commonplace city street." Besides freeing it from utility poles and trash bins, he wanted the "marquies" at the Yarboro Hotel and Boylan-Pearce either to reach all the way to the curb or else to be lopped off.

"It is rather ridiculous to have it stop halfway," dribbling rain onto unsuspecting walkers, Robinson said.

Robinson praised the vistas on Halifax, New Bern and Hillsborough streets. (In the intervening years, one was eliminated, one cut off, and the third afflicted with an S-curve.)

If Robinson's advice had been taken, downtown would have been fitted with beautiful Seattle lights, had public restrooms, and had several diagonal streets.

The perimeter of Capitol Square would also look different. Robinson advocated height limits for new buildings, with the present Court of Appeals building being the highest. Of the tall buildings then rearing up downtown, he said that "they have advertising value; and... tend to empty the other, older buildings; to give the city a mushroom aspect, which is not in keeping with its history and character; to limit greatly the extent of the business district; and to bestow an inflated value on real estate in two or three blocks, while depressing it elsewhere."

(And Robinson was talking about eight-story "skyscrapers"; no need to ask how he would react to First Union's new contribution to downtown dimensions.)

Robinson wanted the height restrictions because, he said, "only by doing so can it keep the lovely old Capitol in scale." He also wanted future buildings which faced the Capitol to have a "required columnar motif," but said that "it is a pity this was not done before the new State office building was planned." (This building which offended the architect now houses the Labor Department and, compared to newer structures, is beginning to take on a little charm.)

As for Capitol Square itself, Robinson said that "its best interests would be served by a well organized opposition to any sculptural additions."

Robinson found a few things in the capital to compliment. Bloodworth Street south of Polk, for example, where the curb-to-curb width was reduced from 42 feet to 34 feet in order to save trees. (He presaged Mr. Hogg in feeling that the city's streets were too wide.)

He suggested that the city obtain a statue of Sir Walter Raleigh, not to go smack in the middle of Fayetteville Street, but in Nash Square in front of the train station, where visitors then arrived. (He attributed the idea to a Genoan statue of Christopher Columbus.) He wanted a bandstand for Moore Square and a new city market.

But then Robinson, as the saying was, "went to meddling." What he said may well have been true, but Raleigh's patriarchs were not interested in hearing, about Pullen Park, that it was "seedy and unkempt," was "full of poison ivy and poison oak," was a "pretty poor apology for a park," and that in general, the architect observed "no privately owned quarter acre garden that was not kept up better."

Robinson noted that in Pullen Park, "the few features which have been put in are not kept up," and then he closed with a zinger: "Within sight are the handsome grounds of the Insane Asylum, to show sane people how their park ought to look."

At a minimum, these remarks did not endear Robinson to the city aldermen, from whose jurisdiction the architect proposed to snatch the park, replacing it with a Parks Commission. Above all, the aldermen did not want to levy taxes to pay for improvements.

Nor was official Raleigh interested in Robinson's suggestion for moving the jail on Fayetteville Street. ("There is no necessity in these days," he wrote, "for having the jail next to the court-house and giving to it a site not only relatively expensive in itself but expensive in its adverse effect on what should be good business property.")

As the city fathers read on, less and less of Robinson's work looked desirable. Who, after all, had funds to rebuild the railroad bridges to make them more attractive? Who wanted to commission a statue of a man wearing tights?

Then Robinson gave them their ammunition: this interloper, this Yankee from Rochester, New York, suh, he proposed that the Confederate Memorial be uprooted from Capitol Square because it queered the sight-line down Hillsborough Street and was overwhelmed by the Capitol behind it.

Robinson suggested that it be moved over by the School for the Blind. And that did it.

Robinson left town with one last telling remark. In response to the city fathers' defense that they could not afford to take his recommendations, the architect pointed out that the city boasted of having the lowest per capita bonded debt of any city in the State.

"This is not necessarily a pride-worthy condition," he wrote, "any more than if a man should boast of having money in the bank, which he had saved by making no expenditures on his house, the roof meanwhile leaking...."

The Woman's Club has not sponsored a city plan since.

Even as the Chamber of Commerce was being implored to do something to halt profiteering on rents during World War I – it didn't – at least one Raleigh firm held the line without urging.

The El-Rees-So Cigar Company, which at the time manufactured 25 million stogies each year, reported that it would hold its price at six cents a smoke despite rising costs in every aspect of its business.

"We will be satisfied to look after ourselves after the war," the owners pledged. They said they would provide Raleigh's fighting men with as many cigars as they could consume.

Mayor T.P. Eldridge, described as a "self-educated man," was forthright in 1922 when the city commissioners finally adopted an ordinance creating a Planning Commission.

"Had there been a municipal planning commission when the town began to outgrow its original limits," the mayor said, "certain conditions which exist to our regret today and which must be corrected tomorrow could not have happened."

He identified narrow and crooked streets, dead-ends, and indiscriminate railroad rights-of-way as problems. Of the railroad cuts, he said that "there is no way to get across without flying."

The mayor criticized Nash Square, the first thing a traveler saw after detraining ("Imagine what kind of an impression!") and kissed off Moore Square as a "place for the display of second-hand wearing apparel."

Eldridge said the city's parks suffered from "neglect and misuse," lamented the lack of playgrounds, and said that if zoning had been adopted in Raleigh earlier, "the citizens... would not have to complain of the annoyance caused by stables, barns and cow lots at their doors."

He also detected that as early as 1922, new streets in the city were being opened not for the purpose of efficient transportation, but for developers who wanted to sell subdivisions around them.

For the first 160 years or so after its incorporation, Raleigh had no city planner.

On the surface, the absence of a planner had a certain logic to it: not until 1923, well after other municipalities in North Carolina had acted, did Raleigh pass its first ordinance for the regulation of land use and zoning. Prior to that time – and many would argue after it as well – the city developed according to where money took it.

Hog pens snuggled up against houses; gasoline filling stations shared the same blocks as ironworking shops with open flames.

If a certain activity became too hazardous – the explosives factory downtown comes to mind – the city would simply discourage similar enterprises in the future. If a condition became too obnoxious – say, a botched development on some floodplain – the city would wait to see whether a private party would initiate a lawsuit. If a public health question arose – over the effects of stables, for instance – the city fathers would cluck their tongues and say that yes, something certainly must be done to slow the building of more stables in the future.

But apart from the original grid of streets drawn by William Christmas in 1792, and violated by the railroads at two corners, Raleigh had no master plan whatsoever.

That situation was supposed to change in 1923 when Mayor Eldridge bullied through the first laws for planning and zoning.

The city brought in an expert from Washington who labored over a series of artful zoning maps which partitioned Raleigh according to building height, population density, and type of use.

The expert worked for about a year on the project. The resulting maps were intended "to furnish guidance for future generations."

They furnished guidance, all right, but for less than four weeks. Then, under pressure from merchant interests, the city board granted the first zoning variance in Raleigh history: it spot-zoned the corners of Glenwood Avenue at Peace Street to permit commercial development. The results are still on view today.

By the time Raleigh hired a planner in 1949, the development horse was long out of the barn in the explosive growth which followed World War II.

The city recruited a planner from the Tennessee Valley Authority; it gave him one draftsman and a secretary as a staff; it stuck him not in city hall, but in the basement of Memorial Auditorium; it provided him with little budget and less authority; and it kept him so occupied with technical work and meetings that he had little opportunity to plan anything.

Further, when planner Herbert Stevens did manage to present some ideas, many in the business community greeted them with ridicule.

Stevens knew as early as 1950 that Raleigh's traffic patterns were totally haphazard. So he fought for a $2,000 appropriation so that Willard F. Babcock of N.C. State could conduct a basic traffic-flow study. Stevens was scorned by the Chamber of Commerce as "the planner who hired a planner."

Then, as it became apparent that nothing was going to check Raleigh's growth to the northwest, Stevens sought to widen Wade Avenue and to improve its intersections. The city board vetoed any funds for land acquisition. Like Fayetteville Street at the end of the 19th century, Wade Avenue had to be improved a section at a time as monies became available.

Frustrated at the delay, Raleigh developer Willie York widened one portion of Wade Avenue at his own expense. A few mornings later, "three signs appeared nailed to a telephone pole at the then existing mudhole. These read Stevens' Slough, Babcock's Bottom, and Carper's Cutoff."

Delays were not the planner's only problem; equally frustrating were projects which seemed to get approved out of nowhere on schedules too short for reasonable analysis.

But by the time Stevens went on to larger opportunities – and given the political environment, it is remarkable that he stayed a year – even the *Raleigh Times* credited him with giving planning a good start.

Stevens and Babcock identified four road projects as essential for Raleigh: three of them were achieved in the form of the Beltline and the I-40 connectors around the city. The most urgent of the four, according to their ranking, was still pending 40 years later: a connector through Boylan Heights so that Western Boulevard would tie into South Wilmington Street.

It has been said," a writer commented in 1935, "that if a man walks each day down Fayetteville Street from the Capitol to the courthouse, at the end of a year's time he will have seen everyone of importance in North Carolina."

Who says that myths do not die? Whether that statement was figuratively true or not when it was made, it could not be said today.

With the one-block relocation of the Legislature, the departure of the Art Museum from downtown, the loss of Raleigh's historic position as the State's banking center, the flight of businesses and law firms to the suburbs

Raleigh

– the list could go on – that man of 1935 would see more muckety-mucks by spending a well-chosen week on Fayetteville Street and the other 51 patrolling Tryon Street in Charlotte.

A few words about rooming houses, those objects of perennial lawsuits by neighbors who believe that they detract from the resale potential of their single-family homes.

It turns out that rooming houses were part of Raleigh from the beginning. Ancestors of the city's oldest families lived in Raleigh rooming houses. In fact, most of the original downtown consisted of homes which took in lodgers, in large part to accommodate the members of the Legislature who arrived each November.

If Raleigh had not had an abundance of rented residential rooms, Fayetteville likely would have been the State Capital since the burning of the State-House in 1831.

Nor did rooming houses cease to play a role after the 1830s.

Former President William C. Friday of the Consolidated University frequented a Raleigh boarding house. So did Jesse Helms. They were comparatively cheap and substituted nicely for the apartment buildings which Raleigh discouraged because it feared the epidemics and fires which arose in tenements in the North.

Of course, all of the city's rooming houses were not up to the standards of those patronized by Friday and Helms. Consider the lodging house of Mrs. G., which was described in a W.P.A. writers' project in the 1930s but somehow was omitted from the city's sesquicentennial memory book.

Located at Wilmington and Cabarrus streets, Mrs. G's house offered a place to sleep for 25 cents a night. Beds and cots were lined up in the halls and in the house's four bedrooms, and each room also contained a double bed which commanded 50 cents per night.

"The lodgers," the W.P.A. writer found, "are usually floaters, habitual drunkards and street bums."

Describing the house, the writer dwelled on the "whitewashed walls of the rooms... almost black from the accumulation of soot over many years." He noted the fallen plaster which revealed lath in many places. He observed that the windows were so dirty that it was difficult to tell day from night.

Mrs. G's house had no wiring and was lit by kerosene lamps. (Imagine those tenants handling kerosene lamps.) Its only plumbing was a single water toilet on the back porch. Although each bedroom had a fireplace, the only stove was in the room occupied by Mrs. G and that room was off-limits to the boarders.

Raleigh

Mrs. G took in about $40 per month from her lodgers and used that to supplement her pension of $300 per month as a Confederate widow.

Proud that she had never taken charity, the landlady was described as having "smutty gray hair, some of which hangs stringy about the sides of her face. She is toothless and a network of wrinkles covers her face. She wears a dark calico dress, a filthy apron and a sweater.

"She frequently mops snuff, which she uses incessantly, from the sides of her mouth and chin with her apron." The writer said that Mrs. G, then in her late eighties, had "never known anything but hard work all her life." She had never seen a play and had attended only two movies, preferring to dip snuff for entertainment.

Mrs. G. had both standards and a good memory. Referring to the makeup which Raleigh women wore in the 1930s, she said that in 1880 "ladies did not use paint and powder those days, only the women of the red light district."

She recalled the "Pattyrollers" in Raleigh during the Civil War, when the theft of food became a problem in town.

"When they got evidence of a thief," Mrs. G related, "the Pattyrollers would take him into the woods, tie him to a tree, and wear him out with a horsewhip." She said that the same punishment was meted out to those who purchased stolen food, and that the same penalties applied "whether they were black or white."

"And they didn't go around wearing masks, either," Mrs. G summarized in a taunt at the K.K.K. which was attempting a resurgence in Wake County in the 1930s.

Mrs. G had been in Raleigh when General Sherman paid his respects. Her clearest memories were of Sherman's troops cleaning out the farms around the city, taking everything they could find to eat. She also reported that Union troops, a few nights after the occupation, arrested, summarily tried, and hanged a black man for raping a white woman.

Mrs. G had little trouble with her boarders. "My prices are so cheap," she told the W.P.A. writer. "They don't expect much."

Many more such buildings... will be needed in the future to meet our parking needs."

With that endorsement, the Chamber of Commerce in 1953 welcomed the first 435-car parking deck to downtown Raleigh. (The number is now up to five with more on the way.)

The Chamber also recommended the construction, if that is the word, of large surface parking lots on the perimeter streets of downtown. Within a few years, so many of the lots appeared that an urban planner singled them out as the main reason why downtown had "a derelict look."

The question of how many shopping centers is enough may have been crucial in the 1991 city council elections, but the centers have been a topic in Raleigh ever since Willie York bought an option on 160 acres from Annie Cameron Smallwood and put together Cameron Village.

The project received immediate accolades as the prototype of a "regional shopping center." It was commended in national studies because, in addition to stores such as Sears, it also incorporated cleaners, pharmacies and markets so that it was a daily resource for people who lived in its surrounding neighborhoods. (Neither was it set back behind six-lane boulevards; customers actually walked to it.)

As for its successors, Raleigh proceeded as if no one had ever read the 1940s book entitled *Mistakes We Have Made in Developing Shopping Centers*. Not that alarms were not periodically set off.

"Care should be taken to locate small neighborhood centers about a mile from established competing centers," a 1950s study recommended. (The operative word is "small"; larger shopping centers were to be proportionately farther apart.)

Of particular concern to one local planner in 1951 were "larger built-up strip centers." These creations, which in the last 40 years have become inescapable on roads leading into the city, were described as disasters from the standpoint of traffic control.

"They sometimes develop into so-called 'hot spots,'" the study found, in which their traffic "adds to the general congestion" and their presence "substantially slows down interregional traffic on highways." (The author failed to mention the effects on traffic of the shards of glass and chrome which decorate their intersections.)

In 1952, the Chamber of Commerce condemned its own proposal for a modern city produce market on the grounds that it would represent "socialism."

More and more cars used up more and more of the available space," a writer from the British Broadcasting Corporation wrote about Raleigh's downtown in 1964.

"I do not think anyone had planned this – it just happened."

The commentator said that downtown Raleigh was developing a "vast parking lot belt." Noting that "the volume of trade... known as 'downtown trade'... was standing still, while that in the suburbs boomed," he said that the city's decision to venerate the car had produced a "motorized exodus."

Downtown sales – which dropped from 83 percent of total sales in the city in 1954 to 62 percent in 1960 – were in trouble.

"Of course you can get a lot under one air-conditioned roof in the suburbs," he wrote, "and one wonders what the effect of this might finally be."

How did Raleigh happen to trail other cities in the State with regard to developing public housing?

In 1965, the chairman of Raleigh's redevelopment commission told an urban planner that "the federal government has no business telling us what to do or how to do it" and that he was "personally opposed to the concept of renewal."

And the chairman of Raleigh's planning commission confided to the same interviewer that he was "against the government's supplying people with their housing. Let them do it themselves."

Urban researchers found in 1966 that "there is in Raleigh about 100 times as much land being developed into suburbs as there is land being *considered* for *possible* urban renewal."

In his study, *Fat City Follies,* Richard Toppe traced the rapid growth of North Raleigh beginning in the late 1960s.

North Raleigh pioneers, he found, had moved there because of "the rural and pastoral attributes of the landscape. There was less of everything – shopping centers, houses, offices and traffic." Further, the pioneers had freedom from city taxes.

By 1978, however, Toppe said that the pioneers he interviewed "find themselves well within the city limits that have grown out to engulf and incorporate them." The result – and Toppe hadn't seen anything yet – was "the transformation of the Northern community into the very type of urban-suburban place that they had avoided when they chose to move there."

Residents of Boylan Heights had no reason to be surprised that their neighborhood split in the 1991 referendum concerning the proposed thoroughfare across their southern boundary.

"Over the years," a landscape architect wrote in 1986, "the city has been forced to jerry-rig various traffic connections through Boylan Heights." He set about to interview every resident who would come to the door about their opinions on the quality of traffic through the neighborhood. The responses indicated that "the auto and noise – the two greatest threats to personal privacy" were both at work.

On Lenoir Street, he found a "pulsing sensation. It is a rhythm which rigidly meters on-foot street crossings and porch conversations...." The rhythm was produced by the street's stoplights and resulting surges of traffic.

"In effect," the architect concluded, "what the city did was rezone Lenoir – the street itself – to the status of a high-speed thoroughfare symbolizing nothing common or vital to life in the neighborhood."

The city's planning policies are moving in opposite directions. While the downtown struggles for growth, the suburbs rapidly expand."

Jeff Adolphson made that observation in 1986 after he studied a ten-year trend in the city's retail office space.

Downtown retail space had dropped by 44 percent for the period, going from 197 to 111 stores. And although downtown office space increased by 75 percent in the same period, office space in the suburbs expanded so much faster that the downtown's share of total city office space declined from 51.9 percent to 29.5 percent.

Sizing up downtown, Adolphson concluded that "for a city that uses the imagery of a forest haven... the overall appearance of Raleigh leaves much to be desired."

Indecent Exposure

Raleigh's earliest newspapers contained practically no local news. On the other hand, everyone in the city knew at the speed of sound what their neighbors had done.

(As the proverb goes, a lie can travel around the world before the truth can put its pants on.)

The early newspapers had four-page editions. They were crammed each with political and military intrigue from Europe, transcripts of Congressional debates, semi-official proceedings of the Legislature, political tracts, page after page arguing the merits of deism, and an occasional curiosity such as George Washington's will. (All of the capital's papers printed it in full over a period of weeks; he was the Great Testator.)

No one seemed to care that the news was an average of six weeks old, unless the story involved a felon who might be heading toward Raleigh at the speed of a stolen horse.

The early newspapers used local events as a filler when floods delayed the arrival of the Northern papers from which they printed extracts. Given the condition of roads around Raleigh, delays were frequent.

When someone committed news in Raleigh and the editors decided to publish it, it usually was a report of a marriage or death. (The two were grouped together in that order.) Rumors of slave uprisings in the area, duelling (which was condemned by the editors but dwelt on with salacious interest), and an occasional boisterous celebration made the local papers.

The journals printed pseudonymous letters to the editor. "The Hermit of Wake" wrote in so often that he should have owned a word processor. Sometimes the letters and resulting editorials had a little bite.

Raleigh

One besieged Congressman was accused of forsaking the voters in favor of "his Lord and Master, Natty" – that's colonial politician Nathaniel Macon the writer was describing. Another was accused of "tailoring his religion to his politics."

A third local office-holder was said to have "a mind as confined as a broad-backed coat." Then there was a personal attack on a letter-writer who was said to have "a face that would be dangerous for a pregnant woman to look at."

The press in Raleigh was concerned about paying its bills. When a toast was drunk on July 4, 1800 in praise of the First Amendment, it was for "freedom of the press without licentiousness." The newspapers picked up the tab.

The march of progress.... The capital's best-known early newspaper, the *Raleigh Register*, used to print an issue every minute on its Ramage press. (The device was inked by hand using deerskin sacs filled with absorbent wool.)

Today's *News and Observer* can publish 50,000 newspapers of 72 pages each in one hour without stretching the capabilities of its presses. Even when an allowance is made for breakdowns and maintenance, the *N&O* produces more pages of news in 30 seconds than the *Register* did in a year.

The city's first lost-and-found advertisement gives an idea of how small the early capital was. The ad in 1800 reported "A Large House Door Key... lost some days ago" and offered a reward for it at the newspaper office.

If the early capital's system of paid informants seems intolerable today, it should be remembered that personal privacy was never very high on the city's list of concerns.

Local newspapers published the grades of students; they printed the names from the city's hotel registers (No, there was not an abundance of Mr. and Mrs. Smiths); and they listed the letters left unclaimed at the Post Office.

As the decades proceeded, invasions of privacy continued.

Newspapers published the name and address of each arriving patient at what is now Dorothea Dix hospital, and at a time when more of a stigma attached to mental disabilities. The papers routinely printed not only the names of victims of sex crimes in Raleigh, but also their physical descriptions and whereabouts.

When the U.S. government first began to collect income taxes, if a Raleigh resident wanted to know what he had paid as compared to his neighbor, he could find out by opening the morning paper.

The case of John Owen would be just another old-fashioned murder on Fayetteville Street except for what it teaches about trials and publicity.

Just a messy murder – a wooden bludgeon, an empty cash drawer, a suspect who cured his financial woes overnight but lacked an explanation of where he got the money – it turned into a media circus in Raleigh in 1810.

The convicted murderer, John Owen, was described in the Star as "idle, rude in his manners, vulgar and profane in his conversation." When he was sentenced to hang for the murder of shopkeeper Patrick Conway, the *Star* clucked that "good may grow out of evil, and poor Owen, though lost himself, may save others by the warning of his example and fate."

Perhaps so, if the *Star* had stopped there. But the newspaper, in common with others in 1810, printed a full transcript of Owen's trial, containing raw opinions about his character, and peddled them for sale in Raleigh while the case was pending on appeal. When the State Supreme Court ordered a new trial, the first thing Owen's lawyers did was to seek a change of venue on the grounds that the Star had contaminated public opinion in the capital.

"The violent prejudices of the people," they argued, "the highly distempered state of the public mind.. and the uncommon exertions of some to convict him" were grounds for moving the retrial to "any county but Cumberland." Despite arguments by the prosecution that "prejudice against Owen is as high in any county in the State as it is in Wake," the retrial was moved to Smithfield.

Owen, after failing in one attempt to escape, feigned heart trouble. Months passed while he was "seriously indisposed" in the jail. (It is a reflection on local travel in 1810 that a physician stated that Owen "may be removed to Smithfield with safety, provided he can be conveyed in a covered carriage or cart, in fair weather, and one or two days are allowed for the journey.")

The accused escaped before his journey to Johnston County. Two other accused murderers went with him; they cut through the ceiling of their dungeon, bypassed the Negroes in chains in the next cell, and escaped through the lightly-secured debtor's apartment on the jail's second floor.

"The prison of this city is now without a single tenant," the *Star* bemoaned.

With Owen on the lam, the *Star* reported what it really thought: "This earth," it wrote, "does not contain a more vile wretch than Owen is believed to be... *There can be no doubt of his guilt.* There is not a more hardened, inhuman and profligate monster in existence." (And these were the *news* columns.)

Granted, Owen's behavior had been tacky – a cabinet maker by trade, he had built the coffin for the late Mr. Conway after measuring his warm corpse the night of the murder. After his arrest, he billed the victim's estate for his labor.

But even the *Star,* in opposing Owen's delaying tactics before he fled, revealed something about the strength of the State's evidence.

The case, it reported, consisted of "a long chain of circumstances linked together by thirty witnesses, one of whom might drop off (by the time of the Smithfield trial), and the prisoner's objective would then be attained."

William Scott, the Keeper of the Raleigh Prison, tracked Owen as far as Virginia. But despite a $100 reward for his capture, the escapee "disappeared among his relatives."

Owen's escape did not deter the *Star* and its competitors from printing detailed accounts of subsequent trials in Raleigh and the resumes of the accused. The practice was a taxing one. Owen's trial had lasted more than 20 hours straight, ending about daybreak when the jury retired. By that time, the Star said, its reporter "was too much fatigued by watching nearly twenty hours sitting, to take any notes" of the prosecutor's summation.

But the newspaper said it agreed with everything the prosecutor had to say.

If the nation's critics ever hold a competition for the most florid editorial ever written, Raleigh has a contender.

The mercifully short-lived *N.C. Beacon and Metropolitan Omnibus* printed the following description of the first passenger train to grace the capital in 1840:

"What a lively joy did the queer 'cheow' of the first locomotive in Raleigh awaken in every heart!" said the journal.

"Merry faces were seen at every turn, the birds sung merrily in the tree-tops, and the martins came hurrying from the sunny South to see the pleasing sight...

"All hearts filled with delight, as belching and coughing, the machinery commenced its evolutions. 'Pfw, pfw – all right, go ahead – pfhst, cheow, cheow, cheow, cheow, cheo, cheo, che, che, ch, ch – clack – che, ch, ch, ch – get off the track...."

Then the *Beacon*'s editor went poetic: "There they go rumbling, see the wheels tumbling, passengers fumbling (in their pockets for tickets), engineers grumbling, pine-knots a'crumbling.

"The water is frying, the sparks are flying...."

That's enough. (Was there a Famous Writers' School in 1840?)

But the *Beacon* did have better days before it expired.

"The fellow with the blear eyes," it once wrote, "dirty paws and a black heart who stole our letter-box on Sunday night, had better return it or he may find himself exposed. He was seen in the act."

Aw, pfhst.

In their competition to win the State printing contract, Raleigh's newspapers often used the kind of sarcasm which one associates with WRAL-TV's comments about *The News and Observer*.

(WRAL does not disparage the *N&O* as much since the departure of Jesse Helms as the station's commentator and the death of A.J. Fletcher, the station's founder. Oddly enough, Fletcher and Josephus Daniels of the *N&O* had been friends and collaborated early in this century on cleaning up corruption in the Wake County courthouse.)

But back to the past. In 1810, William Boylan of the *Minerva* wrote about his competitor at the *Register* that "if I were not fearful of offending Mr. Gales, I would publish a list of the errors made by him in printing the laws of 1808. Some of these errors have rendered passages perfect nonsense, and others again entirely change the meaning."

(Joseph Gales ought to have responded that some of the laws of 1808 were perfect nonsense with or without typographical errors.)

The joys of newspaper ownership.... Upon its failure, the owner of *The Live Giraffe* newspaper said that all he had gotten out of his investment in publishing was "a dinner now and then at a hotel free of cost, provided a half column was devoted to the landlord's ham and eggs."

(Newspapers in Raleigh today pay for their own food critics' meals.)

Nineteenth-century courtship in Raleigh often was conducted through breathless letters. (And if that were still the case, students would learn better English.)

Raleigh

Major William H. Bagley, for instance, wrote almost daily in the 1860s to Miss Adelaide Worth, daughter of the State Treasurer and Governor who was Bagley's employer. Addie, whom the Major addressed as "Little One" and "Child" in his correspondence, wrote back seemingly as often.

Their dozens of letters, back and forth, are almost enough to make an archivist doze off or ask, "Won't these people ever get married so they will quit communicating with each other?" Doze off, that is, until finding a letter in which Major Bagley, alone in his room at the Cooke Hotel with something which the couple coyly referred to as "Uncle Campbell," begins a description of what he is doing in bed with a set of ladies' undergarments which his sweetheart had given him. They married soon thereafter.

But if Major Bagley had his frustrations, he at least was a less soupy letter-writer than another young man in Raleigh two decades earlier.

Some wag, described as a "friend" of the man's, obtained one of his love letters. He published it – name omitted – in the *Microcosm*.

After referring in his first sentence to Pegasus, Hybla, Parnassus and Shakespeare, the lovestruck author cut loose:

"Oh! my lovely Helen!" he wrote. "Thou are *the true Venus!* the *Minerva!* the garden of Thesperides!! Oh! my honey duck!! my sugar loaf!! my tea pot!!" (Let's face it, the man had oral tendencies. Major Bagley could have used some of his "ohs" to help his own saga along.)

As the editor of the *Microcosm* observed, "there is but one step between the sublime and the ridiculous."

That step was also crossed with a vengeance in a practical joke played out on Moore Square.

It seems that Raleigh was home to a socially-challenged young man (translation: a nerd) who was mooning over a certain young lady and practically following her around town.

The woman seemed to ignore him, so after several weeks, one of his "friends" suggested that he write her a love letter. The friend even volunteered to draft it and to take the signed missive to the post office.

Several days after mailing the letter, what purported to be a response came back from the woman.

She was enthralled with the young man, she said. She lived for the sight of him passing by her house, she said. If only he would pause outside and strike a pose against a tree, her heart would palpitate, she said. The young man took to lingering on her corner and continued his assisted correspondence.

The barrage of letters which followed – with the woman's replies all written by a gang of forgers who met at a tavern and raised the ante with each week's "mail" – ended with the woman agreeing to marry the young man in a hasty midnight ceremony in Moore Square. No one was to disclose the event for fear of reprisal from the woman's father.

On the appointed night, after a candlelight service presided over by a "justice," the groom turned to his bride. She drew aside her veil to reveal not only a conspiratorial grin, but a fully developed set of whiskers and a cigar.

The *Microcosm* reported that after a few weeks, assault charges against the groom were dropped. The young man who was the butt of the joke had not exactly gotten over it, but he did cease his pursuit of one particular woman.

It had all been done with letters.

Why newspapers fail.... According to the Rev. Whitaker, the *Metropolitan* newspaper collapsed in 1854 "for the reason that the subscribers did not know how to pronounce the name of the paper.

"They said they just couldn't do it, and they were opposed to having a paper coming into their homes they could not pronounce the name of."

Until Raleigh's newspapers fathomed what the State had gotten into, there was occasional satire in their reports about the Civil War.

The *Standard*, which had resisted secession up until President Lincoln tried to muster Southern troops to put down the rebellion in South Carolina, printed a poem which rewrote the lyrics of "The Old North State Forever." In the new version, the State's enemies were no longer foreign and the "witlings" became "Yankees."

The newspaper also published an extended "Obituary of Uncle Sam."

"A high authority has said," the obituary began, "concerning the dead, say nothing but what is good; a better guide would be to say nothing but what is *true*. Had this latter rule been observed, the reproach against mankind of – 'as lying as an epitaph' – might have been avoided."

The local writer then began to expound on his vision of the truth about Uncle Sam:

• "The truth is, he never had a sound constitution. There were inherent elements of weakness and conflict in it."

• "One Dr. Patrick Henry predicted (at birth) that he would be very greedy, absorbing and consuming the substance of the land."

• "Uncle Sam was... neither a judicial nor an impartial father... consequently, his children did not live happily together."

• "Uncle Sam was a great land speculator, and acquired immense farms in the West and South... Many of his children resided in the South and found

Raleigh

by actual experiment that they could not work their lands to advantage themselves; they therefore purchased Negroes and found that they could work the lands to the advantage of both. But Uncle Sam, under dictation of his Northern children, resisted this natural, profitable and benevolent system...."

- "He sometimes entrusted (his constitution) to mere pretenders to the healing art, to quacks, in fact... he elected one Abraham Lincoln, a creature of his Northern children, to be overseer of his whole domain. This was a great insult and a great injury...."

- "(O)n the 15th of April, 1861, head overseer Lincoln gave an order for 75,000 assistants to join him, for the purpose of whipping his Southern brethren into strict submission to his ill gotten authority.

"This prospect of brethren shedding each others' blood was too much for Uncle Sam to bear, in his senility and imbecility, which had been annually increasing. *He died the very day the bloody order was issued.* Requiescat in pace."

It was nice, light journalism. But the biggest laugh came in a news story from October, 1860, entitled "High Prices for Negroes."

Reporting on an average price of $768 per slave at a Raleigh estate sale, a newspaper observed that despite the impending Presidential election, "these prices show that the institution is at present in no danger."

The capital appreciates a native son... Under the headline of "Too Good, We Fear, To Be True," the *Register* printed a report in 1862 that Andrew Johnson had been killed in Tennessee. "We most devoutly hope that this dispatch tells the truth," the *Register* remarked.

Stories about the visit of Sherman's Army notwithstanding, the greatest risk to Raleigh during the Civil War came not from Union soldiers, but from Confederates. (That is, except for routine household fires in that era of poor fire protection.)

In September of 1863, Raleigh was the locale of what is officially termed "The Military Riot." It started as an argument over newspapers.

Some of Benning's troops, who had hitched rides into Raleigh on the roofs of train cars, found out in local taverns that the *Standard* newspaper had opposed secession and was lukewarm about the course of the war. (Incidentally, the newspaper was also raking in profits from the printing of Confederate documents.)

The Georgians marched on the *Standard* office and "destroyed" it. The

Raleigh

next morning, a group of citizens retaliated by wrecking the operations of the *State Journal*.

Governor Zebulon B. Vance wired Jefferson Davis in Richmond that "the town (is) filled with soldiers, threatening murder and conflagration." In addition to planning to torch downtown, Vance advised Davis, the Confederates were preparing to burn all bridges and trestles into the city.

"They even threatened my life if I interfered with them," one of Vance's cables read. "This thing is becoming intolerable."

Vance rode through the capital on horseback for 60 hours in an effort to prevent further mayhem. Hearing nothing from President Davis, he played a last card.

Vance cabled Davis that he was "faced with the humiliating task of trying to defend the laws and peace of the State against our own bayonets." He threatened to recall North Carolina's troops to defend their own property.

"The distance is short to either anarchy or despotism when armed soldiers, led by their officers, can with impunity outrage the laws," Vance concluded.

Davis at last issued an order for all Confederate soldiers to keep out of the City of Raleigh. In a few days – "the damages being equal to both parties" from demolition of the newspapers – calm returned.

What Vance had termed "the most frightening consequences" did not occur.

Reporting on a severe storm which struck Raleigh in 1863, the *Register* said that "a vast number of birds, especially robins, flocked to the neighborhood of houses and were seen in numbers in almost every street.

"Vast numbers," the item continued, "paid the penalty of misplaced confidence in man's humanity when his palate comes in conflict with his benevolence." Two weeks earlier, the newspaper had printed a paean to a local delicacy, robin redbreast pies.

Ad hominem journalism reached its low point in Raleigh in the late 1860s, when an entire newspaper, *The Holden Record,* was printed each week in an effort to vilify W.W. Holden in his approaching campaign for Governor.

The newspaper was designed, among other things, to convince blacks that Holden was a deep-down racist. It charged that he had changed his reg-

Raleigh

istration to Republican "for no other purpose than to save his neck from the gallows."

Quoting a statement allegedly made by Holden in 1861 – "Who will plot for the heads of Abe Lincoln and General Scott?" it went – the *Record* said that Holden was the instigator of Lincoln's assassination. It accompanied its charges, week after week, with a cartoon of Holden offering $100,000 to an eager John Wilkes Booth.

The newspaper ceased publication when Holden was elected.

What made the front page as news in 1872? The *Daily News* reported that the Green Front restaurant on Hargett Street had received "by express a mammouth sea turtle," and that the proprietor would be selling soup, both ala carte and carry-out for families.

(Actually, the same circumstances might make Page One today, but the focus of the story would be on the restaurateur's arrest.)

And Jesse Helms thought people disagreed with *him*.... Josiah W. Turner, the editor of the *Daily Sentinel,* used to take such controversial positions that he kept a loaded, cocked revolver on his office desk, pointed at the front door. (He needed it.)

In 1872 in Raleigh – apparently in the belief that canceling one's subscription was an insufficient display of contempt – some residents resolved their disagreement with a news publication the old-fashioned way: they blew it off the face of the earth.

"The *Sentinel* Office Blown to Atoms! A Damning Act of Fiendishness and Crime!" were headlines in the capital's surviving newspapers.

At 1 a.m. about a month before the elections, editor J.W. Turner's newspaper building on Fayetteville Street exploded with such force that timbers from its roof landed more than 100 yards away. The explosion was so strong that the building did not catch fire, because in an instant there was nothing flammable left.

(This was unlucky for Turner, whose insurance policy had covered fires but never contemplated a bombing.)

At the bottom of the rubble, under a twisted press, police found a remaining quantity of gunpowder with a defective delayed-action fuse.

Accusations began immediately. Turner and other Democrats placed the blame on Radical Republicans who advocated the reelection of the hated President Grant. The Republicans, however, responded that they had been winning too many elections lately to resort to any tactic which might create a backlash of opinion. They alleged that Turner had detonated his own operation.

The *Sentinel* continued to print abbreviated editions on the presses of its competitors. All that is certain is that Grant did carry Raleigh and that after the bombing, Raleigh never again had a newspaper like Turner's, which used typeface as small as the bottom of an eyechart.

With only two general newspapers in Raleigh today, it is difficult to believe that at one point in the 1800s, the city had 20 newspapers at the same time.

Some were intended to promote a particular viewpoint in an election campaign; more often than not, they disclosed their bias openly in shameless efforts to raise money. None lasted more than a few years.

But their mastheads are eternal. A few of Raleigh's more interesting newspapers, all preserved on microfilm, were:

The Rasp.
The Hayseeder.
We Know.
The Blasting Powder.
Beans.
The Negro Expositor.

G.O.P. Chairman Jack Hawke just possibly sensed this.... When what is now the *N&O* got a new editor back in 1876, he made a promise to the newspaper's subscribers:

"We will labor earnestly and faithfully," he wrote, "for the advancement of the Democratic Party and for the good of the State, which we believe to be one and inseparable."

No history of Raleigh can be complete without lingering over the fistfight on Fayetteville Street between the publishers of the *Minerva* and the *Raleigh Register.*

(All right, sports fans, let's go to the videotape! Wham! Boom! It's the *Minerva* in Round One by a TKO, the fine minus the costs of court donated to the Academy.)

But there was another brawl in the Capitol building between editors of two newspapers in the 1880s. And as in the bout between Boylan and Gales, Messrs. Samuel Ashe and Josephus Daniels got into their contretemps over the State printing contract.

"I was an eyewitness," a Raleigh historian recalled, "to the most famous fisticuff in the annals of our state – between the late Captain S.A. Ashe and Ambassador Daniels."

The historian, who had been a legislative page at the time, said that "Captain Ashe was State Printer, which was the most remunerative office in the state. Editor Daniels aspired to be his successor.

"Bad feelings had been engendered and when the two met at 1 a.m. at the bottom of the steps leading to the rotunda, there was a sharp exchange of the most naughty words, and Captain Ashe swung a wild haymaker which landed...."

Daniels did not swing back at the aging Ashe; nor did he press charges. He did, however, win the printing contract, and a few years later, he owned Ashe's newspaper.

The *N&O* was called the "Nuisance Disturber" as early as 1890, four years before Josephus Daniels and friends bought it at auction.

The bluenoses in town who think it is a "mob action" for N.C. State students to disrupt Hillsborough Street would do well to reflect on two spectacles in Raleigh in 1898.

These celebrations had nothing to do with winning a basketball game; they were for the victory of the White Supremacy ticket of the Democratic Party in the only election in Raleigh which clearly bordered on violence. (Men carrying shotguns walked the streets.)

Election night 1898 started in front of *The News and Observer* office, which displayed illuminated returns and an electric sparking rooster, which was then the Democratic Party symbol. Once a majority was secure, the revelers surged into the surrounding streets.

As the *N&O* described it, "bonfires crackled and blazed while jubilant Democrats crowded about them like Indians in a war dance."

Full barrels of pine tar were ignited, marchers got hold of "tin horns, tin pans, drums, flat boards and bells," and they hooted through downtown and residential streets alike until 5 a.m., when the saloons opened. (All without a parade permit, and much of it within Raleigh's still combustible fire district.)

Josephus Daniels thought the evening was so delectable ("fires smoldered in every street at day-break") that he raised money for an encore: a larger statewide celebration two weeks later. Its headquarters was the mayor's office.

"In every respect," Daniels editorialized about the second demonstration, "it eclipsed anything this city had ever before seen." The *N&O* described the crowd lifting Daniels onto their shoulders, more tar barrels set afire, bonfires made with tree limbs and assorted kindling taken from yards, torchlight parades, 150 white men on horseback, more than 2,000 marchers, fireworks, musicians, more white men brandishing pitchforks, and catchy banners such as "No more crucifixions on colored crosses" and "Hurrah for Wilmington." (Where after election night, a white mob killed eleven blacks, incinerated a black-owned newspaper, and then swore in a mob leader as the provisional mayor.)

Among Raleigh's spontaneous entertainments were burning drapes on a triumphal arch built in front of the Capitol, turning in false fire alarms in order to hear the sirens, setting fires in the streets, and vandalizing the State Institution for the Deaf, Dumb and Blind by chiseling the name of its sole black board member off of that building's cornerstone.

Daniels pronounced all this to be harmless stuff and great fun. He intoned of the Democrats, "WE are the party of Peace and the party of Law and Order."

(Of course, Josephus was a sport. A month earlier, he had written that "a horse race appeals more to men perhaps than any other one thing, a dog fight always excepted, and it is not at all to the discredit of the men." With attitudes like that, who knows whether he would have been stimulated as much by college basketball as he was by "ending Negro domination forever"?)

Presumption of innocence rides again.... The *N&O*, reporting on a forthcoming trial in 1898, wrote in its news columns about the accused that "of his conviction at that time and his subsequent punishment, there can be no doubt. The evidence against him is overwhelming."

Josephus Daniels was not unscathed as he ranted through the 1898 campaign. "A Political Pimp and Monopoly Slave," is how *The Progressive Farmer* referred to its competitor. Clarence Poe also opined that the *N&O* was made up of "gross, indecent, foul-mouthed slanderers," starting with the boss.

Raleigh

Had Poe stopped there rather than explaining his reasoning, he might look more heroic.

But writing about the *N&O*'s campaign to smear James Young, the *Farmer* observed that Daniels had looked the other way as "Jno. Manuel and Berry O'Kelly were appointed overseers of the roads" and "white men work(ed) under them or hire(d) substitutes."

With reference to a black sheriff's deputy who arrested a white woman in Garner and ordered her to walk back to the jail in Raleigh, Poe said that the *N&O* needed to adopt a new corporate jingle:

"Selah! Let the band play, 'There's a new coon in Town, and Demmys sent him round.'" (*The Progressive Farmer* was Raleigh's most liberal journal in the 1898 election.)

Anne Gales Root, when she died in 1911, left a scrapbook filled with anecdotes about her years in Raleigh. Herewith are some of the more printable ones:

• Mary Jones Joyner, when asked by her father to fetch some wire from the cellar in order to repair the front fence, cut down her family's new telephone lines.

• Mary Smedes referred to wedding invitations as "begging tickets."

Many of Mrs. Root's anecdotes were written down in dialect.

• Asked whether her husband was a Baptist or a Methodist minister, the cook for one Raleigh household replied, "No'm, he ain't a reg'lar preacher, he's just a licentious preacher."

• "Boss, if you builds dat road, you sho will enchant the value of yo' property," went one quotation. "De nex' mawnin' we heard dat hospitalities had deceased," went another about the end of the Civil War. "Yo' dress sho' is purty, but seems lak yo' face don't become it," went a third.

• With regard to the possibility of an untimely death, Mrs. Root quoted a servant as observing that "when you puts on yo' shoes in de mawnin', yo' dunno who's goin' to take 'em off at night."

For generations, Raleigh's media never hesitated to use dialect when reporting the remarks of any minority group.

Back in 1918, the *Raleigh Times* reported a conversation at Camp Polk; one recruit was insisting to another that he had to ship out to Europe; the most offensive words are omitted.

"Yeh, you is goin'," the first recruit said. "When President Wilson tells you to go you'll go. Ain't he done took an hour uv daylight away from de

Raleigh

Lawd and give it to the people, and ain't he done took de railroads away from de people an' give 'em to his son-in-law? When he tells you to go, you'll go."

The *Times* also ran an article commending the citizens of Raleigh for buying Liberty Bonds. It quoted a local Chinese merchant as saying about his purchase, "Yes me wanter help Melica."

"I would like to call a meeting in collaboration of the papers in the three states," wrote Frank Daniels as he prepared for a newspaper convention in 1938, "to see if some plan could not be worked out to increase the circulation revenue of all papers."

The scheme which Daniels had in mind was as straightforward as any which inspired the Congress to enact antitrust laws.

"If all papers advance their prices 5 cents per week," he suggested to publisher Gordon Gray, "there will be no relative change in the position of the newspapers in their respective communities."

(All Daniels omitted was that the blame should be placed on the rising cost of newsprint or ink.)

Gray told Daniels that although he would sit in on such a meeting, he would not raise his prices in Winston-Salem because he had recently done so twice. The plot appears to have fizzled.

But Daniels ultimately resolved his concern about yardstick competition in Raleigh when the *N&O* bought out the *Raleigh Times*.

And as a consistent newspaper owner, Daniels later lobbied the state's congressional delegation to relax antitrust regulations so that more newspapers could acquire their ailing fellows. The title of that legislation may seem ironic in light of what happened to the *Times:* it was called the Newspaper Preservation Act.

The *Raleigh Times* in 1942 offered Junior Commando armbands to boys 15 years old and younger who wrote letters to the newspaper explaining that they were "doing something to aid the war effort."

It took fewer than two weeks of *Viewpoint* editorials in 1960 for Jesse Helms to be criticized as a "negative thinker" – his words – who was against everything and for nothing.

So Helms took occasion in *Viewpoint* No. 8 to recite a few causes that he believed WRAL-TV viewers should join with him in supporting.

"You can be for," Helms said (the underlining was his), "laughing in the face of any candidate who pretends that an increase in the social security rate is not the same thing as a tax increase." (Helms should have a hilarious time in 1992.)

However one feels about Helms, the occasional times that he turned his attention to Raleigh produced some memorable results. (An average of one Viewpoint per month was about local developments other than the deaths of friends.)

Need some society news? Helms once revealed that "in Raleigh there are at least two groups of young ladies who have stopped playing bridge and are, instead, devoting their time to study groups on Communist tactics and economics.... Nothing could be more commendable than this." (A message to these women: it is safe to take up Goren again.)

Or perhaps new insight was needed into the N.C. State basketball point-shaving scandal? Helms disclosed that one fixer's "weakness is no greater than that of the clergyman who makes a forgery of the Word of God by transforming the pulpit into a forum for doctrinaire politics and philosophies."

(The Rev. W.W. Finlator is not sure whether Helms was talking about him or not. But locally, a minister or professor who was attacked by Helms wore it as a badge of honor in the style of those enshrined on President Nixon's enemies list.)

Commentator Helms may have surpassed himself in his coverage of Raleigh in *Viewpoint* No. 251. The editorial began as a paean to the Broughton Caps football team which had just brought home the State 4-A championship. But by the time he had finished his discourse, Helms had shifted from the playing field into his Sunday School classroom for the analogy of Joshua at battle of Jericho, and then to a plea that the high schoolers' aggressiveness be applied to the war against international communism.

"Whether I win or lose this election, I want to render to the people the service of ridding them of what I can only describe as a disgrace to the honorable profession of journalism."

Well, Congressman Harold Cooley lost that election in 1966 and later fell one vote short at the Federal Communications Commission in his effort to terminate the broadcasting license of WRAL-TV. But 25 years after the fact, what made the veteran chairman of the House Agriculture Committee so indignant?

Cooley and his opponent, a young fellow named Jim Gardner, had appeared in 1966 at a forum on the campus of N.C. State University.

Gardner's campaign obtained a tape of the proceedings, his public relations squad edited it down to resemble a head-to-head debate, and they put it on the airwaves. Cooley sounded terrible and looked like he needed a makeover from Brown-Wynne Mortuary. Gardner looked vigorous and well-informed.

Cooley said he was convinced that WRAL-TV had conspired with Gardner in editing the tape and putting it on the air.

Gardner remarked that "I wish that we had been able to show the entire two hours," because "Cooley looks bad from beginning to end."

As for Jesse Helms, he denied any role in editing the tape and said that Cooley was "knowingly tampering with the truth." Helms added that "if Mr. Cooley feels he flunked his screen test... it would have been more graceful for him to have chalked up the sad experience as a bad performance on his part and then sought to improve his public image."

Now for some truth. Gardner's people edited the tape not at WRAL, but at Channel 11 in Durham. WRAL in Raleigh *did* edit one tape for a candidate in the 1966 election, however. That candidate? Harold Cooley.

The ex-congressman pursued WRAL hard at the FCC. But in the Cooley collection in Chapel Hill, amidst a heap of depositions and memoranda about the N.C. State tape, is a note from Cooley's lawyer. He is trying to figure out what will happen if it becomes known that WRAL took a tape of Sam Ervin, Luther Hodges, Terry Sanford and Dan Moore and edited it down into a campaign commercial for Cooley. Without charge.

Cooley must not have thought that anyone would find out. He reasoned that Jesse Helms would be the last one to spill the beans. On that point, at least, the former chairman was correct.

The price of a free press.... In the late 1960s, the *N&O* ran a nondescript story about the suspension of the beverage license of a dive on Hillsborough Street named The Scene.

The article contained excerpts from testimony at an A.B.C. board hearing. They contained allegations of the sale of drugs near the premises and the immoral conduct of certain patrons in the club's parking lot. The club owner promptly sued the *N&O* for libel. He alleged that although the published excerpts were contained in the transcript, they had not been the basis for suspension of his beverage license.

The owner also objected that the *N&O* had failed to include in its story other testimony from the record which cast The Scene in a better light. (Note: who would want to see that club in anything but darkness?)

According to his attorney, the club owner was a prototypical graduate student at N.C. State. The value of his investment had been gutted by the *N&O*'s article, the lawsuit said. Three colleges had declared The Scene to be off-limits for their students, it said. (The schools denied it.) Business had turned lousy and no one wanted to buy the club, the complaint said.

The *N&O* backed its reporter and refused to apologize. The newspaper won the lawsuit at the earliest possible moment in U.S. District Court.

As the owner of The Scene began a series of unexpected appeals, the *N&O* repeated its victory at the second, third and fourth next earliest moments. The case lasted for years. The Scene ran out of appeals when the U.S. Supreme Court decided that it had more interesting arguments to hear.

What did the successful defense of the libel suit cost the *N&O*?

At the time, the *N&O*'s libel insurance contained a $10,000 deductible, so the newspaper paid that amount in legal fees. The insurance company picked up about $3,500 in additional costs. There is no documentation about what the lawsuit cost the plaintiff and the taxpayers.

And now for the latest murder-arson-stickup-abduction from... Fayetteville!"

If that seems increasingly like the content of WRAL-TV's news broadcasts, there may be a plausible explanation for it.

Thirty years ago, WRAL had a staff of about four news employees, yet it presented as many as seven live programs each weekday. Today, with more than ten times the people and a news budget estimated at $12 to $14 million, the station offers less coverage of Raleigh than it did in 1962.

What happened? Among other things, WRAL began to focus on Fayetteville, whose military personnel have turned into one of the largest viewing markets in North Carolina. But WRAL faced a problem: unless a television station is smack next to a military post, the TV ratings bureaus discount their audience estimates to exclude many personnel whom they regard as transient.

So the "Big Five" set up what is called a "local presence" in Cumberland County. Its intent was to bolster WRAL's claims for larger audiences, which in turn lead to higher advertising revenues, which can lease another helicopter to film in the station's next target. The effect was a watering down of coverage in the capital, where the station is licensed.

WRAL's move had some amusing results. Not long after it created the "local presence" to the south, an observer remarked that the station was showing so many fires in Fayetteville that the city must be in ashes. It developed that a correspondent paid by WRAL was also a rescue worker who used his portable camera when he responded to calls.

Of Hootch And Bawds And Chicken-Pecks, And Cards And Frolickings

Gambling, bootlegging, narcotics, prostitution, loansharking and payoffs – Raleigh had them all by 1800. The difference between 1800 and today is that back then, some of those activities had not been declared illegal, and all of them were more or less out in the open.

So how has Raleigh loved thee, Rhonda Sue Vice, over these last 200 years? Hang out that "Do Not Disturb" sign and let me count the ways.

If early Raleigh was not awash in whiskey, its newspapers certainly were confused.

The *Minerva* and the *Register* regularly inveighed against booze, calling it "the inlet of all evil" that could "turn Patriot into Beast." Many reports of crimes in the city included information about alcohol being an accessory before the fact.

(Not to give the newspapers unadulterated credit for taking the moral high ground: both accepted liquor advertising and both doled out drinks to State officials in their efforts to win the State printing contract. And their editors joined in drinking all of those toasts at public celebrations.)

Local citizens in 1800 formed a society called the "Ice Water Regulars" and staged alcohol-free outings reminiscent of efforts at today's high school proms.

But ideas about the treatment of alcoholism were, well, those of 1800. Other than an instant religious conversion, the most mentioned method of reforming a drunk was to dose him with enough opium so that he would float through a cold-turkey withdrawal.

Raleigh

As a new town in 1800 with only 669 residents, Raleigh's morals seem to have been about one step removed from those of a mining camp.

Bars stayed open until dawn; card games were available at all hours; brothels and streetwalkers operated without much interference; opium was one of the recreational drugs of choice; and the city did not have a church.

But beyond those failings, the early residents of Raleigh made their mark even when they were in their own homes.

The crime of bastardy was both rampant and well-documented. When what today are referred to as "births out of wedlock" occurred in the capital, an accused father could be hauled into court and placed under bond, which usually was $200. The same happened to mothers who declined to name their bed partners.

The city was propelled by a desire to keep illegitimate children "free and clear from becoming in any wise chargeable to the parrish." Courts had little patience with parents who fell behind in their child support payments.

(A man named Horatio Darley was held to be $15 in arrears, was jailed, was hired out by the county to work the roads, had all of his net pay assigned to his progeny, and was not released until he was two months ahead on his payments. He stayed in jail for more than a year.)

In several instances in early court records, more than one Raleigh lothario was bonded in connection with a single illegitimate birth. (Whether this was the mark of extraordinary friendship or reflected the absence of blood tests, or both, is not clear from the proceedings.) Local women also produced more than one illegitimate child from the same or different fathers.

The existence of bastardy cases in Raleigh is not as unusual as their frequency.

In the years surrounding 1800, Raleigh averaged more than 22 documented cases per 1,000 population per year of children born out of wedlock.

To begin to place this statistic into context, in the years since the State has kept track of birth rates, Wake County topped out in total live births at 26.8 per 1,000 population in 1954 and had a rate in 1990 of 16.4 total live births per thousand.

To place it further in context, the illegitimate births which can be documented from about 1800 are only those which resulted in a dispute and came to trial.

Further, no such births among blacks would have appeared in court dockets in 1800, because nearly every black in Raleigh was a slave. The children of slaves, whether born in or out of wedlock, were considered only as assets on the balance sheets of the city's slaveowners.

No, these bastardy cases were among white people, and that fact pushes the ratio up to nearly 40 contested cases per year per 1,000 freemen and freewomen.

Last, all of this activity took place on fewer acres than are contained in an average country club development.

How could she possibly have earned a living?... The *Raleigh Register* in 1800 printed an editorial describing a "slut" who inhabited one of the new city's whorehouses.

"She is all grease," the newspaper declared, "and I know not what use to put her to, but to make a lamp from her, and run from her by her own light. I warrant her rags, and the tallow in them, will burn a Poland winter. If she lives till Doom's-day, she'll burn a week longer than the whole world."

Raleigh was the center of the State's prohibition movement through the first part of the 19th century.

At one point, a new business opened on Fayetteville Street: the Temperance Hotel, where the owners converted their public house to one which served "only water and the most limpid refreshments."

Does this sound familiar?... Men who bought whiskey in the early days of Raleigh were required to wrap their purchases in paper before going out onto the street.

Although the capital's liquor merchants could sell on credit – a half-pint was the smallest amount – the Intendant had enough experience with arguments over hootch so that each citizen's credit was limited to $4 per month.

Twenty years before Legislator Robert Potter lost his last faro game as a public servant, a local newspaper posted the following warning in its editorial columns:

"*Gamblers.* You are cautioned not to appear in Raleigh during the insuing session of the Legislature, under pain of incurring the punishments which the law prescribes. Signed, A Magistrate."

A week later, the newspaper printed a similar advisory for "*Swindlers.*"

Describing a local campaign for sheriff in 1838, William A. Jeffreys chortled in a letter that the winner had used the right ammunition.

On election day, the candidate went to his opponent's headquarters and threw "a copious shower of cider barrels... jugs, decanters, black bottles, tumblers and wine glasses from the door of his office..." out into Fayetteville Street.

The exposed opponent, Jeffreys wrote, could only "ride up and down braying like a jackass."

"Every body who has smoked," the *Microcosm* editorialized in 1838, "can bear testimony to the fact that it produces dizziness, tremors, enervation, stupefaction, loss of appetite, indigestion...." The list went on until it reached "a reduced production of bile" and a jaundiced complexion.

The newspaper, in tones which the U.S. Surgeon General would use 140 years later, said that smoking "is deleterious to health and often shatters, if it does not entirely break down the constitution."

(These days it is the non-smoking ordinance which is accused of harming the Constitution.)

"This... would be loosening another screw in the machinery of married life, marring its operations, weakening its obligations, and producing discord and confusion, when peace and concord ought to reign."

Well, the State Supreme Court knew a fishy arrangement when it saw it. In this case, it was a wife-bartering deal in Raleigh in 1841.

The surnames of the litigants really do not matter. It is enough to say that it was the first time the Justices addressed the doctrine of the Dreaded Mother-in-Law, and as far as cases from Raleigh are concerned, nothing has happened since to surpass it.

The plot: Lucy had a daughter named Anna, who was married to John, who led "somewhat of an itinerant life." Lucy was also shacked up with a wealthy man to be called Westy; the two got along for years in Raleigh without a marriage license. In the summer of forty-one, Lucy and Westy conceived of a plan which would save Anna and her infant daughter from "perishing" with poor John, whom they thought was "lazy" and "did not provide for his family" as the Dreaded One thought he should.

Their idea was that Anna and her child should come to live with Lucy and Westy. John would be asked to sign away all rights to his family, and in return, Westy would promise to give the child a college education. John would be able to visit his wife and cohabit as often as he wanted, but no longer than four days at a time, because the Dreaded One did not want to be there when he came calling. And who Anna entertained in the house when John was not there was none of his business.

John signed the agreement. His wife and daughter disappeared into the wealthy man's house. From time to time, John would drop by and cohabit with Anna, and after a few years, he decided he wanted his wife and daughter back. Westy and the Dreaded One refused and both sides reached for their lawyers. The wife-barter arrangement was about to move into court, a distance of no more than three blocks.

The case would have made for salacious reading in the 1840s if any of Raleigh's newspapers had chosen to report it.

John sued Westy and his mother-in-law, charging that they had unlawfully enticed away his wife and stolen the benefits he should have received from her companionship and dowry. He was also concerned about what Westy might be doing with his wife and have in mind for his growing daughter. He asked for $3,000 in damages and delivery of his family.

The Wake County Superior Court, which at the time could usually be relied on to side with the privileged (well, the laws were stacked on the side of the privileged), ruled against husband John.

But the State Supreme Court took one look at the transaction and held that John had not entered into a valid contract. If anything, the Court said, John had given Westy "a license to harbor the wife and child" which John could revoke at his pleasure.

Holding that damages were appropriate, the Court ordered a new trial. It had been eight years since Anna and daughter had moved to the big house.

There are several ways in which a modern researcher can react to the absence of any record of the new trial ordered by the Supreme Court. One way is to assume that the parties reached an out-of-court settlement, but county documents should still contain a notice of remand. Another way is to chalk it up to the incompetence of the Wake County courthouse, which in 1849 did not bother even to index its minutes.

But the best way is to reflect on the information which is available and to let the matter rest. As CP&L Chairman Sherwood Smith once said, there may not always be a solution to every problem, but there is an outcome.

Mrs. Lucy Bryan's letters from 1851 provide a snapshot of alcohol abuse among Raleigh's well-to-do in that era. (So do the minutes of the Superior Court, but in less vivid detail.)

"Old Tom _____ is in the land of the living and drinks as much liquor as he can hold," she wrote about one of the city's patriarchs. She added that his son "furnishes a house and servants for the old scamp," who had gone so far around the bend that he no longer chased women.

Of a local dowager, who thought that she would not survive a hangover, Mrs. Bryan recounted that "Old Mrs. ___ gave all the directions about being buried, where she was to be buried, and what in, and sent for a woman to come and shroud her. Then the old lady got better."

R aleigh is the worst place for boys that I ever knew," Mrs. Bryan wrote in 1852.

"The majority of men are of the meanest sort – they will entice William (her son) to drink and gamble – some are fathers themselves – there is a number of eating establishments that are bad places for young men."

Her concerns about her 16-year-old son were overstated: William needed no enticing at all.

Mrs. Bryan in another letter confided that her son had taken to getting drunk on weekday afternoons, but that after being confronted, he had taken the pledge. "Please do not mention this," she wrote, "as William would be mortified."

During the State Fairs of the 1870s, roulette wheels and other games of chance were licensed by the Fair managers, but "skin" games were run off after the first account of their presence hit the newspapers.

Raleigh's bars operated 24 hours a day, seven days a week while the Fair was in town. The *Sentinel* reported in 1874 that "saloons were three deep at night with frantic calls for the beverage...."

The prohibition forces tried a new tactic in 1874, asking voters to close the city's saloons for one year as an experiment.

Raleigh, they said, had been "cursed by licensed dram-shops" since 1795 (a neat distinction, since before the city was chartered, the saloons needed no licenses), and a one-year shutdown would be "for the good of the rum-ridden majority."

The arguments that year continue to resonate. To the objection that "prohibition has been a failure" when tried, the drys said that "there is, of course, no statute law which is not sometimes violated. The real question involved is 'What are the results?'"

Charging that liquor caused most of the "pauperism" and crime in the city, the drys had no use for the claims that prohibition would cause the city to lose $4,500 in annual license revenue and that "sixty business houses... will be made vacant." Their retort had a kick in it:

"One hundred men will be thrown out of employment if Prohibition succeeds, they say. Alas, how many have you not only thrown out of employment, but out of decent society and irretrievably ruined in the last twelve months?"

On referendum day the drys lost again.

If the presence of homeless people on the 100 block of Fayetteville Street causes an image problem today, Raleigh had concerns on that block as far back as 1877, not counting the legendary mud, dust and gunplay.

How sophisticated could it have looked for two merchants to stage a rooster fight in mid-block at 11 a.m., even if the squawking, clawing birds did attract a crowd which virtually emptied the downtown businesses?

(Cockfights were a local tradition. The *Observer* proudly announced a contest in the spring of 1877 between roosters from the two Carolinas, "21 cocks the show, $1,000 the main and $50 the battle.")

How dignified did it look to have runaway steers charging down the street? Or nearly a dozen runaway horses and wagons, as were reported in 1877? Or men gathered in the 100 block willing to gamble on whether one horse might outrun another if they unhitched them and fired a pistol?

And once visitors avoided the livestock and made it safely into the Capitol, what did they find there?

"It is very wrong," the *Observer* chided in 1877, "for boys to play cards on the dome of the Capitol, when they are so kindly permitted by Col. Turner to visit as often as they please."

Of politics and liquor... In 1877, prohibitionists lost another referendum to close down Raleigh's many saloons.

The strategy of the "wets" closely resembles those which are ascribed to "Landslide" Lyndon Johnson and others during this century.

"The Prohibitionists entered immediately into the battle," wrote the *Observer* about election day, "and did a good work polling their entire vote at the outset. That was also their downfall, because the 'Wets' or 'License' men held back, and patiently awaited to see what amount of votes they would need to offset the votes already cast on the dry side."

They had their target before noon. Then, "the Oberlin delegation," described as "about 50 able-bodied colored voters," appeared at the courthouse and voted as a bloc for continued saloons. (Both saloon jurisdiction and voting extended outside the corporate limits.)

Crowing about the results, which were 1,248 to 480, one pub owner on Fayetteville Street told the pastor of the First Baptist Church, "they pray mit you, but they drink mit me."

There was one cigar left in the box," the *Observer* reported in 1878, "and there were two young hopefuls struggling for it."

According to the newspaper, "the first little boy clutched it, but he said consoling to his brother, 'Never mind, Dick. I'll smoke on it till I get sick, and then you can finish it.' And the heart of the other little boy was comforted."

Raleigh's *laissez faire* outlook toward gambling – except from the pulpit, where a few ministers questioned even their own churches' fundraising methods – may have seemed over in 1886 with a high-stakes raid on Fayetteville Street.

Miller's was an establishment which offered liquor, wine, beer, cigars, billiards, a lunch and dinner buffet, and a few other extras which eventually bothered the authorities. It was located, as Judge Walter Clark described it, "next door to the principal hotel in the capital of the State, and immediately opposite to the United States courthouse and post office, and under the very shadow of this court house."

Miller's was painted a "glaring red," was "brilliantly lighted with the electric lamp," and according to Judge Clark, "no means (were) left unemployed to make it attractive to the unwary." (Including card games, roulette and dice.)

As he was handing down a sentence on the proprietor, Clark described Miller's as a profitable enough business so that its owner had bought the premises for $13,000 and advertised on the front page of the *N&O*. (On appeal, Miller protested that he owed a mortgage.)

In a plea bargain, Miller pleaded guilty to one out of five counts of running a gambling house (the gaming rooms were upstairs and Miller took a percentage). Clark then shocked him by fining him $2,000 and giving him the maximum 30 days in jail for that single count.

As the State Supreme Court later put it in rejecting Miller's appeal, Judge Clark had the discretion to levy almost any fine he saw fit.

It seems that Miller's defense attorney had stated in court that his client was "a person of means," and although the lawyer had made the remark in an effort to get Miller's bail reduced, Clark seized on it. Further, Clark said, "no expression of an intent to discontinue his illegal business came from him" or the lawyer. Clark decided to make Miller an example.

He justified the fine by saying that a smaller sum "would have no effect on the defendant. He would make it back again in a few nights."

Clark added that "some one has said that the old-fashioned way of stopping a man on the highway and with a loaded pistol demanding his money was more honorable than this modern way of stripping one of it without an equivalent, for the highwayman at least risked his person to obtain his booty. But the Court is not called upon to pass on that question."

With that, "probably the most elegantly furnished and handsomely equipped bar in the State" went out of business.

Former Governor W.W. Holden wrote Judge Clark in praise, remarking that "for months and months that foul gambling house has glared upon the main street of our city, inviting young and old men to bankruptcy, desperation and ruin...."

The gambling, of course, moved around the corner.

Students of prohibition might reflect on what happened in Raleigh when liquor was banned by a 60-vote majority in 1886.

Although arrests for various stages of drunkenness did diminish (drunk and disorderly; drunk on the streets; drunk and down; drunk in the Market; drunk in the Capitol; drunk on Sunday) from about 300 per year to about 150, the police chief reported that "the people of the city have been more bellicose during the past year than the year before."

Nor had liquor consumption ceased. When they were granted several weeks to close out their affairs after the referendum, the city's liquor dealers "offered their wares at low prices."

According to the mayor, "all who desired to so purchase and were able to do so, supplied themselves just before the law took effect with much larger quantities than they were accustomed to keeping on hand. Doubtless there was a great deal of treating done by them after the law was in operation."

The mayor said that "there have been some clear evasions of the ban" – he singled out unneeded prescriptions which were issued by pharmacies – and that there were still barrooms "within two miles of the Capitol" but outside of the city limits. However, he said that Prohibition's effect had been "salutary for day laborers and blacks."

Prohibiting the sale of liquor in Raleigh also had an unintended consequence: "Gambling," complained the mayor, "cannot be suppressed and vice is now on the increase."

(All of the city's laws pertaining to gambling had focused on businesses which allowed card games where liquor was sold. With no more liquor sales, there was no control over gaming until the city applied for help from the next General Assembly.)

Raleigh's chief of police cited the gambling traffic when he asked for funds to hire detectives. He said that he could not recruit enough informers because "the service is considered very dangerous."

Within a year of the ban, arrests for drunkenness in Raleigh had not only rebounded, but they exceeded those made when the city still had all its saloons.

Raleigh's first experiment with Prohibition ended on July 2, 1888, two years after it had begun. On that afternoon, city hall issued 24 licenses for saloons. It appears that all of them opened at the stroke of midnight.

In 1893, the city's liquor dealers petitioned the city board and asked them to investigate drug stores and groceries which were acting as fronts for whiskey merchants outside of the corporate limits. The dealers had trouble matching the low prices of the moonshiners, whose product smelled so "mean" that a section of Wilmington Street was known as "Cologne."

If Miller's was the pinnacle of vice in Raleigh during the last century, its lowest common denominator may have been a person arrested in the 1890s:

"His place of business is back of the Soldier's Home," a newspaper report read. "He has for a long time been a sort of peripatetic saloon, walking around with his pocket full of whiskey bottles, selling it by the drink to whomsoever cared to buy. Now he is in the county jail."

One person's entertainment in the capital has on occasion looked like another person's concept of vice.

In 1905, the Rev. Whitaker was discussing games of chance at the State Fair, which had been deplored for the umpteenth consecutive year. Whitaker startled his congregation by remarking that gambling was only natural at the Fair, because "in order to popularize our State Fair it was necessary to make it up as nearly as possible after the model which modern society is molded."

The minister then trained his remarks at Raleigh mothers, who with "progressive euchre, whist and other games are learning their children to gamble" as well as "how to sip punch and guzzle champagne."

Whitaker expanded beyond bad maternal influences, however.

He noted that "in church festivals, when they introduce fish-ponds, grab bags, dice throwing and other games of chance," members were "filling the minds of children with the idea of getting something for nothing."

Continuing in this vein, Whitaker said that in some Raleigh churches at the turn of the century, "a pile of biscuits would sell at twenty-five cents each because it was known that one of them contained a five-dollar gold piece." (The author has bitten into biscuits which only had the *consistency* of ones with metal centers, but without any money.)

The Rev. Whitaker concluded his homily by recommending an amendment in the text of the Lord's Prayer.

"Lead us not into temptation," he said his version would go, "except in certain cases wherein we have educational interests, and wherein, also, the mothers are becoming gamblers and punch guzzlers for society's sake."

No records could be found of the proceeds of his church's next fundraiser.

Raleigh was selling whiskey out of a dispensary on Exchange Place when Carrie Nation bustled through town in 1907 and managed to offend the city's establishment in just 36 hours.

By the time she appeared in Raleigh, Nation was no longer chopping up saloons with an axe. Instead, she sold souvenir hatchet lapel pins at a quarter apiece. But her rhetoric did not seem to have lost any punch and she saw her targets with clarity.

The dispensary, voted in after so many years of struggle, was "a regular hell-hole," she began. "And these goody-goody church people put it here – so good that the devil loves them."

She singled out several Raleigh men who worked there, including a popular Sunday School teacher, and accused them of being participants in the evil of merchandising liquor.

"If that Snellings ain't a mean hypocrite," she said, "he acts like one." Nation lobbied in two speeches at Pullen Park for prohibition in the capital.

But Carrie Nation spent more time in Raleigh assailing perceived vices other than alcohol: dancing, the Masons, pool rooms, and her new enemy, the sacrosanct cigarette.

Of dance classes ("Or hugging schools, I call them," she said), Nation proclaimed that "I warn all boys against marrying ball room girls. I tell them if the girls practice hugging strange men before marriage they are likely to have the same taste afterwards."

The Masonic orders made Nation's list of vices because of their secrecy, which she found at odds with Biblical prescriptions for marriage. "A Mason swears to know something all his life that he will not tell his wife," she warned.

Lewis' pool hall on Fayetteville Street drew her ire because it had a "perfectly nude female" portrait hanging on one wall.

She wondered aloud to Raleigh audiences why Mr. Lewis did not get his own wife or daughter to pose for the odalisque.

But smoking was her fixation in 1907. Speaking of a recent hailstorm which shredded tobacco crops west of Raleigh, Nation said that "when I see a field of tobacco, I always pray to God to send a storm or something to smash it up."

Calling the American Tobacco Company "a regular cancer," Nation noted that "by the way, they are building a memorial church now to old man Duke. I say they ought to put a memorial window in that church made of Bull Durham tobacco and Durham's Mixture."

Somewhere along the line, the *N&O* had enough. In its news reports, it said that "Nation dealt out a lot of big talk, sense and nonsense," and that "one reaches the conclusion that she is a nonentity."

The newspaper waited until she had left town to print those words. It also reported that the hated Raleigh Electric Company had paid Nation a $35 appearance fee – the utility figured on recouping the honorarium with streetcar fares out to Pullen Park – and estimated her take from the hatchet-pin sales.

Nation left Raleigh with a final request that boxing promoter Don King could not have phrased better: "I want you to agitate and hatchetate," she said.

Raleigh's saloons in 1908 were absolutely, positively required to close at 5 a.m.

Although they were forbidden to do business of any kind on Sunday, many opened at 12:01 a.m. on Monday in order to ply their trade until daybreak.

Raleigh

Public hangings were not the only customs to disappear from Raleigh in 1908. That May, the State adopted prohibition.

The *Raleigh Times* lamented that "the Old North State is now scheduled to become the 'toddyless Sahara' for which the prohibition forces have long labored." Raleigh itself had voted 771 dry to 694 wet.

Two days after the election, the *Times* gleefully revealed that two ostensibly sober citizens had been arrested for gambling on the referendum. One was "a sanctificationist" who had been "so confident the right would prevail in the election Tuesday that he was ready to back his judgment. He gave odds, it is said, of two to one."

(And he was bound over for trial for $100. It was a contrast from the election of 1898, when the *N&O* used its front page to encourage betting on that outcome.)

"The present generation," an observer wrote in 1930, "has scant conception of the situation which existed in Raleigh 45 or 50 years ago.

"Vice flourished in forms which would be tolerated no-where today. Streets there were in the heart of the city down which no woman would walk and preserve a stainless name," he continued.

"There were from 30 to 40 licensed saloons; a grog shop for less than every 300 of population. These places were open on Sunday and their hours were still unrestricted."

"The ladies as a rule truly ran away if they saw us coming."

That may be what the commandant of Camp Polk experienced during World War I, but he had obviously run into the wrong ladies.

Camp followers were arrested for prostitution at the Giersch, Belmont and Yarborough hotels. At the Yarborough, Federal officers handcuffed a "noted aviatrix" in her hotel room with five soldiers.

They escorted her back to New Jersey, where she faced a morals charge even worse.

Acting in concert, the U.S. Department of Justice, military police and the city police divided wartime Raleigh into "vice zones" and conducted regular raids throughout 1918, until the camp closed.

The time: the Roaring Twenties. The place: 229 East Martin Street, the home of the Raleigh Cafe. The crime: operating a den of iniquity.

The Raleigh Cafe must have been quite a joint. In its eating room downstairs, a patron could listen to a stream of profanity from the owners as he watched sundry sleazy characters walk to the rear of the restaurant. In the back room, he could get a drink, place a bet, or make an assignation for one of the dozen or so prostitutes who rented the rooms upstairs.

Out front, in case the patron did not like the accommodations upstairs, he and his "date" could take any of a series of taxicabs which ferried customers to and from the establishment. Then came the raid.

"I made my living like all other sporting girls," said one of eight witnesses who turned State's evidence in return for a *nol pros* on charges of prostitution.

One of her co-workers testified that the flavor of the language in the eating room was so pungent that she would not repeat it in front of the decent people on the jury. She made her point, as did six other hookers.

One of the cafe's owners, trying to get off the hook, turned on the others and swore that he had been bamboozled and had no idea about the activities in the cafe. He was as stunned as the jury, he maintained.

In turning down his appeal after the jury refused to believe his alibi, the State Supreme Court observed that "... he could not help but know (not being a blind man) the character of the women and the character of the place the partnership was engaged in running."

Each owner received six months on the county roads for running their operation wide open for nearly two years.

Dr. Wilmoth Carter of Shaw University recounted that "the whites had their red light district on one side of the street there where Crosby-Garfield (school was in the 1930s), and the colored had theirs as close to them as they could get, the reason being that they could get more money out of white men."

In 1954, the *Raleigh Times* took occasion to compliment the refurbished Nash Square downtown, and in the process it disclosed more about the square's prior condition than it had in years of news stories.

"Not long ago," an editor wrote, "the winos ruled unhindered and the ladies of the night openly plied their trades once shadows fell over the oaks. It was almost worth one's life to negotiate the park after nightfall."

The newspaper wrote that before the city installed lights, "hoodlums and shady ladies completely took over and used the square for public display of their law-defying nocturnal antics."

Those people simply fell behind the curve of urban development.

Changes in Nash Square made doing business there difficult for all but the stalwart rats. Between the lights and the new municipal building, the relocation of the bus and train stations, and the razing of several hotels, the square not only lost its ambiance for vice, but also much of its clientele. Once again, the vice simply moved.

(Nash Square, incidentally, had a long tradition for sowing oats. The *Observer* in 1877 fretted that if a broken culvert in the square were not repaired, it would "drown the city oat crop" which was grown in the square to feed the city's workhorses.)

The operators of two alleged bawdy houses last night said they were closed. One said she and her girls were going to the beach."

What precipitated that *N&O* report in 1940 was a discourse by Dr. Carl V. Reynolds, director of the State Board of Health, that Raleigh cathouses were the source of more than 40 percent of North Carolina's recent cases of venereal disease.

(Only Fayetteville, with its vice emporiums which flanked Fort Bragg, exceeded the capital's record. Fayetteville's newspapers were amused when the U.S. Army, in possession of Dr. Reynolds' report, threatened to make Raleigh off-limits for soldiers or else to install condom dispensaries and station military police on the city's streets.)

Dr. Reynolds placed the blame on the Raleigh police department for what he called an "indifferent attitude" toward prostitution. The *N&O* concurred, calling for the "substitution of action for alibis" by police and observing that "members of the Raleigh police force are neither blind nor deaf. Few of them are dumb, either literally or figuratively ... but they can be said to be good at waiting."

Police chief J. Bryan Winder defended the city's honor. He claimed that "not a week passes without some prostitutes being apprehended" in the capital. He accused Dr. Reynolds of being "on a crusade" and suggested that the physician was complicit because he had not revealed the locations of the v.d. dens.

Chief Winder was not Dr. Reynolds' only critic. A second city madam, announcing that she was going out of business after 29 years at the same location, said that she was "greatly embarrassed" and denied that her girls had spread any disease. And, she added, "I have enough health certificates to plaster the doctor's house."

A special grand jury got into the act. It concluded only that the police should "go after (a) the clandestine, independent white woman streetwalker

Raleigh

and (b) the colored women operating out of the small houses in certain sections of the city."

Chief Winder went after the clapboard houses first, raiding five establishments one night and arresting six females. He blamed media publicity for the fact that three houses were empty when his officers stormed them.

Dr. Reynolds credited that same publicity for the fact that the incidences of venereal disease soon dropped off in the capital.

Today the fire of law must sometimes be applied to the Sodoms and Gomorrahs that have sprung up along our highways."

With that explanation, Judge R. Hunt Parker – the future Chief Justice of the N.C. Supreme Court – sentenced a man in Raleigh to two years on the roads for operating 5,258 illegal slot machines. The sentencing ended the court term in 1940 in which Judge Parker disposed of more than 500 cases involving the capital's dirty linen, ranging from gambling and prostitution to tax evasion and election rigging.

Up until Judge Parker ordered his machines smashed, Joseph Calcutt had a lucrative business. He paid taxes on income of more than $4.5 million from the slots, of which some 600 were in Raleigh, for the years 1937, 1938 and 1939. He also paid the State Department of Revenue more than $105,000 for licenses on the slots. After the department pocketed the money, the state prosecuted Calcutt for altering the machines so that they violated the anti-gambling Flannagan Act.

(Calcutt had used some of his proceeds to lobby the legislature to weaken the state's laws on prohibiting one-armed bandits. In one session alone, he spent today's equivalent of $84,000 to influence legislation – at least that was the amount he reported.)

In handing down his sentence, Judge Parker declared that Calcutt "shall not...directly or indirectly, in any way, form, shape or manner ...either through himself or anyone else...have anything to do with politics in the State of North Carolina for three years." (Parker's wording touched so many bases that the State Supreme Court reversed his decision because it deprived Calcutt of rights of citizenship for what, after all, were misdemeanors.)

How big was the slots business in Raleigh during the Depression?

Besides Calcutt, other local entrepreneurs held licenses for an additional 489 machines. Using Calcutt's confessed revenues as a gauge, Raleigh's slot machine industry would have taken in today's equivalent of more than $5 million per year.

And how pervasive was the gamblers' influence? At one point in Calcutt's trial, Judge Parker learned that the defendant was operating slot

Raleigh

machines in Fayetteville even as he was standing before the bench in Wake Superior Court.

Parker ordered the courtroom sealed and telephoned the State Bureau of Investigation, which descended immediately on roadhouses in Cumberland County which contained as many as 100 machines each.

By the time the raiders arrived – less than a half-hour later, with Judge Parker's courtroom still locked – all the machines had vanished. Eyewitnesses reported that they had been hauled away by people using trucks, cars and even wheelbarrows.

Our Special Guests

If a state capital should by all rights be the center of dealmaking, Raleigh sewed up the prize back in 1792.

Consider the coup of Joel Lane, "the father of Raleigh," who sold the State land for the city at a time when conflict of interest was an infant theory.

Lane sold his property in a negotiated rather than a competitive sale, but that was not unusual because the State was comparing several different tracts within 10 miles of Isaac Hunter's tavern. Neither was it unusual that Lane was a prominent planter.

But Lane was also a State Senator, and if that situation was not sticky enough, he also happened to have been the State's land agent.

It was Lane who entertained the site purchase committee late into the night at his plantation the night before the selection. (To deflect persistent reports that Lane got the committee drunk, historians have tried to point out how early the committee members arose the next morning and how far they traveled on horseback.)

But Lane may not have needed to lubricate the committee; he had at least one ringer on it, Willie Jones. And so he was able to adjust his asking price after the members ate and drank at his home, likely with full knowledge of other sellers' positions.

After the successful sale, Lane helped to steer desirable Raleigh lots to influential political insiders, including members of the site committee. He even loaned money to some so they could effect their purchases and did not press them for repayment. Lane also sent slaves to work for committee members free of charge. And he obtained a buyback option on a portion of

Raleigh

the land which he could exercise at a future date if he perceived that it would be profitable.

All in all, it was a resourceful start for the center of North Carolina politics. It is certain that if the process were duplicated today – say, on the proposed state air cargo complex – grand juries would hear presentments on the subject.

As a result of the sale and rumors around North Carolina that it was rigged, bad-mouthing Raleigh became an immediate pastime in 1792. But shenanigans do have their pluses: if the land purchase had been played straight from the beginning, Fayetteville might have been the capital, a result too horrid to contemplate. Not every state Capitol has to overlook a river.

The original State-House, which students from Broughton High School early in this century described as resembling a "dog kennel," had its detractors even in the 1800s.

It was "a large building of brick and wood where the present capitol so majestically stands," one historian wrote, with "no ornaments to relieve its huge ugliness."

The State-House "was used for a variety of purposes," the essay continued, "and when not graced with the assembled wisdom, was a house of worship on the Sabbath, and a theatre or ball-room during the week."

(The Capitol was also home to trapezes and high-wire artists. By the time it burned in 1831, observers were convinced that the structure would have fallen in of its own accord a few years later.)

Not only were blacks, women and those with low incomes discriminated against in early Raleigh, but so were those to whom society referred as The Unfortunates.

Take orphans, for instance; those who were lucky enough to inherit property had tiers of law to protect them and guardians to channel their assets into circulation. But orphans who were poor or had no near relatives were regarded as a burden to the taxpayer.

Such orphans were sold by the Superior Court into apprentice bondage until they reached at least the age of 21 years. They then were given six dollars and "a suit of cloathes" and turned loose into the world. Most were hired out for $500.

Enough court records survive to show that Raleigh's apprentices were promised training in some trade. "The Art and Mistery of planting and farming" was popular. Masters also pledged to teach their hirelings how to read and write.

But in some apprentice bonds from early Raleigh, the masters undertook no obligation other than to furnish food, shelter and the most basic garments. William Boylan, for instance, simply did not fill in the blank on the State form in which he was supposed to promise to make his apprentices literate. (He may have assumed that working on a newspaper would accomplish that task.)

Apprentices were also subject to lawful beatings by their masters. (One apprentice from Raleigh named Andrew Johnson ran away from his master and ended up as President of the United States.)

The other major group of Unfortunates consisted of the mentally ill.

In the days prior to what is now Dorothea Dix hospital, these people were housed in the Fayetteville Street jail or else at the county Poor-House unless they were hidden from view by a relative or some understanding parishioner like William Boylan.

At the jail, the mentally ill were housed in one of four "apartments;" the possible combinations of inmates is boggling.

Each apartment in the "gaol" was exclusive: the Criminals' Room; the Debtors' Room; the White Female Prisoners' Room; and the Negroes' Room. The last was a dungeon which was equipped with chains.

Like any other prisoners, the mentally ill – one cannot call them patients, because they received no treatment – were expected to supply their own clothes and bedding and received each day "a pound of wholesome bread, one pound of good roasted or boiled flesh," and water.

Those who managed to avoid the jail fared somewhat better at the Poor-House. There, they were required to work on the profit-making county farm, where one of the cash crops was a plant known as cannabis. But at least they received some fresh air and the therapeutic effects of gardening.

Thirty-five years before the State-House burned, local bigwigs were at a party at Peter Casso's tavern when "a negro announced that burglars were forcing an entrance in to the State-House."

The felons were seeking to steal or set fire to records in order to conceal what became the James Glasgow land fraud. A slave of one of the conspirators was captured and hanged.

Rather than getting the rope himself, Secretary of State Glasgow suffered the ignominy of seeing his name stricken by the General Assembly from the county which since then has been named Greene.

Raleigh

Planned Parenthood is by no means the first organization to try to assume a role in the development of families in Raleigh.

In 1800, the General Assembly thought that relations between the sexes were so estranged that it took up a bill "for the further taxation of bachelors, and to forward the population of the State by encouraging and promoting matrimony."

At the time, Raleigh had about 85 families "and an equal number of bachelors." The city's bachelors already paid property taxes which were four times those of married men. (So much for complaining about a "marriage penalty" in post-Colonial tax codes.)

Despite all these encouragements, urban growth continued to lag in the city and would not accelerate until the next wave of immigration from Europe.

Debate over whether to build a penitentiary in Raleigh may have started early, but the original arguments have a contemporary tone.

In 1802, Representative Henry Seawell of Raleigh argued against spending any money for a prison.

"The man who undergoes the ignominious punishment of a Prisoner under the abject bondage of a Master," he told his colleagues in the House of Commons, "will... lose all the finer features of his nature and be rendered unfit for society. This institution would therefore create a new order of beings."

Seawell was a conservative. One of his fellow members agreed that the $300 which was proposed for a study of the prison was inappropriate.

"You propose to lavish it on criminals," he told the sponsor of the appropriation, "while the forming walls of your unfinished college buildings, which you have deserted and neglected, stand to reproach you."

Another opponent said that supporters of the prison were deluding themselves if they thought that the institution would be self-supporting. (Connecticut had built its first prison atop a lead mine and was turning a profit from convict labor.)

"All who calculate on it being a source of profit," Calvin Jones said, "are assuredly preparing disappointment for themselves. They will awake from their illusion when they see crime and taxes multiply together."

The bill's sponsor, not willing to be portrayed as a coddler of criminals, pointed out that his penitentiary bill did "not propose a plan for the reformation of convicts." Rep. J.G. Wright also acknowledged that although North Carolina lacked lead deposits such as Connecticut's, our prisoners could manufacture shoes and thus reduce imports from other states.

Raleigh

With that remark, the debate turned to whether the use of convict labor would amount to unfair competition for North Carolina's businessmen. The bill was defeated.

One of North Carolina's original three justices of the State Supreme Court, Samuel Spencer of Anson County, became renowned in Raleigh as a polygamist. After he retired, Judge Spencer became further renowned when he died from injuries he received when he was attacked by a wild turkey.

Others have lost more money, but the bicentennial award for Unluckiest Contractor goes to William Bragg, whose breakfast was spoiled as he watched the State-House go up in smoke in 1831.

Hired by the Legislature to renovate the State-House and to plate its roof in order to "render the same fire proof," Bragg was "at the eve of completing it in a very masterly manner, perhaps unequalled by any undertaking of a similar kind in the United States." His work would have been finished "in a few hours," wrote the committee which heard testimony on the origin of the blaze.

Whether the fire was caused by one of Bragg's subcontractors who admitted carrying hot coals onto the roof between two wooden shingles, or by a soldering pot which overheated the planks beneath the new zinc roof, or was the "act of an incendiary which we have no evidence," the committee never concluded.

But the legislators did conclude how they wanted to treat Bragg.

Aside from reimbursing him his $2,000 performance bond – a gesture which was conditioned upon Bragg's waiving all rights to any other payments – the Assembly paid Bragg "the sum which he has expended for materials used in covering the Capitol lately destroyed by fire; but he should not be paid the full sum specified in the contract, nor shall he be paid for the skills, labour or attention bestowed in the performance of the work."

(It could have been worse. The investigating committee had recommended paying Bragg "the value of the work as it was received" – that is, nothing.)

Out of all the problems created by the 1831 fire at the Capitol, many citizens in Raleigh focused first on the loss of Canova's statue of George Washington.

Raleigh

The State-House had scarcely quit smoldering when the Legislature was handed a "Report Relative to the Statue...."

"Limited in their means," the report described North Carolinians, "plain in their habits, and economical in their expenditures, on this one subject they had indulged a generous magnificence."

The report urged the State Treasurer to write a check payable to Mr. Ball Hughes, who promised for $5,000 to restore the statue so that it would be "perfect, durable and with all its original grandeur and elegance." (Hughes lit out with the money and fragments of the never-restored artwork.)

The legislative panel, encouraged by Raleigh proponents, murmured that the Canova work "bade (even) the most thoughtless and inattentive to inquire and reflect."

(More than thoughtless people had cause to reflect when they first glimpsed George in his toga, and what they thought they often kept to themselves.)

(In his journal for 1823, the Rev. John Ravenscroft observed that the statue "would answer better for any of the Roman consuls – being neither a likeness (of Washington) in features or in Costume – the Carolinians however very touchy on this point.")

Citizens in Raleigh held Fayetteville in low regard long before the sleaze strips, used car lots and pawn shops appeared there as a consequence of Fort Bragg.

(And to be fair, by ignoring the advice of every city planner since A.C. Hall in the 1950s, Raleigh's city council has approved so much strip development that the arteries leading into the capital look strikingly like those in Cumberland County.)

When Fayetteville tried to become the capital in 1791, its advocates predicted that Raleigh would never become more than a "catchpenny village" – that is, a low-rent clip joint. Local residents had put those comments aside when the media in Fayetteville refreshed their memories in 1831, immediately after the State-House burned.

In words which were less than sympathetic toward Raleigh's loss, the *North Carolina Journal* wrote that the blaze "has awakened a keen hope" that the capital would move to the banks of the Cape Fear River.

"The opinion of a very numerous and intelligent portion of the citizens of the state," wrote the newspaper, "has constantly been expressed in favor of Fayetteville."

High-minded politicians from Cumberland and adjacent counties set

Raleigh

about to secure the votes needed to block appropriations to rebuild the Capitol in Raleigh. They agreed to support an amendment to the State Constitution which would give western North Carolina more equal representation in the General Assembly. In return, Fayetteville demanded that the westerners back its bid to supplant Raleigh.

Equally high-minded politicians from Raleigh tried to encourage the Legislature to remain there. They used incentives such as reduced rates at rooming houses, free meals and liquor, and compliant women. (It must have been a glorious time to be a legislator.)

Fayetteville's attempts to barter democracy nearly succeeded.

Before authorization was passed to rebuild in Raleigh, pro-Fayetteville members won two votes outright and lost others by small margins.

In the opinion of Raleigh citizens, Fayetteville had not only been tasteless in seeking to take advantage of the fire, but it had been graceless in defeat. At the close of the debate, the *Journal* in Fayetteville had predicted what would happen if Raleigh remained the capital:

"North Carolina," the editor wrote, "will have then sealed her own condemnation to poverty, and her renunciation of political consequence for many, many years."

One of Raleigh's cherished anecdotes in the 19th century was told by Governor Zebulon B. Vance.

Writing about one of his predecessors, Vance said that a certain North Carolina governor had ridden from Raleigh to South Carolina to attempt to negotiate a border dispute.

When he arrived, the governor told his counterpart that "I am tired and sleepy and hungry and sober." The governor of South Carolina said that he could remedy all of those ailments and the two sat down on the veranda with a jug of whiskey. They fell asleep in the afternoon sun.

When North Carolina's governor awoke, he looked into the disapproving eyes of South Carolina's First Lady and muttered, "It's a damn long time between drinks" before reaching again for the jug. With that, she brought all conviviality to an end.

"Yes, the Governor of South Carolina had a wife," Vance would recall, "as all good Governors should have, on the principle of the old maxim that he who aspires to govern should first learn to obey."

Someone in 1833 took the trouble to classify the 199 members of that year's Legislature.

Raleigh

All were men, of course, with 147 married and 52 single. As for occupations, 145 were farmers, 31 were lawyers, seven were merchants, six were physicians, six were unemployed, two were blacksmiths, one was a tailor and one a tavern-keeper.

An all-night card game in Raleigh on Christmas, 1834 ended the career of a man who, it is hoped, was the State's most unusual legislator.

Rep. Robert Potter, at the time the freeholders of Granville County reelected him to the House of Commons, was a convict. In a petition to unseat him, his disgruntled opponents described Potter as a "person of wicked and malicious disposition."

The petitioners may have had a point; among other offenses, Potter was behind bars for castrating an "aged and feeble" minister and his 16-year old relative. Potter excused his action by asserting that the two had been sleeping with his wife while he was down in Raleigh representing the public interest.

Although he should have killed the younger one outright, Potter said, he had chosen a different "punishment" because he thought that "the eunuch and whoremaster" would keep quiet.

(Who knows what the voters of Oxford hoped Potter would do in trimming the State budget? His indictment had begun, "With a certain knife, which he... in his right hand, then and there held....")

Able to be elected but unable to serve if he remained a convicted felon, Potter wangled a pardon from Governor David L. Swain. The Governor also sought to keep Potter alive long enough for the session to begin.

"It has lately been suggested to me," Swain wrote, "that in the present highly excited state of the public mind, tranquility may be promoted by dispensing with the condition regarding (Potter's) appearing in person" in Oxford to pay a fine.

The House met in Raleigh to hear the anti-Potter petitions.

They included references to "inhumane and savage treatment" and other allegations that Potter had married "for the sake of money or property" and his wife had had to look elsewhere for companionship.

Potter, however, claimed that he had exercised restraint: "Do I live in a community," he wrote his constituents, "which places a higher value upon the blood... upon the carcase of a man, *than upon the purity of the marriage bed? Good God!*"

The House of Commons threw out the petitions. It said that "as relates to the moral disqualifications of the sitting member, it would be a dangerous

Raleigh

precedent for this House to vacate the seat of a member upon such grounds... There is no standard of moral excellence, and if it is once admitted that we have a right to go into such inquiries, when are we to stop?"

Indeed. Which brings Rep. Potter, on the prowl in Raleigh, to a faro game which opened at 6 p.m. on Christmas Day in a rented room on Morgan Street.

Potter swiftly lost $40 to Raleigh gamblers. Upset, he insisted that the game continue while he rounded up some more money. He soon returned and resumed losing until by morning, his funds were gone – an estimated $2,800 in current money.

Potter then "snatched up the money and thrust it into his pocket."

In the scuffle which followed, Potter pulled out a pistol and then drew his trusty knife. Word about Potter's exploits being what it was, the gamblers let him leave and then complained to the Wake County legislative delegation.

A short inquiry followed. Potter maintained that the other players had conspired to cheat him. Likely as that was (and the House pondered hard over whether to believe any testimony by admitted card sharps, none of whom were later charged by the sheriff or Intendant with a crime), the House by then had seen enough of Robert Potter.

A week after the game, the House expelled Potter by a vote of 62 to 52. The explanation was that Potter had reflected discredit on the Legislature. Potter by then had misplaced the money he grabbed from the card table.

(Note: The next minister to confront an official named Robert Potter also suffered a painful outcome. His name was the Rev. Jim Bakker.)

As the General Assembly packed up following the 1837 session, an editorial revealed how much the Legislature's visits still meant to the local economy.

"We can say for our citizens, that they will breathe many an anxious wish for their return, before we shall again be blessed with a sight of the members."

For those in Raleigh who like to bash the Legislature, there is this opposing view of the city from a respected Whig Senator in the 1840s:

"I can only say I am in tolerable health," he wrote his wife, "anxious to get home, have a lower opinion of mankind now than I ever had before."

Raleigh

State government may have been in debt in 1846 – "This is true," wrote the *Standard*, "but when will the State be out of debt? Will someone be good enough to tell us *that?*" – but the Legislature at last found money to fence in Capitol Square.

Although the new Capitol was acclaimed as the finest in the nation to that time, the citizens of Raleigh threatened to trash it. They routinely used the square "so that the sheep, and the hogs, and the cows, and the horses... come up and stick their noses in at the windows, and the wagoners crack their whips and jingle their bells..." all while the General Assembly was in session.

Combined with the mammoth stacks of firewood which leaned against the building – and which Raleighites used to steal – the animals gave the Capitol a less than cosmopolitan look.

After an initial defeat for the fence appropriation, the *Standard* lamented that "we fear the winds of the Twentieth century will blow upon an unenclosed Capitol."

The vote was reversed and the Capitol got a splendid iron fence, but the *Standard* was ultimately correct in its fears.

Several generations later, the Capitol fence and gates were removed. Most of the fence now surrounds the old city cemetery, although some sections were sold by a junk dealer on South Wilmington Street.

(Today, neither sheep nor horses nor legislators congregate on the open square. But there are occasional hawks which dine on urban pigeons.)

By 1846, legislators had more choices in where they roomed during the session, but all of the out-of-town members stayed in one of ten hotels or boarding houses within three blocks of the Capitol. (Their residences were listed in that year's legislative directory.)

Writing about his breakfast companions at his boarding house, one Senator confessed that "I have no inducement – in fact no wish – to form acquaintances. I do not even know my right and left-hand neighbour at table and I am sure they set me down for a vain self-conceited dolt."

The Senator had to break off his letter because "the alarm of fire is now given." After ten minutes, he resumed his correspondence by reporting that the fire had been in a chimney.

"I am very glad it is no worse for the wind blows from the North West," he said. "It would be very difficult to arrest the progress of a fire in any part of Raleigh."

Raleigh

"Money traps are set here to catch every sixpence," a legislator wrote to his wife about Raleigh in 1848, "and baited with every possible thing that can procure the patronage of any class."

Rep. Alexander C. McIntosh's letters home give varied impressions of the city when it had 4,500 inhabitants.

"A man can associate himself with whatever class suits him," he wrote at one point, "from the highest to the most abandoned of men." In other letters he remarked on Raleigh's beauty in the snow, when the greenhouses behind many residences were filled with orange trees.

Concerning the capital's stores, he wrote that the establishments on Fayetteville Street offered "very fine goods" of "considerable taste," but that "a great many fancy articles would not sell at all in country stores." He speculated that "it would take two dollars here, to one in the country, for a person to live on, and keep up anything like a respectable appearance in dress."

McIntosh was not impressed with what he felt were Raleigh's affectations in fashion. "The women at church and public places," he wrote, "look like it would spoil them to touch or handle them."

(As the legislative session dragged on, McIntosh's frequent references to Raleigh's women began to grate on his wife back in Taylorsville. "There was a little more of the breast and arms naked than would look becoming in the country," he wrote about one party at the Governor's Palace.)

Describing that party, McIntosh said. "I set out in company with many others, having first taken the precaution to leave our hats at the room of a friend close by. We proceeded bareheaded to the Palace. This precaution is necessary for it is very often the case that a man goes away bareheaded or at least without his own hat."

When he reached the Palace, McIntosh found a main room outfitted with "chairs, sofas, seats, piano, richly carpeted floor, rich chandelier, etc.," and a second room which was similar "with the addition of a side board furnished with Good Liquors." The Governor offered the legislators a buffet table in a third room; the fare included meats and game, five different presentations of oysters, and pound cakes "in abundance."

A fourth room was set aside for dancing with "3 or 4 *colored brethren* in one corner with the violin and other instruments of music."

McIntosh reported that at the buffet, "persons stand around or crowd around the table, and help themselves without ceremony and those who crowd hardest generally fare best."

He told his wife "you will no doubt say in the country we would very likely call that a frolic. Well I think so too – I can see no difference.

"If it is *wrong* to drink and dance and cavort in the country, to do the same thing in the Governor's (P)alace will hardly make it right. There is a marked difference in people here and in the country. I enjoyed myself very little." (He attended two more parties the next week.)

On Sundays, McIntosh would leave his "sedate" rooming house to attend one of the city's churches. "It is different at some houses here," he wrote about rooms for legislators, "especially where a good many young members board – they drink some, fiddle, dance and cut all sorts of things."

About the churches, McIntosh observed that "surely if the people of Raleigh are lost it will not be for want of Preaching."

The city of 4,500 was not enjoyable for the Representative.

He wrote that the country "offers opportunities for calm reflection and retired meditation, not known, nor enjoyed, at least by me in the bustle of city life."

After the State Lunatic Asylum opened in 1856, Superintendent Edward C. Fisher asked the Legislature for funds so that he could fence in the grounds.

The purpose of Fisher's request was not so much to keep the original 90 patients in, but to keep the residents of Raleigh out.

According to the superintendent, the institution was subject to "the constant liability of hourly intrusions of those who are drawn hither by curiosity or as it is believed in some instances, by worse motives."

(These people must have not heard the expression, "He's not so bad off that we could have him committed, but if he was already *in* there, we'd have a hell of a time getting him out.")

Dorothea Dix may have provided the last impetus for the State to provide for its mentally ill, but as with any institution, the new hospital in 1856 needed a shakedown period.

Superintendent Fisher wrote that he preferred the use of "personal restraint" in transporting new patients to the hospital rather than the use of "personal deception and false representation."

"One of the inmates of the Asylum at this time," he reported, had been lured to Raleigh "under the belief that upon his presentation to the Governor of a spurious (petition)... he would receive immense sums of money."

When he learned the truth upon reaching the Asylum, "the disappointment of the poor deluded man can be more easily imagined than described." Dr. Fisher said that such tricks caused "total want of trust towards those who had accompanied them" and hindered the patients in their progress.

Raleigh

Over generations, when people in eastern North Carolina would say of someone, "Oh, he's gone to Raleigh," they likely were referring to Dorothea Dix Hospital.

Mrs. Lucy Bryan, writing in the late 1850s about an individual she clearly did not care for, said that "he had better send up here and engage lodgings in the Lunatic Asylum."

During the first 30 years after the Asylum opened its doors, patients were often committed for more than the classic mental disturbances.

"Religious excitement" and "religious fanaticism" were the diagnoses of several patients each year, and women were committed to the hospital for a malady which could only have been PMS. On a per capita basis, citizens of Raleigh led the state in admissions.

The accounting reports of some of Raleigh's institutions show clearly what happened to prices near the end of the Civil War.

(Inflation looked like that of any other third-world country faced with war and economic pandemonium.)

At the Institution for the Deaf and Dumb and the Blind, here is what happened to wholesale food prices, using the low end of the scale:

Flour went from $30 per barrel in 1863 to $200 per barrel in 1864. (In today's dollars, the 1864 price was about $27.80 per pound.) Corn went from $6 per bushel to $10 over the same period; bacon went from $1.25 per pound to $5; and beef went from 50 cents per pound to $2.

As for pharmaceuticals – and the school's superintendent reported that he had a "healthy" population of students – expenses for medicine rose from $34.50 in 1963 to $962.70 in 1864.

Towards the close of the Civil War, the Confederacy's desperate conscription of Raleigh men into Camp Holmes forced some local patriots to show their loyalty with their checkbooks.

(These men were physically ill, not just suffering from quayle-like tendencies.)

"The fact is notorious," the State Supreme Court wrote, that "this practice of considering every man *not bedridden*, fit for service, has driven thousands of invalids to resort to substitutes to save themselves from death by the hardships of service."

Raleigh

Although they had survived the Confederate military riot, people in Raleigh were still agitated as General Sherman was rumored to be nearing the city.

"The people are very much alarmed here," Mrs. Walter Howell wrote to her son on March 20, 1865. "They think the Yankees will get to Raleigh."

Mrs. Howell reported that "some are moving out and some are hiding and bur(y)ing their things," but that the city faced a more immediate problem: Confederate troops in the capital were "impressing and confiscating everything in sight."

Along with other homes in Raleigh, Mrs. Howell's had become a convalescent ward, with two wounded enlisted men in her parlor.

"How we are pestered," she wrote without a hint of wartime romanticism. "I cannot tell when we shall get shut of them."

She complained that tending to the soldiers interrupted her from hiding valuables.

(Mrs. Howell's letter tends to disprove one remark about Confederate soldiers in Raleigh: that judging by their titles after the war, no one from the capital had a rank below that of lieutenant.)

In prose which presaged Sinclair Lewis, Senator Leander Gash wrote to his wife in 1867 about a boisterous session in the State Capitol:

"... We got on a drunk yesterday," he informed her about the Legislature. "The House gave way about twelve and the Senate failed about one o'clock. It is positively disgraceful.

"Some of those rich old colts from the East," he continued, "gave a general treat on the East portico of the Capitol furnishing the best liquor – ice – lemons and sugar and before we old fogies knew that anything was wrong the whole (C)apitol was in an uproar."

Gash said that "the House soon... crowded in the Senate chamber. And many senators like old uncle _____ being drunk themselves."

He related that "those in a jovial mood seemed to think that it was the smartest senate that ever sat.... I got up to reply to a gentleman but on looking around and seeing his condition I sat down without opening my mouth."

That some chips in the marble steps of the Capitol were caused by whiskey barrels may be legend, but Samuel A. Ashe – a veteran by the time of Reconstruction – wrote of liquor-drinking in the Capitol as a matter of fact.

In his *Reply of North Carolinians to the Committee of Bondholders*

Raleigh

(the New Yorkers were still trying to get paid on defaulted Reconstruction bonds), Ashe wrote in 1905 that one Scalawag had "established in a room in the west end of the Capitol a free bar where all who chose to drink and smoke caroused at his expense....

"And so," Ashe wrote, "with wine and women, he and his friends led a gay life, debauching all who longed to be debauched in those first months after the ushering in of New North Carolina."

Raleigh's W.W. Holden was the State's only governor to be impeached, but the State Supreme Court had kind words for his service as Provisional Governor in the months after Appomatox.

The Court said that it was "fortunate that the Union appointed Holden in order to "give the wheels of government a new start."

"Far from being a usurpation," the Court advised, Holden's appointment "was a discharge of duty in its mildest form." The Court speculated on what might have happened to North Carolina if the Union had treated secession and warmaking as acts of treason, which it was entitled to do.

Raleigh was in a regular fix when Holden took over as Provisional Governor.

"No one of the State officers was bound by an oath to support the Constitution of the United States," the Court explained, "and consequently no one of them was qualified to discharge the duties of their respective offices.

"There was no Governor, no members of the General Assembly, no Judges. Every office in the State was politically dead, and the effect (was) the same as if they had all died a natural death.... Here, then, was a state of anarchy."

The first special tax bonds to be sold for the construction of Central Prison were found by the courts to be unlawful and fraudulent.

The original prison, built on land purchased in 1870 from Kate Boylan, had 268 convicts in twelve temporary cells which were "made of heavy logs each cell 18 feet square."

As the stockade fence rotted at the bottom, prisoners uprooted the poles and replanted them upside down. Prisoners escaped repeatedly over the ever-diminishing fence.

Raleigh

As Central Prison became permanent ("The prison built itself," reported *The Prison News,* from its adjacent quarry), its population reached 343 convicts; of that total, 267 were illiterate, 208 were minors, and 63 contracted scurvy when a drought struck the State's vegetable crop.

Prisoners were budgeted four cents a day for food and made their own shoes and clothes. The cost of the original cells, $177 each, would be about $1,375 today.

By 1873, Central Prison was so crowded that inmates had only 216 cubic feet of air space apiece and their natural mortality rate was 4.5 percent. The prison's physician reported that "the only warmth in winter, save that from clothes and blankets, is derived from overcrowding...."

In the 1870s, the prison in Raleigh was not the worst place that a man could land in the State's criminal justice apparatus.

Each year, the State sent about 200 men to labor on the Spartanburg and Asheville Railroad, then being cut through the mountains. (Under the "convict lease" system, the State tried to turn a profit on its inmates.)

Of the 224 sent to the railroad from Raleigh in 1875, 22 died; the next year, 18 died out of the 185 sent.

In 1909, the Legislature decided that local county jails were better for the "safety and safekeeping" of convicted felons than was the sieve-like Central Prison. It ordered that all persons who were scheduled for execution be confined in their home counties unless they either had no appeal pending or had been sentenced for the crime of rape.

(Indeed, although murderers led the procession of inmates who have been executed in Raleigh, rapists would be a close second if so many had not been lynched at the local level.)

Central Prison was preparing for its role as execution site for the State.

The first electrocution did occur at Central Prison in 1910, but only because the condemned man received four separate stays of execution before "the current was given by the Prison power plant."

The man would have been executed sooner, but the New York firm which manufactured the electric chair kept having problems with its circuitry and repeatedly delayed delivery.

Raleigh

For those who are certain that the *N&O* is a bleeding-heart, left-wing publication, consider the newspaper's stance on a "prison mutiny" in Raleigh in 1887.

One afternoon that year, Central Prison's black inmates mistakenly got the impression that guards had murdered a fellow prisoner. They refused to return to their cells and began amassing a pile of bricks in the prison yard for self-defense.

Under the headline "The Gloved Hand not for Convicts," the *N&O* expressed outrage that inmates had been allowed to present a "grievance" – in this case, an objection that the guards had turned into killers.

The *N&O* said there was a "danger of undertaking to treat convicts like Sunday School scholars;" added that prison authorities had "temporized" for too long before moving to regain control; and stated that any reluctance whatsoever by the inmates to obey orders should be greeted with "nothing less than a shooting down."

The prison's officials did not rush the convicts as the *N&O* advocated. When instead they produced the "murdered" inmate, who was alive and bandaged, the prisoners returned peaceably to their cells.

But although the mutiny did not produce gunfire, it did provide cocktail party chat for members of the Governor's Guards, a volunteer Raleigh militia unit. The affluent, all-white Guards had been sent into the prison and posted with rifles during the insurrection. Fearing the worst, they were posted around the prison yard when the prison's gas lights failed.

Guards and mutineers alike were plunged into darkness. For weeks in Raleigh the question was who had been most terrified through the night, the Guards with their rifles or the prisoners with their bricks.

In *The Prison News* in 1926, Superintendent George R. Pou warned his guests to "remember flogging has not been abolished. I am opposed to corporal punishment, but if you prisoners prefer 'black aggie' to the present mode of punishment, you will hardly be disappointed."

Pou also sent the prisoners a Christmas message which remarked that it was their own fault that they were behind bars and that the guards would all rather be pursuing more upscale lines of employment.

By 1927, the State Board of Charities and Public Welfare could report an "Alarming Increase of White Prisoners" in Raleigh. (Their percentage had risen from 32 percent of Central Prison's inmates in 1915 to 40 percent in 1920 to 62 percent in 1925.)

The Board ascribed the corresponding decline in the percentage of black prisoners to the success of the State's education program which had been begun in 1901 by Governor Charles Aycock, the White Supremacy candidate.

"There is a shudder that chills one," the editor of the *Observer* wrote in 1878 after a tour of the Insane Asylum, "as he steps from the bright, free world into this den of animals that is indescribable.

"The faint line that marks the mental and moral boundaries of sanity and insanity, few of us can trace perhaps, but the physical barriers that shut in the man and shut out those upon whom the curse has not fallen are bold, real and awful."

Traveling circuses that hit town, with or without a camelopard, had nothing on the trial in 1889 of Dr. Eugene Grissom.

The superintendent of the Insane Asylum, Dr. Grissom was accused of cruelty to patients, sexual romps with female attendants and inmates, and misappropriation of hospital property.

By the time the Asylum board's formal inquiry was over – with dozens of lawyers and witnesses and testimony spattered across the front pages of Raleigh's newspapers each day – everyone involved in the proceeding was somehow smeared.

"He jumped on a poor, demented creature while held down by strong men," went one complaint of cruelty against Grissom, "and stamped him in the face." Not at all, replied the superintendent; he had merely pressed his foot against the man's throat until attendants could restrain the patient.

Dr. Grissom also had rationales for every occasion on which he strapped patients for days to their beds, although testimony in the hearing suggested that other states had discarded the practice decades before.

Grissom defended his flinging of a dipperful of water into the face of a patient who was the daughter of "one of the most highly cultured and refined families in Eastern North Carolina." He said she had become hysterical and that he had "frequently resorted to throwing water in the face for the purpose of producing a mental impression." (His technique worked; when she told her parents, they became indignant.) All the while during the hearing, the newspapers published the names of the patients.

But on to the sexual allegations. Asylum staff members volunteered that they had been spying on Dr. Grissom. For days, the trial focused on what could or could not be viewed through keyholes and peepholes in examination rooms and matron's quarters, and how long Grissom had been closeted alone with various women.

Dr. Grissom was alleged to have been particularly aggressive toward one nubile, pristine attendant who was so shocked by his advances that she quit the Asylum and moved away from Raleigh. Then a letter was introduced into the evidence; it was written by one of Grissom's subordinates to the poor, exiled nurse.

It wasn't so much that the subordinate sent her money that put a different light on events. It may not even have been that he urged her to perjure herself against Grissom. What really stirred Raleigh's pulse about the letter was his manner of expressing himself.

"There will be times when we will forget all but the pleasure we have together," he wrote. "We must hope for the best and if we pull through all right and no one ever finds out it won't make any difference." So much for the credibility of two key witnesses.

As for the misappropriations, the Asylum records did show missing turkeys, hams, chickens and produce. But Dr. Grissom countered that the provisions had been used to feed dignitaries and therefore saved scarce funds for treatment.

Grissom's eight-member board exonerated him on a split decision – three voted him guilty of immorality and two of cruelty and embezzlement. With the acquittal, Raleigh's newspapers turned manic.

Josephus Daniels organized a mass meeting at Metropolitan Hall the night after the decision. "I now declare to you in the sight of God that I believe the verdict not to be in accordance with the testimony," he shouted. "I shall never be satisfied until this verdict is reversed and this man is made to step down and out of this position which he is totally unworthy to fill."

Through the *Chronicle,* Daniels attacked the Asylum board, revealing that its chairman, Dr. E. Burke Haywood, received fees for examining patients at the hospital. The newspaper pounced on two other board members who had business ties to Grissom, several who were close friends of the superintendent and socialized with him, and three who had received some of the disputed turkeys. Moreover, Daniels said, Dr. Haywood's son was one of Grissom's defense attorneys.

Daniels concluded that the board was so entwined with Grissom that it could never repudiate him. He organized a second "indignation meeting."

Although several newspapers picked up Daniels' call ("LaGrange gives three cheers for the indignation meeting," was a typical report), others questioned whether the Raleigh crowds were behaving like louts with no regard for due process.

"High-handed justice stalking through the streets," was how

Goldsboro's newspaper termed the Raleigh movement. The *Charlotte News* observed that "there is no liberty where juries are to be denounced."

Daniels backpedaled and insisted that he had not meant to impugn the board's motives. He revamped his argument to the effect that guilty or not, Dr. Grissom's effectiveness had been ended by bad publicity. The editor also began to nag at Governor Daniel G. Fowle for not taking a public stand on whether the Asylum board should sack its superintendent.

Of course, repudiating Grissom would also have reflected on the majority of the Asylum board and on Chairman Haywood. And the chairman, in yet another interlock, was an in-law of the Governor's from his first marriage. The Governor remained silent for weeks.

Then Governor Fowle achieved what was called a tactical masterstroke. He offered Dr. Haywood the chairmanship of the State's new board of public welfare. In order to accept the honor, Haywood had to resign as chairman of the Asylum. A similar offer to another board member created a second vacancy. Dr. Grissom saw what was coming, resigned, and left politics after someone fired a shot at him in the State Capitol.

Anyone who read the small print in the *Chronicle* could have smiled the next year. When Daniels made his annual boast about his stable of learned and eminent citizens who were the *Chronicle*'s correspondents, one name was no longer on the list: Dr. Eugene Grissom.

Public officials in Raleigh will complain about coverage in the media for as long as there are reporters, but none of them lately has had to endure what Rep. J.T. Phillips – one of our special guests – did in 1898.

What the *N&O* did to Phillips was either a crucifixion or accurate reporting, depending on the point of view, but this is what it wrote about the man it called "Juice Taker":

"We have always advocated the superiority of the sober man as a lawmaker," the *N&O* intoned after describing Phillips being dragged unconscious from a baggage cart at the Yarborough House.

"He may not be as picturesque or even as brilliant, at times, as his tanked up contemporary, and certainly he is not as susceptible of nasal embellishment or decoration," the *N&O* went on, but the sober legislator was "safer and steadier."

In case anyone missed the point, the *N&O* added of the sober man that "nobody pulls him out of the gutter at night or out of the guard-house in the morning."

(Phillips had not challenged reporters to follow him around and predicted that they would find it boring.)

Raleigh

Historians of the State Capitol remember 1898 as the year in which agreement was reached to rip out the iron fence, grade the grounds and lower the stone sidewalks to meet the new contours. But the Capitol that year was notable for another change in its appearance.

Dead dogs – mostly expensive pointers – began to appear each morning on the dewy Capitol lawn. After several weeks, suspicion fell on the Rev. J.L. Burns, who was Keeper of the Capitol.

Burns had become annoyed at dogs entering his domain. He had threatened to kill them if their owners did not prevent them from using the grounds as a toilet. Moreover, the Capitol's night watchman had recently bought a bottle of strychnine from a pharmacy on Fayetteville Street.

When autopsies found that the dogs had died of strychnine poisoning, the Rev. Burns was arrested and brought to trial. The watchman testified that Burns had ordered him to go buy the poison.

The sheriff found an unopened bottle of strychnine in Burns' desk in the Capitol. (No defense attorney offered the simplest explanation: that Burns kept the poison in reserve not for pointers, but for lobbyists.)

Matters looked grim for Burns until someone decided that his trial would detract from the rabidity of the White Supremacy campaign which was then underway. The trial was adjourned and never resumed.

Burns left the Capitol staff and presumably the dogs again went about their business.

During the Spanish-American War, the *Charlotte Observer* printed this dispatch concerning military contracts in the State capital:

"All the men who bake bread for soldiers by contract give a pound of it for one pound of flour, the gain being in the extra weight of the water used.

"A Raleigh baker who knew this rule," the Observer continued, "refused to furnish more than 13 ounces of bread for 16 ounces of flour. As a result he is not baking just now, another man being given the contract."

By the early part of the Twentieth century an alleged motto for State employees had gained enough currency to appear in the *Raleigh Times:* "Few die; none resign," was the watchword.

Attention in 1991 may have been directed at the First Union Plaza, but debates over encroachments on Capitol Square date back to at least 1905.

The *Charlotte Chronicle*, commenting on the brick pile which now houses the State Labor Department, wrote that "in no way can money be as utterly wasted as in bad buildings."

The newspaper argued that "if any money is to be expended, let it be upon the capitol building itself. It would be a shame to encroach on the limited space of Capitol Square by the erection of other buildings. Besides, it would be extremely bad taste from an architectural standpoint."

(Well, no one cared in 1905 what those pedants from Charlotte thought. At least the plan which would have done most to detract from the Capitol – to add two wings to it so that it would have resembled the U.S. Capitol – was shelved.)

"Why Not Electrocution?" read a headline in the *Raleigh Times* in 1908.

The *Times*, in its editorial, made a graphic case against continued hangings at the city quarry. Noting that hanging "is both painful and barbarous," it quoted a physician's report of a typical execution:

"The heart continued to beat for 13 to 15 minutes after the springing of the trap, and there were conscious efforts to breathe, struggles of the manacled hands to free themselves and reach the strangling neck and bitter contortions of the feet, tied though they were, to free themselves and find support."

"A horrid and repulsive picture?" asked the *Times* about its depiction of scenes at the city quarry. "Yes, but a more repulsive and barbaric practice.

"Far be it from us," the *Times* continued, "to advocate the abolition of capital punishment. The time may come when this will be expedient in North Carolina, but as yet, it is absolutely necessary that the death sentence be sanctioned by law even though it not be invoked by juries as often as it ought to be."

The *Times* rallied behind the proposal for an electric chair at Central Prison.

(As the Rev. Bill Finlator might put it, no persons who have undergone the death penalty are available to tell which is the least painful approach. Central Prison got its electric chair, which in turn was discarded several decades later for the more "humane" gas chamber. Witnesses immediately noted that the gas chamber produced the same lengthy strangulations on a regular basis which had happened when nooses slipped at the city quarry.)

Raleigh

For years the wardens of Central Prison were adversely affected by their duties which involved executions.

Alcoholism, crime, early death – all of these befell those who carried out the lawful orders of the State. The case of Thomas Sale in 1916 is perhaps the lowlight.

Sale, who according to the *Greensboro News* "had killed so many prisoners he could not execute any more," reached his limit one evening. A man who was said to "mope and worry" for days before an electrocution, Sale had to preside over a double execution. (The State later performed a triple in 1934; on the other hand, citizens near Pittsboro hanged four at once from a tree.)

After the bodies were pronounced dead and removed, Sale "shambled over to his office."

He "picked up his pen to write the date 1-28-16 and fell dead on his desk." Sale "smeared ink over the page left for the death certificate."

In the present-day Statehouse, on the walls which flank the central staircase, are bulletin boards which direct the public to the locations of committee meetings and members' offices.

During the 1970s, the time and place for meetings of the Senate Committee on Wildlife were listed as "8:30 p.m." at the "Club of the Eight Lords", a watering hole which was then in the basement of the Velvet Cloak hotel.

During the 1960s, a State Senator was in his office on the first floor of the Legislative Building when he learned that the House was working mischief on one of his bills.

Preoccupied, he strode out of his office towards the House side of the building. About six seconds into his journey, he stepped into a sunken fountain up to his knees. As the Senator looked up, he saw a tour group of public school students who were observing him as if he were a grown man in a suit standing in a pool of water.

The Senator forded the fountain like MacArthur returning to the Philippines. Dripping wet, he climbed out, grinned, and addressed the students.

"So much for the myth that legislators can walk on water," he said, and disappeared into a stairwell.

Bibliography

Books and reports

Abernethy, Elizabeth. *Historical Facts of Raleigh*, Raleigh, N.C., 1938.
Adolphsen, Jeff. *Federal Square Program*, Raleigh, N.C., 1986.
Amis, Moses. *Historical Raleigh*, Raleigh, N.C., 1913.
Anonymous. *The Negro and His White Allies*, Raleigh, N.C., 1903.
Associated Charities of Raleigh. *Annual Report*, Raleigh, N.C.,1905.
Battle, Kemp P. *Address on the Occasion of the Centennial of the City of Raleigh*, Raleigh, N.C. 1892.
Battle, Kemp P. *Address to the City of Raleigh on July 4, 1876*, Raleigh, N.C., 1876.
Boyd, Daniel L. *Free-Born Negro: The Life of John Chavis*, Princeton, N.J., 1947.
Brauer, Stephen W. *Testing Siebert's Proposition II: A Civil War Case Study*, Chapel Hill, N.C., 1968.
Brown, Hugh V. *A History of the Education of Negroes in North Carolina*, Raleigh, N.C. 1961.
Cantwell, Edward. *The North Carolina Magistrate*, Raleigh, N.C., 1856.
Capital City Cycle Club. *Constitution and By-Laws*, Raleigh,N.C., 1894.
Capitol Broadcasting Company. *Viewpoint* and other editorials, Raleigh, N.C., 1960-?.
Carolina Power & Light Company. *Report to the Stockholders*, Raleigh, N.C., various.
Carroll, Grady. *The City of Raleigh and the Civil War Experience*, Raleigh, N.C. 1979.
Carroll, Grady. *They Lived in Raleigh*, Raleigh, N.C., 1977.

Raleigh

Carson, Douglas. *Horticultural Therapy at Dorothea Dix Hospital*, Raleigh, N.C., 1977.

Carter, Dr. Wilmoth. *Shaw's Universe: A Monument to Educational Innovation*, Raleigh, N.C., 1973.

Carter, Dr. Wilmoth. *The Urban Negro in the South*, New York, N.Y., 1961.

Cathey, Cornelius O. *Agricultural Developments in North Carolina, 1783-1860*, Chapel Hill, N.C., 1956.

Chamber of Commerce and Industry. *Raleigh, North Carolina, within 15 hours of New York City, The ideal winter home for semi- invalids and pleasure seekers from New England*, Raleigh, N.C., 1897.

Chamberlin, Hope. *History of Wake County, North Carolina*, Raleigh, N.C., 1922.

City of Raleigh. *Annual Reports of the Mayor and Officers of the City of Raleigh*, Raleigh, N.C., various from 1883-1910.

City of Raleigh. *The 18 Year Police Protection Plan for Raleigh, 1977-1995*, Raleigh, N.C., 1977.

City of Raleigh. *Hillsborough Street Task Force Report No. 1*, Raleigh, N.C., 1982

City of Raleigh. *Rules and Regulations for the Government of the Raleigh Police Force*, Raleigh, N.C., 1882.

Coon, G.L. *North Carolina Schools and Academies, 1790-1840.*

Covington, Nina. *Guidebook of Raleigh, Raleigh, N.C.*, 1917.

Cunningham, H.H. "Edmund Burke Haywood and Raleigh's Confederate Hospitals," *N.C. Historical Review*, Raleigh, N.C., 1958.

Drury, J.R. *Industrial Survey of Raleigh*, Raleigh, N.C., 1953.

Eckler, A. Ross. *Census Statistics for Local Use*, Raleigh, N.C. Advertising Club, 1954.

Edmisten, Linda W. *J.W. Willie York; His First Seventy Five years in Raleigh*, Raleigh, N.C., 1987.

Edmonds, Helen G. *The Negro and Fusion Politics, 1894-1901.*

Elliott, Robert N. Jr. *The Raleigh Register 1799-1867*, Chapel Hill, N.C., 1955.

Eplan, Leon S. *Annexation Policy Considerations for Raleigh, N.C.*, Chapel Hill, N.C., 1953.

Fesperman, Edward L. *Hand-Book of Things You Ought to Know about Raleigh*, Raleigh, N.C., 1908.

Fletcher, Fred. *Tempus Fugit*, Raleigh, N.C., 1990.

Fletcher, James F. *The Origin and Development of the Carolina Power & Light Company, 1881-1925*, Chapel Hill, N.C., 1938.

Gangemis, Marie E. *Transition in Abeyance: Urban Growth in Raleigh, North Carolina, 1880-1900*, Chapel Hill, N.C., 1975.

Gaskins, Karl S. and Nordman, Theodore P. *Housing Development in Raleigh*, Raleigh, N.C., 1966.
Glenton, Mary V. *The Story of a Hospital*, Raleigh, N.C., 1923.
Goss, Jerome. *Factors Affecting Urban Renewal in Three North Carolina Cities: A Comparative Analysis*, Chapel Hill, N.C., 1968.
Harris, Linda A. *Raleigh Historic Properties Inventory*, Raleigh, N.C., 1978.
Haywood, John. *Duty and office of Justices of Peace and of sheriffs, coroners, constables, etc.*, Raleigh, N.C., 1808.
Hendrick, Burton J. *The Teaching of an American*, Dunwoody, Ga., 1970.
Hess, Timothy. *Crabtree Creek Development*, Raleigh, N.C., 1983.
Hicks, Frank A. "Negro Business in Raleigh," *The Home Mission College Review*, Raleigh, N.C., 1930.
Hogg, T.D. *The Streets of Raleigh: Their Condition and the Remedy*, Raleigh, N.C., 1881.
Hunnicutt, F.H. *Hot-Shot Truths About Raleigh City Affairs*, Raleigh, N.C., 1917.
Johnson, Ronald V. *Evolution of a Community Open Space System: Raleigh, North Carolina, A Case Study*, Raleigh, N.C., 1986.
Jordan, Graydon Wright. *A History of Wake County Schools*, Chapel Hill, N.C., 1943.
Lawrence, Robert. "Some Boyhood Recollections," *The Uplift*, Concord, N.C., 1944.
Lemmon, Sarah McC. "Raleigh – An Example of the 'New South,'?" *N.C. Historical Review*, Raleigh, N.C., 1966.
Lockmiller, David A. *History of the N.C. State College of Agriculture and Engineering*, Raleigh, N.C., 1939.
Lowry, Sheldon G. *Differentials in Morbidity and in the use and cost of health services in Wake County, North Carolina*, Lansing, Mich., 1934.
MacDonald, Francis. *It's the Best Place I Have Ever Lived! Cameron Park: A Study of Neighborhood Images and Myths*, Raleigh, N.C., 1975.
Martin, Francois-Xavier. *A treatise on the powers and duties of a sheriff, etc.*, New Bern, N.C., 1806.
Martin, John A. *A Study of Proposals for Hillsborough Street*, Raleigh, N.C., 1984.
Mathews, Donald G. and De Hart, Jane S. *Sex, Gender and the Politics of ERA, A State and the Nation*, Oxford University Press, 1990.
McKenna-Klute, Linda. *Design Review in Historic Districts*, Raleigh, N.C., 1978.
McLaurin, Melton A. *The North Carolina State Fair, 1853-1899*, Greenville, N.C., 1963.

Mental Hygiene Clinic of Raleigh and Wake County. Various reports beginning in 1954

Morgan, Gwendolyn S. *A Study of Thirty-Four Third Grade Children in Wartime*, Chapel Hill, N.C., 1944.

Murray, Elizabeth Reid. *Wake: Capital County of North Carolina*, Raleigh, N.C., 1983.

Nichols, J.C. *Mistakes We Have Made in Developing Shopping Centers*, Washington, D.C., 1945.

North Carolina Conference of the United Methodist Church. *Early Methodist Meeting Houses in Wake County*, North Carolina, Raleigh, N.C., 1979.

North Carolina General Assembly. *Report by Commission to Investigate Charges of Fraud and Corruption*, Raleigh, N.C., 1872.

North Carolina Ordnance Department. *Consolidated Statement, 1862-1864*, in the North Carolina Collection, Chapel Hill, N.C.

North Carolina State University. *Chancellor's University-Neighborhood Report*, Raleigh, N.C., 1983.

Olivia Raney Library. Rules and Regulations, Raleigh, N.C., 1901.

Olmsted, Frederick Law. *A Journey in the Southern Slave States*, New York, N.Y., 1856.

Parker-Hunter Realty Company. *Cameron Park: Its Purposes, Its Attainments and Its Future Outlook*, Raleigh, N.C., 1914.

Pathak, Chittaranjan. *Growth Patterns of Raleigh*, Chapel Hill, N.C., 1963.

Peebles, Wilma C. *School Desegregation in Raleigh, North Carolina, 1954-1964*, Chapel Hill, N.C., 198_.

Pilot Cotton Mills, Inc. *Time Book A*, Raleigh, N.C., 1893-1896.

Potter, Henry. *The office and duty of a Justice of the Peace, etc.*, Raleigh, N.C., 1816.

Potter, Robert. *To the People of Granville County*, Oxford, N.C., 1832.

Raleigh Academy. *Laws of the Raleigh Academy: with the Plan of Education Annexed*, Raleigh, N.C., 1811.

Raleigh Academy. *Prospectus of the Raleigh Academy and Mrs. Hutchison's View of Female Education*, Raleigh, N.C., 1835.

Raleigh Chamber of Commerce. *Facts and Figures about RALEIGH*, Raleigh, N.C., 1925.

Raleigh Chamber of Commerce. *Planning for Raleigh's Future*, Raleigh, N.C., 1953.

Rebellion Records. "Military Riots at Raleigh, North Carolina," 1864 in the North Carolina Collection.

Riley, Jack. *Carolina Power & Light Company, 1908-1958, A Corporate Biography*, Raleigh, N.C., 1958.

Robinson, Charles M. *A City Plan for Raleigh*, Raleigh, N.C.,1913.
St. Augustine's College. *St. Augustine's College, a Record of 50 Years*, Raleigh, N.C., 1917.
St. Augustine's College. *Impressions of St. Augustine's School*, Raleigh, N.C., 1906.
Sesquicentennial Committee. *Raleigh – Capital of North Carolina*, Raleigh, N.C., 1942.
Shaheen, Donald G. *Contributions of Urban Roadway Usage to Pollution*, Washington, D.C., 1975.
Small, Milton C. III. *Urban Design, Raleigh, N.C.*, Raleigh, N.C., 1966.
Smith, Glenda. *Neighborhood Identity: A Source of Citizen Participation*, Raleigh, N.C., 1976.
Smith, Mary Phlegar. *Municipal Development in North Carolina, 1665-1900*, Chapel Hill, N.C., 1930.
Sparer, Burton. *A Technique to Determine Space Requirements for Neighborhood Shopping Centers in Raleigh, North Carolina*, Chapel Hill, N.C., 1951.
Stuchell, James E., Jr. *The Role of the Urban Planner in the City Government of Raleigh, North Carolina: A Case Study*, Chapel Hill, N.C., 1960.
Swain, David L. *Early Times in Raleigh*, Raleigh, N.C., 1867.
Taylor, Hon. John Louis. *A charge delivered to the Grand Jury of Edgecomb Superior Court etc.*, Raleigh, N.C., 1817.
Thiem, James E. III. *Privacy and the Art of Model Airplane Construction*, Raleigh, N.C., 1986.
Toppe, Richard. *Fat City Follies*, Raleigh, N.C., 1978.
Underwood, Larry R. *Montague Square*, Raleigh, N.C., 1983.
Unknown. *The Case of Raleigh for the University Medical School of North Carolina*, Raleigh, N.C., 19XX.
Unknown. *Financial Status of Raleigh Teachers*, Raleigh, N.C., 1934.
Unknown. *City of Raleigh: Historic Sketches*, Raleigh, N.C.,1887.
Unknown. *A Proposal for the Location of the North Carolina School of Science and Mathematics*, Raleigh, N.C., 1978.
Unknown. *Raleigh Illustrated*, Raleigh, N.C., 1910.
United States Senate. *Document No. 92, Utility Corporations, 70th Congress, 1st Session*, Washington, D.C.
Vickers, James. *Raleigh City of Oaks, An Illustrated History*, Raleigh, N.C., 1982.
Vissering, Jean E. *The View from the Sidewalk: Three Walking Tours of Downtown Raleigh*, Raleigh, N.C., 1976.
Walser, Richard. *The Watauga Club*, Raleigh, N.C., 1980.

Warner, Michael K. *Southside*, Raleigh, N.C., 1966.
Warner, Peter C. *A Community Mental Health Subcenter*, Raleigh, N.C., 1966.
Waugh, Elizabeth. *North Carolina Capital*, Raleigh, N.C., 1967.
Waynick, Capus. *North Carolina and the Negro*, Raleigh, N.C., 1964
Webster, Daphne. *A Study of Potential Impacts and Possible Land Management Techniques: Within the Proposed Falls Lake Regional Watershed*, Raleigh, N.C., 1976.
Whitaker, Rev. R.H. *Whitaker's Reminiscences, Incidents and Anecdotes*, Raleigh, N.C. 1905.
White, Daphne A. *Cemeteries in the Landscape*, Raleigh, N.C., 1986.
Williamson, Hugh. *History of North Carolina Vols. 1 and 2*, Raleigh, N.C., 1812.
Winstead, Timothy F. *Building Design as a Contributor to Urban Space*, Raleigh, N.C., 1983.
Wright, Robert S. *Lake Lynn Road Townhouses*, Raleigh, N.C.,1982.

Newspapers and periodicals

(The following publications are available on microfilm, microfiche, and in some cases on actual paper at the State Library, the Search Room of the State Archives, the North Carolina Collection at the University of North Carolina, the D.H. Hill Library at N.C. State University, and the Duke University Library. In instances where the names of newspapers changed through the years, only the most familiar listing is given.)

The Asheville Citizen
Beans
The Biblical Recorder
Blasting Powder
The Carolinian
The Caucasian
The Charlotte Chronicle
The Charlotte Daily News
The Charlotte Observer
The Chronicle
The Daily Dispatch
The Daily News
The Durham Herald
The Evening Times

Raleigh

Everywoman's Magazine
The Goldsboro News
The Greensboro News
The Hayseeder
The Holden Record
The Journal of Commerce and Industry
The Independent
The Live Giraffe
The Microcosm
The Minerva
The Niles Register
The News and Observer
The North Carolina Anvil
The N.C. Beacon and Metropolitan Omnibus
The North Carolina Journal
The Oak City Item
The Observer
The Oxford Public Ledger
The Post
The Prison News
The Progressive Farmer
Raleigh Magazine
The Raleigh Register
The Raleigh Times
The Rasp
The Sentinel
The Spectator
The Standard
The Star
We Know
Wilmington Messenger

Wake County records

(The best source for these records is at the Search Room of the N.C. Division of Archives and History.)

Appointments of administrators, executors and guardians
Apprentice bonds
Bastardy bonds

Raleigh

Census records
Civil action papers
Clerks' accounts of minor lunatics
Condemnation proceedings
Constable bonds
County home accounts
Criminal action papers
Criminal dockets, Superior Court
Deeds
Deeds of Trust
Divisions of dower
Divorce records
Ejectments
Election records
Equity minutes dockets, Superior Court
Estates records
Execution dockets, Court of Pleas and Quarter Sessions
Fraternal organizations records
Grand jury reports
Inventories and settlements of estates
Land entries
Ledgers
Lunacy proceedings
Marriage bonds
Minutes dockets, Superior Courts
Minutes of the Court of Pleas and Quarter Sessions
Miscellaneous records
Mortgage deeds
Personal accounts
Railroad records
Records of county workhouse
Registry of licenses to trades
Road records
School census (white and colored)
School records
Tax records
Trial dockets
Wills general index

Raleigh

State of North Carolina records

(Materials from the foregoing depositories plus the libraries of the N.C. Supreme Court and N.C. General Assembly. The records were reviewed for materials concerning the City of Raleigh for as long as the respective bodies kept records since 1792.)

General Statutes of North Carolina
Constitution of the State of North Carolina
Public, Private and Local Laws of the State of North Carolina
General Assembly session records
General Assembly committee reports
Charters of the City of Raleigh
Journals of the North Carolina State Senate, House of Commons, and House of Representatives
Opinions and case files of the North Carolina Supreme Court
Reports and case files of the North Carolina Court of Appeals
Governors' papers
Governors' letters
Governors' pardon and commutation books
Office of the State Treasurer, receipts and warrants books
Office of the Secretary of State, corporation records
North Carolina Department of Agriculture records
North Carolina Department of Public Instruction records
North Carolina Utilities Commission records
North Carolina Railroad Commission records
North Carolina Lunatic Asylum, Insane Asylum, Dorothea Dix Hospital records
North Carolina Institution for the Deaf, Dumb and Blind records
Governor Morehead school records
North Carolina Penitentiary, Central Prison records
North Carolina Highway Commission, Department of Transportation records
Committee on (Civil War) claims decisions
Committees and commissions on the State Capitol records

Raleigh

Private collections

From the Search Room of the N.C. Division of Archives:

Associated Charities of Raleigh
Bickett papers
Bennett T. Blake papers
J.G. Blount papers
Willis G. Briggs Collection
Stephen S. Burrill Diary
Busbee Collection
Collins papers
Emma D. Conn papers
David L. Corbitt papers
Calvin J. Cowles papers
C.C. Crittenden papers
Allen T. and Theodore F. Davidson papers
L. Polk Denmark Collection
W.H. Dietrick papers
Episcopal School of North Carolina
Thad S. Ferree papers
Gales papers
L.S. Gash papers
Marmaduke James Hawkins papers
Daniel H. Hill, Jr. papers
William Hill papers
Charles L. Hinton papers
Hodges Collection
Holeman Collection
Jeffreys Collection
Crabtree Jones papers
Lewis papers
Nell Battle Lewis papers
Little-Mordecai Collection
Charles Manly papers
Alonzo T. Mial papers
Fred A. Olds papers
Clarence H. Poe papers
Mrs. Millard Rewis papers
W.L. Saunders papers
Dr. Henry B. Shields papers

Raleigh

Simpson-Biddle Family papers
John Steele papers
Gertrude Weil papers
William Sidney Wilson papers
Worth papers
Jonathan Worth papers

From the Southern Historical Collection at the University of North Carolina, Chapel Hill:

Allen-Simpson papers
Rufus Amis papers
Alexander Boyd Andrews papers
Samuel A. Ashe papers
Badger Family papers
Bagley Family papers
Daniel Moreau Barringer papers
Battle Family papers
Jesse S. Bean diary
Edmund Ruffin Beckwith papers
Henry Lewis Benning papers
John Bragg papers
Willis Grandy Briggs papers
Bryan Family papers
Marion Butler papers
Bennehan Cameron papers
Cameron Family papers
John D. Cain papers
David Miller Carter papers
Joseph Blount Cheshire papers
William John Clarke papers
Walter S. Clemence Diary and papers
Edmund J. Cleveland Diary
Anne Cameron Collins papers
Charles A. Cooke papers
Harold Dunbar Cooley papers
Mary Farrow Credle papers
Moses Ashley Curtis papers
Adelaide Daniels papers
Frank Arthur Daniels papers
Jonathan Worth Daniels papers
Josephus Daniels papers

Raleigh

Theodore F. Davidson papers
Ferebee-Gregory-McPherson papers
Thaddeus S. Ferree papers
Stephen Frontis autobiography
Gales Family papers
James Carson Gardner papers
William Gaston papers
Grimes Family papers
Hawkins papers and books
Ernest Haywood Collection
John Haywood papers
Thomas Devereux Hogg papers
E.V. Howell papers
Susan Nye Hutchison Diary
Joseph Seawell Jones papers
Drury Lacy papers
George William Lay papers
Edward McCrady L'Engle papers
Lewis papers
Peter Mallett papers
Manly Family papers
Richard Sharp Mason papers
McIntosh Family papers
Elvira E. Moffitt papers
Mordecai papers
Robert Treat Paine papers
Joseph and William Peace Account Books
Pettigrew Family papers
Polk, Badger and McGehee Family papers
Elsie Riddick papers
Riddick Family papers
Marmaduke Swaim Robins papers
Anne Gales Root papers
Royster Family papers
Thomas Settle papers
Cornelia Phillips Spencer papers
Walter Frank Taylor papers
Alfred Moore Waddell papers
Richard Gaither Walser papers
John W. and William A. Williams papers
Jonathan Worth papers